Rethinking Misrecog
Struggles for Recognition: Critical Theory Beyond Honneth

Douglas Giles

Insert Philosophy
Praha

ISBN: 978-1-7358808-1-5

Insert Philosophy
Italská 209/17
Praha 120 00
Czech Republic
InsertPhilosophyHere.com

To my Spouse, who never fails to recognize my true self.

Table of Contents

Introduction

Human integrity owes its existence, at a deep level,
to the patterns of approval and recognition.

- Axel Honneth[1]

Considerations of the causes of and correctives for social injustice are increasingly vital topics. Social recognition plays a vital role in both social injustices and efforts to overcome and prevent them. Axel Honneth's influential accounts of recognition and struggles for recognition contain important insights into these topics. Unfortunately, some of Honneth's concepts are narrow and need expansion for them to be useful in considering social injustices and responses to those injustices. This book presents important and, to my mind, necessary correctives and additions to Axel Honneth's view of recognition to give the concepts of recognition, misrecognition, and struggles for recognition more explanatory power. I seek to address problems within recognition theory by clarifying the roles of misrecognition and struggles for recognition in human behavior. Rethinking misrecognition and struggles for recognition can lead to a more robust and relevant critical theory.

Following Honneth and others, I accept that recognition is integral to individuals' self-realization and to social justice, and I accept Honneth's idea that struggles against injustice are often struggles for recognition. Those who seek justice seek not only material changes but also a change in their place in society. Workers striking for better pay and working conditions are also fighting for recognition of their needs, dignity, and moral right to just compensation for their labor. Women who have fought for the vote, property rights, equal pay, control of their bodies, and similar causes have been seeking a change in society's recognition norms to include women as full members of society. The Black Lives Matter movement seeks not only the end of violence against blacks but also

[1] Axel Honneth, *The Struggle for Recognition: The Moral Grammar of Social Conflicts* (London: Polity, 2003), 131.

recognition as human beings. The movement's name itself is an explicit appeal to recognition: They are seeking recognition that their lives also matter.

Recognition has been cast by some, most notably Charles Taylor and Honneth, as public political struggles between social groups, but recognition is also at the heart of interpersonal relations. Mutual recognition enables friendship, romantic partnerships, and other relations of care, but the guiding norms of recognition also facilitate less-personal relations by socializing us into our culture's normative expectations for individuals' roles and behaviors. The importance of recognition in individuals' lives and in social justice movements makes it a vital element in social and critical theory. One of my main tasks in this book is to illuminate the foundational importance of interpersonal recognition in struggles for recognition.

This study will begin with Axel Honneth, harvesting his insights to craft a foundation for understanding injustice and struggles against it. This study also builds on that foundation and goes beyond Honneth's conceptualizations. It opens up new possibilities for critical theory by focusing on the vital social roles served by intersubjective recognition. A number of excellent scholars have put forward improvements to Honneth's conceptualizations, and this study seeks to advance the study of recognition a step or two further with some friendly amendments and corrections to Honneth's work. My goal is to enhance the understanding of recognition and misrecognition so they are more useful in diagnosing and correcting social injustices. To do this, we need to build on Honneth's ideas and go beyond the shortcomings of those ideas to craft a new critical theory of interpersonal relations.

Perhaps Honneth's clearest summary of his project is this:

> Essentially, my idea amounts to the hypothesis that all social integration depends on reliable forms of mutual recognition, whose insufficiencies and deficits are always tied to feelings of misrecognition, which, in turn, can be regarded as the engine of social change.[2]

Honneth has attempted to show that subjects' experiences of misrecognition cause moral injuries, a psychological suffering that leads to feelings of moral indignation over having their intuitive notions of justice violated. Moral feelings of indignation are, Honneth claims, the motives for social resistance and rebellion that contribute to social change and moral progress.[3] Honneth therefore calls for struggles for recognition to be the guiding thread of critical theory.[4] In his oeuvre, he has developed a critical theory linking subjective moral experiences of suffering, intersubjectivity, and normative intent that attempts to avoid structuralism and totalizing analysis.

By "recognition" Honneth refers to "attitudes and practices by which individuals or social groups are affirmed in certain of their qualities."[5] There are two keys to Honneth's concept of recognition. The first is that individuals are socialized into a lifeworld of recognition norms that denote what behaviors and contributions by human individuals should be honored and what behaviors should be censured. The second is that receiving recognition on the basis of these norms enables an individual to develop a positive relation-to-self, his or her sense of place in society, and most importantly his or her autonomy to be able to determine and realize his or her own desires and intentions freely. Thus, individuals desire and need to both receive and give recognition to achieve their ends in society. For Honneth, justice is linked very closely to how, and as what, subjects mutually recognize each other and to what extent society's relations of recognition support intersubjective relationships of mutual respect[6] and grant all members of society the opportunity to participate in institutions of recognition.[7] Thus, Honneth's view of justice extends beyond the

---

[2] Axel Honneth and Nancy Fraser, *Redistribution or Recognition? A Political-Philosophical Exchange* (London: Verso, 2003), 245.

[3] Honneth, *The Struggle for Recognition*, 131-139, 161-163. Axel Honneth, *Disrespect* (Cambridge, UK: Polity, 2007), 71.

[4] Honneth, *The Struggle for Recognition*, 144.

[5] Axel Honneth, "Grounding Recognition: A Rejoinder to Critical Questions." *Inquiry: An Interdisciplinary Journal of Philosophy*, 45 (4), 2002, 505.

[6] Honneth, *Disrespect*, 71, 130.

[7] Axel Honneth, *The I in We*, trans. Joseph Ganahl (Cambridge, UK: Polity,

distribution of labor and the distribution of resources while including them in the quality of social relations and the personal integrity of all members of society.[8]

A number of philosophers have criticized the concept of recognition in general and specifically Honneth's use of it in social theory. To mention just a few: Nancy Fraser agrees with Honneth that recognition is central to critical theory but says Honneth has a monistic framework in which a properly differentiated account of recognition is all that is required for critical theory. She further charges that

> Honneth overextends the category of recognition to the point that it loses its critical force. Inflating that concept beyond all recognition, he transforms a limited but precise instrument of social criticism into a bloated and blunted catchall that fails to rise to the challenges of our time.[9]

Lois McNay accuses recognition theory of binding agency too tightly to identity and relying on a reductive notion of power that neglects how social structures outside intersubjective interactions condition human experience.[10] Danielle Petherbridge similarly argues that Honneth attempts to transform Foucault's notion of power/struggle into a concept of recognition/struggle but that this move fails largely because he does not include an adequate account of power in his recognition theory.[11] Patchen Markell criticizes recognition as an impossible and incoherent idea requiring a world of mutual transparency and invulnerable identities in which struggles for recognition are part of the problem rather than the solution of identity-based injustice.[12]

2012), 61.

[8] Fraser and Honneth, 177-183.

[9] Fraser and Honneth, 201.

[10] Lois McNay, *Against Recognition* (Cambridge: Polity Press, 2008).

[11] Danielle Petherbridge, *The Critical Theory of Axel Honneth* (Plymouth, UK: Lexington Books, 2013), 92-93.

[12] Patchen Markell, *Bound by Recognition* (Princeton, NJ: Princeton University Press, 2003).

Some of these critiques of recognition have merit, and I agree there are flaws in Honneth's account; however, I still believe recognition is a highly useful concept if we can address its shortcomings. This study will amend recognition theory and answer some of its shortcomings through an analysis and rethinking of two important concepts: misrecognition and struggles for recognition. I believe that Honneth is correct about the importance of recognition in individuals' lives, how the denial of recognition can motivate social resistance, and how that resistance can lead to normative change. I will show how Honneth's conceptualizations of misrecognition and struggles for recognition are too general and therefore lack sufficient detail and clarity to explain social injustices and individuals' responses' to injustices. Despite the shortcomings in Honneth's recognition theory, his voluminous writings provide us with a wealth of detail and insights on which I wish to build in directions that Honneth did not travel, attempting to illuminate how individuals experience recognition and misrecognition and how they struggle for recognition and justice.

There are a number of aspects of Honneth's large volume of work that I am not addressing in this book. I am not undertaking a genealogical study of Honneth's philosophy, an extensive reconstruction of it, or an analysis of his historical and macrosocial theories. I am also not engaging in meta-questions about critical or social theory. My aim is to explore a particular set of questions and problems arising from Honneth's work, attempting to solve them so as to provide a phenomenological foundation of misrecognition that can help shed light on the causes of injustice. I should also add that my focus is not on a "politics of recognition" or politics of misrecognition because I think that focusing on the experiences of individuals is the path to enhancing our understanding of social injustice. I will argue that thinking in terms of group identities is a contributor to misrecognition and injustice.

This book is composed of two stand-alone but connected parts. In Part One, I critique Honneth's account of misrecognition and provide an alternative view of misrecognition that replaces his account. First, I analyze ways in which Honneth's accounts of recognition and misrecognition are insufficient, especially in terms of misrecognition. I critique Honneth's argument for the separation of recognition into three modes—love, respect, and esteem/solidarity—and reveal problems with this division. Despite the internal logic of his typology, it does not help us to see clearly what is going on when individuals give or withhold recognition. His separation between legal respect as what unifies people under universal rights and social esteem as what differentiates people through distinctive traits does not dully consider the complexities and interconnections involved in legal and esteem recognitions. His restriction of love recognition to the family sphere fails to include the many forms and degrees that intimate relations can take and unduly separates it from solidarity. My analysis reveals that recognition can be described better as behaviors in which individuals and social institutions engage in varying degrees with recognition norms and with other individuals. I then reconstruct Honneth's account of misrecognition, showing that he presents misrecognition as the contrary of recognition, which I argue is lacking in sufficient complexity and detail to describe the phenomena of misrecognition and individuals' experiences of it.

To build a more robust and fine-grained picture of misrecognition, I first critique Honneth's typology of misrecognition as the contrary of recognition. Honneth is correct to understand that recognition is guided by social norms; however, it is not the case that misrecognition is always a violation of recognition norms. The social norms themselves may be at fault either in being intrinsically biased against some members of society or in inadequately reflecting individuals' attributes and needs. Also, if Honneth's typology of recognition is inadequately complex and fine-grained to describe recognition relations, then presenting misrecognition as the contrary of recognition within that typology will also be inadequately complex and fine-grained to describe the ways in which recognition relations can go wrong.

To address these concerns, I develop a multidimensional view of misrecognition that replaces Honneth's binary account of misrecognition as the contrary to recognition without replacing Honneth's conceptions of the value of recognition. The dimensions I identify are the levels of engagement with recognition norms, with other individuals, and with action. The multidimensional characterization of misrecognition describes it as a varied phenomenon that is more than the contrary of recognition. Disengagement from social norms is misrecognition, but I identify forms of engagement with social norms that also lead to misrecognition and result in domination and oppression. One example is what I call "pathological recognition" in which the recognition norms are intrinsically biased and, though appearing to recognize individuals positively, in practice reduce those individuals' social status and autonomy. "Normative discrimination" provides another example, denoting the engagement with a recognition order that designates social groups as having particular traits that should be negatively recognized. Lack of engagement with individuals includes a quotidian forgetfulness of others or deliberate and selective disengagement from others all of which result in misrecognition. I also identify ways that engagement with individuals can result in misrecognition. The action dimension of engagement in misrecognition is the level of action of the engagement with or disengagement from norms and/or other individuals. This multidimensional view allows for a more robust and fine-grained account of what goes wrong in recognition relations leading to misrecognition and injustice. By replacing Honneth's overly simplified account of misrecognition with a more robust, multidimensional account, we can address one weakness in recognition theory and better equip it to address its practical aims of diagnosing injustice.

One complaint about the concept of recognition is that it is limiting and inflexible and maintains, if not creates, injustice and oppression. If recognition means conformity to homogeneity and ideological power structures, then recognition is at best problematic. It is true that some forms of forced conformity are labeled "recognition" by both defenders and critics of recognition, but I will argue that these forms of "recognition" are distortions of recognition that are, in practice, pathological. This identification shows that much of the criticism of recognition is directed at pathological forms of recognition and, therefore, is actually criticizing injustices that are *mis*recognitions, for which healthy mutual recognition is the remedy. Pathological forms of recognition assume that identity is solely group oriented. As I will show, this assumption of group identity is inherently a misrecognition of individuals that leads to injustice.

The injustices of the oppression of women, racial minorities, and workers are better understood, I argue, through the multidimensional view of misrecognition, which sees misrecognition behaviors along dimensions of engagement with norms, engagement with other individuals, and engagement with action. For example, within institutional racism are varieties of misrecognition behaviors and associated varieties of injustices suffered by marginalized groups that are revealed by applying the multidimensional view to individual behaviors. The multidimensional view of misrecognition opens up the complexities of social behaviors by appreciating the conflicts between recognition demands that individuals face and the ways social norms and individual involvements turn into behaviors of injustice.

Part Two of this book is a critical examination of Honneth's account of struggles for recognition—the emancipation from injustice. Honneth sees struggles for recognition as the driving force for historical change. I accept Honneth's statement of the importance to critical theory of struggles for recognition, but if struggles for recognition are to be the "guiding thread of critical theory,"[13] then he needs a fuller account of what is involved in struggles for recognition. To understand better how oppression and other injustices are resisted, and why often they are not, we need a revised account of struggles for recognition and their preconditions that correct some omissions in Honneth's account.

My critique of Honneth's account of struggles for recognition identifies two problems: His premise that emotional experiences of misrecognition motivate struggles for recognition is contradictory without an account of individual agency, and his theoretical reliance on political resistance movements leaves out other paths that responses to injustice can take. I propose the following solutions to these two problems: First, Honneth claims that experiences of injustice will motivate individuals to a

[13] Honneth, *The Struggle for Recognition*, 144.

struggle for recognition, but how can an individual, being damaged by misrecognition and lacking the recognition that Honneth says is necessary for one to be autonomous, have the capacity to struggle for recognition? To solve this dilemma, we need to include some conception of individual agency and responsibility in the undertaking of struggles for recognition. I incorporate the response model of recognition, Christine Korsgaard's concept of self-constitution,[14] McNay's interpretation of habitus,[15] and insights from several other philosophers to give us a conceptual basis for how an individual could develop the oppositional consciousness to respond to experiences of suffering subjectively with a struggle for recognition within a cultural power structure. The ideas that individuals' actions contribute to the constitution of their practical identities—composed of their roles, relationships, and membership in social groups—and that they can act out of that sense of self despite the misrecognition they receive from others, helps resolve the agency dilemma of how an individual undertakes a struggle for recognition.

Second, I take issue with the tendency in recognition theory, not just in Honneth, to consider struggles for recognition predominantly as collective political movements for legal justice. I argue that Honneth incorrectly collapses interpretive structures that inform individuals that they are being treated unjustly with collective political movements against injustice. Although political struggles for recognition are the most accessible to social theory, considering only or predominantly such collective movements creates a lacuna that hides other forms and aspects of struggles for recognition. Most specifically, this theoretical view leaves out the very personal aspects that we can find in struggles for recognition. By decentralizing struggles for recognition from collective political movements and adding the concept of individual agency, we can craft a more robust picture of struggles for recognition.

---

[14] Korsgaard, Christine M., *Self-Constitution: Agency, Identity, and Integrity* (Oxford, UK: Oxford University Press, 2009), Kindle locations 375-377.

[15] McNay, *Against Recognition.*

Instead of connecting struggles for recognition with political resistance movements as Honneth does, I argue there are two types of struggles for recognition:

- Affirmational: The ongoing efforts of individuals to seek recognition that constructs and affirms their personal identities and their place in society. Affirmational struggles attempt to fulfill human needs that are present prior to any particular social interaction and are the constant general condition of being a social individual.
- Transformational: Responses to circumstances or instances of misrecognition that seek to rectify perceived injustices and restore healthy recognition relations. Transformational struggles attempt to fulfill needs caused by feelings of being misrecognized.

The familiarity of continually needing to affirm one's identity and social relations is a resource on which individuals can draw in engaging in transformational struggles against injustice. Placing these struggles in the context of social power relations and the multidimensional view of misrecognition clarifies how individuals respond to misrecognition with varying struggles for recognition.

At the heart of the struggle for recognition is a struggle for authority, Cillian McBride observes[16]—a struggle over the authority and power to interpret and apply recognition norms. Struggles for power and authority over recognition norms and relations play out not only between social institutions and cultural groups but also intersubjectively among individuals and factor heavily in all interpersonal relations, including with whom we choose to have relationships. This insight is central to understanding how any individual responds to experiences of misrecognition—whether to acquiesce, withdraw, or undertake a transformational struggle. Individuals need an interpretive structure to understand the moral content of their experiences and what options of response are available to them. However, struggles for recognition are not

[16] Cillian McBride, *Recognition* (Cambridge, UK: Polity Press, 2013), 136, 152cf.

limited to collective political struggles for legal rights or social esteem; they include struggles over identity, which, though they have personal, social, and political dimensions, are always struggles undertaken by individuals in the service of their own individual concerns. This understanding amends Honneth's account by opening up other phenomena of individual responses to injustice. We can then see that some individuals form and join subcultures to increase potential recognition relations, perhaps separating from others including through subcultural antagonism toward others and the self-recognition that I call "manufactured recognition."

Finally, I deal with another gap in Honneth's theory (and social theory in general): the question of why, if experiencing misrecognition is a prerequisite for struggles for recognition, then how is it that anyone not so injured can join in solidarity with those who have been injured by misrecognition? Why did white people join the American civil rights movement; why do heterosexuals join same-sex marriage legalization movements; and so on? The answer to this gap is to understand that love recognition can extend beyond the family sphere where Honneth places it and that compassion for others can join with a rational understanding that others are being misrecognized. Our individual agency enables us to join others' struggles for recognition, acts that are movements of recognizing other individuals and their transformational struggles as people and causes worth our time and energy.

My expanded view of struggles for recognition takes it beyond identity politics and group political conflicts into everyday social experiences, expanding Honneth's account. Collective social movements and the social changes they engender are best seen as arising from the dynamic social interactions among individuals who, in the context of their own lives, take action. Actions against injustice do not have to be political, organized collective action, and this is significant for social and political philosophy. The insights into struggles for recognition, combined with the multidimensional view of misrecognition, contribute to social theory with a set of conceptual tools that strengthen our understandings of how and why individuals contribute to injustices and respond to injustices. It also casts new light on political movements, social conflicts, and the dynamics of interpersonal relations.

Part One: Rethinking Recognition and Misrecognition

We cannot make sense of social conflicts, and the way our embeddedness in the social world gives rise to moral and ethical dilemmas, without understanding the way that our sensitivity to recognition orients us in the world.

- Cillian McBride[17]

Placing recognition and struggles for recognition at the center of critical theory is, I believe, the best approach, but Honneth's functionalist account of recognition does not capture the full picture of the complexities of recognition. Recognition is an interpersonal social relation, and each individual is embedded in a very complex set of recognition relations that are as varied as the individuals involved in them. I argue that Honneth's theory of recognition is fundamentally correct but lacks sufficient complexity for it to explain the moral experiences of individuals. Honneth's recognition theory provides insights into how individuals are socialized and how responses to injustice lead to social change. However, Honneth lacks a robust account of how the individual experiences and contributes to recognition and misrecognition. This lack is particularly problematic for Honneth given the importance of misrecognition in his account of social struggles. We need a more robust and fine-grained account of recognition relations and what goes wrong in them. To craft such an account, I will first argue for the need to go beyond Honneth's tripartite typology of recognition and then move to the argument for the need to go beyond Honneth's view that misrecognition is the contrary of recognition.

[17] McBride, 8.

1.1 - Rethinking Honneth's Hegelian Tripartite Structure of Recognition

Contrary to Honneth's Hegelian typology, recognition is not simply a matter of separate social spheres of family, state, and civil society but of different types of intersubjective relations. My argument will proceed as follows. First, I establish some essentials of Honneth's account of recognition demonstrating his Hegelian tripartite structure of recognition. I do not dispute that there is a difference between legal recognition and esteem recognition but that one of Honneth's descriptions of the difference—that legal recognition unifies subjects under general norms while esteem recognition differentiates subjects on the basis of a graduated appraisal of particular traits and contributions—is not entirely accurate. Showing that both legal recognition and esteem recognition involve both inclusion and exclusion of individuals, I argue that that something additional is at work in both modes of recognition than what Honneth's typology delineates. I then explore the problems with both Honneth's account of love recognition in the family sphere, and his account of solidarity, which he places in the same civil sphere as he places esteem and work and economic activity. I argue that Honneth's portrayal of solidarity as public and love as private and that they are different modes of recognition introduces unnecessary confusion over affectional bonds such as friendships that obscures some of the ways in which individuals receive self-esteem. From the above, I argue that recognition can be understood as two types of engagements—engagement with norms and engagement with individuals, which manifest in varying ways, including the inclusion and exclusion of others. Using the two engagements, we can unpack what is going on in recognition relations and see that the operative question in recognition is the recognition relations involved and the object of recognition behavior rather than how the recognition can theoretically be mapped to a social sphere. My argument is not that Honneth is incorrect but that increased focus on the aspect of the object of engagement in recognition will improve our understanding of recognition relations and how they can go wrong.

Honneth adopts the concept of recognition from Hegel and states that his intention is to employ "Hegel's model of recognition as the key to specifying the universal conditions under which human beings can form an identity," conceptualizing Hegel's structures of mutual recognition as preconditions for self-realization and as practical conditions for the development of a positive relation-to-self.[18] By "recognition" Honneth refers to "attitudes and practices by which individuals or social groups are affirmed in certain of their qualities."[19] Honneth refers to recognition "in its most elementary form" as the care we take to maintain a fluent interaction with our surroundings with the character of an affirmative, existentially colored style of caring comportment.[20]

Honneth accepts Hegel's position that recognition is essential for providing the conditions under which human individuals can form an identity and a positive relation-to-self.[21] Within Honneth's discussion of recognition, we can trace a path of human development, which, generally stated, posits that through receiving recognition, an individual becomes socialized to the norms of his or her community, comes to realize what capabilities and possibilities he or she has within society, and through this process of socialization into recognition relationships individuals become self-realizing and autonomous. For individuals to be self-realizing, certain practices of mutual recognition must exist; a special type of normative status must be ascribed to individuals; and, finally, a specific form of individual relation-to-self must be developed.[22]

Honneth describes recognition as a socializing movement.[23] Honneth states that

---

[18] Honneth, "Grounding Recognition," 500.

[19] Honneth, "Grounding Recognition," 505.

[20] Axel Honneth, *Reification: A New Look at an Old Idea* (Oxford, UK: Oxford University Press, 2008), 37.

[21] Honneth, "Grounding Recognition," 500.

[22] Axel Honneth, *Freedom's Right*, trans. Joseph Ganahl (Cambridge, UK: Polity, 2013), 105.

[23] Honneth, *The Struggle for Recognition*, 19.

> individuals can become members of society only by developing, via the experience of mutual recognition, an awareness of how rights and duties are reciprocally distributed in the context of particular tasks.[24]

Mutual recognition socially integrates subjects into society's normative expectations of them and what they can reasonably expect of others. We learn to recognize others by internalizing normative attitudes by which we can know ourselves to be socially accepted members of the social lifeworld.[25] The socialization process is ordered by recognition norms:

> Individuals learn in the process of their socialization to internalize culturally specific norms of recognition … These kinds of internalized norms are what regulate how subjects deal with each other legitimately in various social relationships. They regulate what kind of expectations I can have of others, what duties I have toward them and what kind of behavior I can count on from them.[26]

By showing us what behaviors and values we should internalize, recognition helps us to orient ourselves in the social world and helps us learn how to be successful in our social endeavors.

To describe the normative framework of recognition, Honneth turns to Hegel's tripartite structure of the social world. Hegel saw society divided into the institutional complexes of family, civil society, and the state. Honneth says that Hegel has indicated

> for each of these three institutional complexes, how they: (a) contribute to the formation of the subjective capacities that subjects, as members of society, require for actualizing all of their various freedoms; (b) are capable of providing the social roles and responsibilities that can serve subjects as rational goals for their self-

[24] Honneth, "Grounding Recognition," 501.

[25] Honneth, *The Struggle for Recognition*, 78. Also, Honneth, *The Struggle for Recognition*, 68, and Honneth, *Freedom's Right*, 35.

[26] Honneth, *Reification*, 153.

> actualization; and finally (c) provide a necessary and, taken altogether, sufficient contribution to preserving the 'material' conditions upon which the reproduction of modern societies depend.[27]

Hegel's structure of ethical life provides Honneth with an account of normative authority that gives subjects their practical identities, their place in society, and their ethical duties that enable them to attain individual autonomy within the objective ethical order. Honneth argues that the three institutional complexes of family, civil society, and the state must form both subsystems of societal reproduction and stations of individual self-actualization.[28] Honneth's move extends Hegel's tripartite structure of ethical life into a tripartite structure of the individual human being. Honneth holds that human beings have three practical relations-to-self related to certain capabilities that they possess. Each practical relation-to-self is developed in relationships in which one is affirmed or recognized by others according to distinct types of recognition. Thus, there are three forms of recognition that correspond to Hegel's three social spheres—"three forms of practical attitudes, each reflecting the primary aim of a certain affirmation of the other."[29] These three forms he defines as: "Love, (the central idea of intimate relationships), the equality principle (the norm of legal relations), and the achievement principle (the standard of social hierarchy)."[30] Honneth usually refers to these modes of recognition as "love," "respect," and "esteem," respectively. Honneth sees recognition processes as unfolding within the tripartite structure of society developed by Hegel.

Honneth assumes that the internal tripartite structure of three differentiated aspects of self-relation mirrors the tripartite structure of society.[31] Within the subject, he theorizes that there is a genetically primary level of self-relation in which a subject conceives of its needs and

---

[27] Honneth, *The I in We*, 30.
[28] Honneth, *The I in We*, 29.
[29] Honneth, "Grounding Recognition," 506.
[30] Fraser and Honneth, 143.
[31] Honneth, *Disrespect*, 135.

desires as an expressible part of its own person. This valuing of one's needs he calls "self-confidence," and it is a prerequisite for the subject to develop further through the other levels of self-relation. The second level is where a subject relates to itself as a morally accountable subject and learns the value of its own moral judgment, a valuing he calls "self-respect." The third level is where a subject relates to itself as having valuable capabilities, which he calls "self-worth." These three stages he sees as "a sequence of necessary presuppositions under normal conditions" that forms a subject's self-relation.[32] By "self-relation" or "relation-to-self," Honneth means "the consciousness or feeling that a person has of him or herself with regard to the capabilities and rights he or she enjoys."[33] Recognition in each of the three spheres of recognition map to the three practical relations-to-self: the family to self-confidence, the state to self-respect, and civil society to self-esteem. Using this mapping, Honneth believes we can systematically consider forms of misrecognition as the negative equivalents of the corresponding forms of recognition, which allows us to identify the social experiences that would generate the pressures that could motivate struggles for recognition in the social process.[34]

Honneth's reasoning for connections between the subject's internal structure and society's structure makes sense. As McBride observes, if the self is socially extended, then it has multiple layers each entailing its own set of relations. There is the external relationship we have with others and the internal relationship we have with ourselves, and Honneth believes that the external relationship determines the nature of the internal relationship.[35] Receiving recognition in all three forms of social relations—affectionate care, legal recognition, and social esteem—is necessary for human subjects to acquire undistorted and positive relations-to-self. Self-confidence that one's needs and desires have value can only come, Honneth says, from recognition in the form of unconditional care, which

---

[32] Honneth, *Disrespect*, 136.
[33] Honneth, *Disrespect*, 135-136.
[34] Honneth, *The Struggle for Recognition*, 93, 143.
[35] McBride, 12.

legitimately can be expected only from tight mutual bonds of family. Self-worth legitimately can be expected to develop only through understanding oneself as valuable within a shared normative interpretive structure found in concrete communities. Self-respect, however, because it is tied to legal recognition of one's universal rights, is a categorical obligation in all levels of interaction.[36] Honneth holds that particular modes of recognition (love, respect, esteem) are structured by the normative content of particular spheres of recognition, and, therefore, particular modes of recognition can come only from their related sphere of recognition through its particular form of social relation. The typology set down by Honneth is that there are three social spheres that have their respective recognition norms and that there are social institutions that structure and maintain these norms. If the social institutions are healthy, then subjects will receive the recognition they require for self-realization, but if the social institutions are pathological, then subjects will be unable to achieve self-realization.

Combining his descriptions of recognition across his works, I demonstrate Honneth's tripartite structure of recognition as shown in Table 1.

[36] Honneth, *Disrespect*, 139.

Table 1 - Honneth's topology of recognition

Spheres of Recognition (D 131-133)[37] (RR 138-142)	Forms of Social Relations (RR 138-142)	Modes of Recognition (GR 501, 506) (RR 143) (SR 129)	What Is Recognized as Valuable (D 138-139)	Practical Relation-to-Self (D 138-139) (RR 138-142) (SR 129)
Family - intimate relationships	Intimate relationships	Love	Individual needs and particularities	Self-confidence: "My individual needs and desires are of unique value."
The state - legal	Legal and political relations	Respect/equal rights	Moral agency and equality	Self-respect: "My moral accountability and authority is equal to others'."
Civil society - economic	Loose-knit social relations within civil society	Esteem/solidarity	Productive capacities and achievements	Self-esteem: "My capabilities are of concrete value to the community."

Distinguishing his typology from Hegel's, Honneth portrays Hegel's typology of recognition spheres as being an "institutionalist way of thinking"[38] that interprets social institutions too concretely as legally constituted spheres. Honneth criticizes Hegel's understanding of ethical life as falling entirely under the organizational and legislative authority of the modern state whose central institutions represent the only areas of

[37] Parenthetical references are to what I deem to be Honneth's clearest statements of the particular concepts, not the only place he references them. GR="Grounding Recognition," RR=*Redistribution or Recognition?* D=*Disrespect,* SR=*Struggle for Recognition.*

[38] Fraser and Honneth, 145-146.

practice in which subjects can receive the recognition and education that enables their self-realization. Instead of Hegel's insistence that the state, though only the third sphere of ethical life, is also the organizational framework for family and civil society, Honneth sees society as a complex of spheres of recognition offering various forms of social institutionalization.[39] Love, rights, and solidarity are three modes of recognition that set down the formal structural requirements for communicative interaction within which human beings can feel assured of their dignity and integrity. Honneth stresses that he does not go so far as to say that these requirements delineate the particular institutional manifestations in which these modes of recognition may be finalized, but he does specify that they compose "the moral infrastructures which must belong to a social lifeworld if it is to be able to protect its members."[40] So, although Honneth thinks there is variation in the institutional manifestations of the tripartite moral structure, he thinks the structure itself is necessary for the successful functioning of a society. This thought underlies much of his work.

By shifting from Hegel's conception of three concrete social institutions to three less concrete principles of reciprocal recognition, Honneth can show, whereas Hegel cannot, how within the family there is both love and legal recognition, which he says are two types of recognition that should be combined to protect personal integrity. However, he warns against the subordination of familial recognition to the sphere of legal recognition. "If [legal] recognition vanishes then the autonomy of individual family members is threatened; if [care] recognition evaporates, the emotional bond within the family will be destroyed."[41] He illustrates this tension in his comments on the film *Kramer vs. Kramer*.[42] Honneth

---

[39] Axel Honneth, *The Pathologies of Individual Freedom*, trans. Lasislaus Löb (Princeton, NJ: Princeton University Press, 2001), 57, 69-72.

[40] Axel Honneth, *The Fragmented World of the Social*, ed. Charles W. Wright (Albany, NY: State University of New York Press, 1995), 256. See also Honneth's discussion in *Redistribution or Recognition?*, 145-147, where he details the difference he sees between institutional complexes and spheres of recognition.

[41] Honneth, *Disrespect*, 155-156.

says that the main characters, as they go through a bitter divorce and custody battle, show in their actions the social pathology of the lifeworld being subordinated under the medium of law. The father especially, Honneth says, calculates his actions toward his child in terms of his legal status in the custody battle. The film's audience is brought to question whether the father's actions are expressions of true feelings or attempts to conform to legal demands. The parents are compelled by the same law that they invoke to protect their interests to block out their lifeworld of caring family communication and dependencies. Honneth later puts this distinction in harsher terms: "Whoever exercises the individual right to divorce as a means of separating from one's spouse has destroyed any possibility of commonly discussing their separate life paths in the future in light of their shared experiences."[43] To this overly literal interpretation of the division between forms of social relations, I say, from my experiences as a divorced person, this seems harsh and misses the possible desire to separate oneself from a nonbeneficial relationship whose shared experiences are what impedes one's future life path. It is possible that divorce, by releasing the psychological clinging to shared experiences, is the healthy life path for both involved. Honneth's larger point remains, though, when he warns that intrusion of the legal into intimate relationships is a sign of a social pathology. Family members must be recognized as being subjects with universal rights, but in general, he is concerned that the clinging to legal rights is a focus on escaping from communicative obligations. Family members can hide behind the juridical to avoid their other obligations, abandoning existing attachments and replacing communicative obligations with strategic attitudes as soon as legal conflicts threaten.[44]

Because he holds that the subject's relations-to-self mirror the social spheres, Honneth follows Hegel's notion of three degrees in the realization of freedom. First, a subject must experience the recognition of love and

---

[42] Honneth, *Freedom's Right*, 90-91.
[43] Honneth, *The I in We*, 85.
[44] Honneth, *The I in We*, 91-92, 94.

develop self-confidence, and only then can the subject move on to the second stage of experiencing legal recognition and developing individual self-determination. Finally, the freedom of personal self-realization arises from receiving recognition from the community.[45] The subject's freedom is therefore not measured according to the distance the subject can establish between itself and the cultural lifeworld, but according to the degree of recognition it can find in its social environment for its freely chosen goals. Instead of being defined by the scale of distance from all normative bonds, an increase in personal individuality is determined by the degree to which individual differences are communicatively granted by society. Honneth asserts that built into each sphere of recognition are publicly justified normative standards for interaction that shape subjective claims for recognition within communicative relations.[46] Thus, for Honneth, the three spheres of recognition are learned in stages in a formative process of ethical life. The subject is socialized into each sphere, confirmed as a member of society, and assimilated into its communal ethical life. Honneth says that "what is demanded or expected in terms of moral action relates to a circle of subjects whose size varies with the type of recognition at hand."[47] This reference to size relates to Honneth's position that recognition is first learned within the family sphere and that other relations of recognition are "merely filled out at later stages through the acquisition of conceptions about the reciprocal ascription of abilities and rights."[48] The family sphere being the social sphere of smallest scope and the economic and legal spheres being larger in scope, it seems that Honneth believes that if there is love recognition within the family sphere, then other aspects of a subject's social relations eventually and inevitably fall into place.

---

[45] Honneth, *The Fragmented World of the Social*, 226-227.

[46] Fraser and Honneth, 145.

[47] Honneth, *Disrespect*, 139. See also, Honneth, *The Fragmented World of the Social*, 226-227.

[48] Axel Honneth, "Rejoinder," in *Axel Honneth: Critical Essays,* ed. Danielle Petherbridge (Leiden: Brill, 2011), 392. This statement from 2011 shows that Honneth's notion is not limited to his earlier work.

The idea that society and ethical life can be divided into three social spheres is a constant throughout Honneth's work, including his more recent book *Freedom's Right* in which he explores three spheres of social freedom—the personal, the markets, and the public political. Honneth's modes of recognition formally track to his institutional spheres of recognition—the personal, the civil/economic, and the legal—that correspond to Hegel's stages of social development. The question is this: Is recognition's socialization process best described in terms of three social spheres? There are two issues here: How do we describe the sources of recognition behaviors, and how do we describe how recognition behaviors affect individuals? When we consider a particular recognition behavior, does mapping the behavior onto the legal, the civil, and the family spheres of recognition sufficiently illuminate what is going on?

To address these questions, we need to be clear on the concept of what being recognized means and then flesh out what it means in terms of sources and effects of recognition. The first step is to address recognition in terms of communities. Honneth defines recognition in terms of one being socially recognized as a member of a community. Human individuals live within the context of their community. They are not isolated subjects. Individuals become autonomous and self-realizing within a community and because of a community. Mutual recognition affirms individuals who have incorporated society's values into their lives and maintains their inclusion in the community. Individuals learn to perceive in other individuals qualities to which they can respond with the proper recognitional behavior appropriate to their relationships with each person. Looked at in this way, acts of recognition are acts learned through socialization that demonstrate to others the individual's integration into the social lifeworld and enables the individual to see him- or herself as a member of any human community.[49] Social integration is a process of inclusion through stable forms of recognition. One is recognized as a member of the community insofar as one recognizes the other members.

---

[49] Honneth, *Disrespect*, 130.

Honneth defines two communities: political communities and value communities. A political community is composed of legal subjects who are bearers of legal rights and duties that are distributed by their community.[50] In the political community that is the universalizable interests of all members of the society, one can experience legal recognition and form self-respect. In the value community that is the cultural self-understanding and value convictions of a society, one can experience esteem recognition and form self-esteem.[51] This conception links the political community with the legal sphere of recognition and the value community with the civil society sphere of recognition, with the corresponding forms of social relations and modes of recognition.

That Honneth discusses both communities as institutional macrosocial spheres limits the explanatory power of his theory. What is a community? That was a much simpler question to answer in Hegel's time before social, political, and technological changes altered the structures of the family, social democracy, and culture. Ease of communication and travel, the emergence of mass media and more recently social media, increased mobility and diversity, and various other changes have transformed many aspects of human society. Individuals are socialized by their community into their community, but community is now more varied than what is implied by the Hegelian three social spheres that Honneth adopts. Partly as a result of this increased social complexity, the mutual influences between what Honneth calls the legal and value communities are deeper than he accounts for. A deeper analysis is required to understand recognition in our contemporary world.

A deeper analysis of Honneth's connection between his spheres of recognition and the practical relations-to-self shows that his tripartite structure misses several aspects of human social experience, subsuming them under an overly static and monolithic[52] theoretical overlay. A

---

[50] Honneth, *The Struggle for Recognition*, 109.
[51] Honneth, *The Struggle for Recognition*, 87, 90, 122.
[52] Georg W. Bertram and Robin Celikates. "Towards a Conflict Theory of Recognition," *European Journal of Philosophy* 23 (4), 2013, 5.

phenomenological look at recognition shows a more complex picture. Lines dividing the three spheres are more permeable than Honneth seems to credit. My contention is that, in terms of recognition, the intended object of recognition behavior is more salient than the social sphere in which the recognition behavior occurs. To explain this requires an analysis of the difference between legal recognition and esteem recognition.

Honneth's thinking in defending the distinction between legal respect and social esteem is that respect recognition is the empirical application of general norms, whereas esteem recognition is the graduated appraisal of particular traits and contributions as distinct from those of others. In the former, one is recognized as sharing a set of qualities with all other members of one's community[53]; in the latter, one is recognized as being distinct—individuated—from other members of the community.[54] The idea of equal rights entails that all subjects share certain universal human qualities and thus should be granted equal rights with all other members of society.[55] Accordingly, subjects acquire legal rights and develop self-respect by being recognized as possessing the same legal rights and moral accountability as others. Within legal recognition, positive qualities have a universal sense—being a human being entitles one to human rights; being a citizen entitles one to citizenship rights. Political rights, even voting rights defined as one person, one vote, are not addressed to the individual as an individual, but to the citizen as a member of the democratic community of rights. Self-esteem is different for Honneth, involving a sense of what it is that makes one special and unique, and esteeming others involves seeing their unique traits and contributions. Subjects esteem each other as persons of unequal social standing based on hierarchically graded traits and contributions. Social esteem is directed at the particular qualities that characterize people in their personal differences. Thus, legal recognition unifies all individuals under legal norms, whereas esteem recognition differentiates individuals under esteem norms.[56] The

---

[53] Honneth, *The Struggle for Recognition*, 120.
[54] Honneth, *The Struggle for Recognition*, 113. Fraser and Honneth, 146-147.
[55] Fraser and Honneth, 142.
[56] Honneth, *The Struggle for Recognition*, 121-122.

distinction means, Honneth argues, that one can demand legal recognition as being treated uniformly, but one cannot demand esteem recognition because it must be earned by distinctive behavior.

The distinction between the universalizing of legal rights and the individuating of esteem is basically correct but is more complex than Honneth's typology delineates. Delving into this complexity shows that something additional is at work in both modes of recognition—legal respect and social esteem—that makes them more similar than the tripartite structure indicates. Looking first at the legal norms, we see that legal statutes are not always a practice of universalizing. This reminds us that justice is more than an adherence to legal norms, with important consequences for recognition and misrecognition.

Honneth's formula of universal legal respect recognition works only in an ideal society in which all human individuals are considered only under the homogeneity of high-minded concepts such as the Universal Declaration of Human Rights. Honneth would probably defend his view by pointing out that universal rights are a normative value to which society should aspire, made all the more important because society suffers legal inequality. I agree, but the point I seek to make is that as important as moral ideals are, rights themselves are not always unifying but are also often based on differentiating individuals, literally drawing a line between members and nonmembers of a formal community. To be included in any formally defined community is to be respected (in Honneth's legalistic meaning of the term) as a member of that community with all the spoken and unspoken rights and privileges that membership entails. I can demand the rights to which I am entitled as a member of a community, such as a trade union or an interest organization. We think of legal rights in the same way because legal rights are usually tied to citizenship, which is a membership in a political community. The rights of citizenship are denied to migrants who are not members of the political community. Legal recognition is universal only within a differentiated and bounded concept of community differentiated from noncommunity. The recognition of citizenship includes some individuals and excludes others.

There are also justifiable instances of legal differentiation—for example, the "reverse discrimination" of affirmative action. Treating minorities strictly under universal legal standards will not emancipate them from traditional patterns of discrimination. Legal programs sought to help blacks and women in the United States and Dalits and Adivasi in India who had long been legally excluded from equal opportunity in their societies.[57] Laws were passed requiring processes of admission to schools and hiring in jobs to differentiate deliberately on the basis of social class, race, and gender by setting quotas or targets of inclusion of members of oppressed groups. The aim was to emancipate oppressed people from past discrimination by enacting a targeted "reverse discrimination." Certainly, the ideal that underpins these laws is that of universal rights and equal opportunity, but the argument is that unifying the oppressed with the nonoppressed requires a period of differentiation. Some would argue that the programs have helped lower poverty and raise self-respect in oppressed groups, whereas others would argue that the programs only mask deeper social problems of discrimination or are themselves discriminatory by favoring social class, race, and gender over individual merit, creating special rights for certain social groups. In the argument over whether these legal programs are unifying or differentiating, the answer is, both, and this is why the debate is difficult to resolve.

The principles and practices of legal recognition are based on both inclusion and exclusion—legal recognition is universal only among those included by definition. This has implications for recognition and misrecognition and their effects on individuals who are not adequately included in Honneth's account. My contention is that legal recognition is the establishment of inclusion and exclusion of a right and that struggles for legal recognition are not simply appeals to universalizing of legal rights but are challenges to the existing formulation of inclusion and exclusion. For example, rights related to marriage include married couples

[57] A.R., "Affirmative Action: Indian Reservations." *The Economist*, June 29, 2013, accessed November 25, 2016, http://www.economist.com/blogs/banyan/2013/06/affirmative-action.

and exclude nonmarried people who are barred from being legally recognized in tax status, government benefits, and property rights. Only recently were same-sex couples included in marriage rights. The struggle for recognition of same-sex marriage reveals the dual nature of legal recognition as inclusion and exclusion and how appeals to recognition are often found on both sides of legal conflicts. We can legitimately say that legal recognition of marriage rights should be universally extended to all couples and should not be restricted to heterosexual couples. Nevertheless, the U.S. *Defense of Marriage Act* used the concept and language of legal recognition to include and exclude people under a universal definition of marriage. The law stated that "the word 'marriage' means only a legal union between one man and one woman as husband and wife, and the word 'spouse' refers only to a person of the opposite sex who is a husband or a wife."[58] Proponents of the law saw it as defending a universal moral norm of the legal recognition of marriage that same-sex marriages did not respect. Their idea of inclusion was defining marriage as "between one man and one woman" to the exclusion of "one man and one man" and "one woman and one woman." Proponents believed the morally justified social relation and structure of marriage was a heterosexual one and rejected the struggle for recognition by homosexual couples for marriage inclusion. Advocates of same-sex marriage opposed the *Defense of Marriage Act* saying that it wrongfully denied same-sex couples inclusion in the legal recognition of marriage and the rights conferred by it.

The social conflict over same-sex marriage saw both sides appealing to what they saw as universal recognition norms. The question I am raising is this: To what are both sides appealing when they are appealing to recognition? Both appeal to the value of a universal legal standard—what defines legal marriage. The question is not whether legal recognition should go to married couples (both sides agree with that concept) but who are to be included within the community of married people—a difference

---

[58] Defense of Marriage Act. United States Government Printing Office. September 21, 1996, accessed September 1, 2016, https://www.gpo.gov/fdsys/pkg/PLAW-104publ199/html/PLAW-104publ199.htm.

that is a question of value. The conflict is over whether same-sex couples are to be included in the value community of who is entitled to the legal status of marriage. The argument for legalizing same-sex marriage is that same-sex couples should be valued by society in the same way that heterosexual couples are. Those who believe same-sex couples should be excluded from legal marriage also hold homosexuals in poor esteem, and their exclusion of homosexuals extends beyond the legal sphere into civil society.

Questions about who is included in and excluded from legal communities also involve questions about who is included in and excluded from value communities, which Honneth associates with esteem. Esteem recognition is not wholly an issue of differentiation as Honneth's account implies but is another form of exclusion and inclusion. Even in a situation in which I am esteemed for my achievements, I am individuated on condition of my membership in a community. If I am esteemed for writing an exceptionally good PhD dissertation, that is possible only because I was recognized as a member of the community of postgraduate philosophy students at a university that is recognized as a member of accredited degree-granting institutions. My particular achievement was predicated on my sharing the same general characteristics as other PhD students and students within my discipline. Subjects can mutually esteem each other as individualized persons only when they share an orientation to the same values and goals, which Honneth acknowledges.[59]

This unifying framework of esteem is why I *can* demand social esteem in terms of equal treatment. I can say that anyone who achieves a particular goal should receive the honors connected with it. We are due that honor if we have achieved that goal, but that honor can be denied based on discrimination either against a group or against a particular individual, both of which would be misrecognitions. One has every right to demand some types of esteem on the basis of an appeal to collective norms similar to demands for legal recognition. Tenure and promotion are good examples. If one has fulfilled the practical requirements for tenure, then

---

[59] Honneth, *The Struggle for Recognition*, 121.

one can legitimately claim one is entitled to it. Esteem recognition or lack of it is an expression of inclusion similar to that of legal recognition, and inclusion into a community entitles one to any rights associated with community membership. A lecturer granted the esteem of tenure is being included in the community of tenured faculty at the same time he or she is being differentiated from those who lack the qualifications for tenure and are excluded from it. The rights of tenure now accrue to the professor as they apply universally to all members of the exclusive community.

That esteem is inclusion into a social status that is dependent on membership in a value community fits with Honneth's association of esteem with solidarity within the civil sphere. However, this association is problematic for Honneth as is his account of solidarity. Within Honneth's typology, esteem and solidarity fit within the civil sphere of recognition, which is a tenuous gap-filler between legal recognition and love recognition. Theoretically, this civil sphere serves two purposes: It gives subjects the possibility of relating to their concrete traits and contributions in ways that rights and love cannot, and it covers the social territory between the institutions of the state and the family. The problem for Honneth is that the he talks variously of "love, rights, and solidarity" and "love, rights, and esteem," but the relationship between esteem and solidarity is not firmly established. Honneth sees solidarity as subjects respecting and approving each other in each subject's particular qualities as interpreted by means of shared ideas of a good life,[60] which fits with the idea of differentiation in terms of inclusion into a value community.

Still, there seems to me to be a tension between esteem and solidarity. The idea of esteem is a distinguishing of an individual from the crowd of others. This is especially true of honors or awards, which are given to a select few to elevate how they are regarded by others. More general forms of esteem recognition still confer onto an individual a special status and privilege that is not universalizable to the general population. However, solidarity unifies individuals into a group identity and value community. Honneth gives the example of war creating "spontaneous relationships of

---

[60] Honneth, *The Struggle for Recognition*, 89, 91.

solidarity and sympathy across social boundaries."[61] True, war is an experience of great strain and sacrifice that brings people into common cause, but Honneth's contention that war creates a new constellation of values in which accomplishments are newly esteemed seems overly optimistic, especially in the long term. Women filled many work roles during World War II, but their contributions were not esteemed—at least compared with those of men, who remained differentiated with a higher social status—and women's lesser social position remained after the war. Also, the relationships of solidarity in war are more matters of survival or of hostility toward an enemy than an expansion of mutual recognition across social boundaries—solidarity in war is a violent form of inclusion and exclusion.

Honneth's hope for solidarity is that it is a form of recognition that can provide the communicative basis on which individuals who have been isolated by legal misrecognition can unite within the context of an ethical community.[62] He sees solidarity as a necessary prerequisite for shared activity in the public sphere; therefore, he counts as being morally just whatever is capable of promoting social attitudes of solidarity.[63] Mostly, Honneth associates solidarity with the civil sphere, though he also links it to the family sphere, referring to the family as a community of solidarity.[64] This certainly makes sense because any social unit regardless of size must interact in solidarity to maintain itself as a social unit. Honneth places family in a separate sphere that he refers to as either "family" or "intimate relations," the corresponding mode of recognition being love. To this third mode of recognition, love, I now turn.

Honneth defines love relationships as primary affectional relationships that "are constituted by strong emotional attachments among a small number of people."[65] This is a good definition with which to start, but Honneth focuses his inquiry, on the one hand, on the institution of the

---

[61] Honneth, *The Struggle for Recognition*, 128.
[62] Honneth, *The Struggle for Recognition*, 24.
[63] Honneth, *Freedom's Right*, 39.
[64] Honneth, *Freedom's Right*, 165.
[65] Honneth, *The Struggle for Recognition*, 95.

modern family as established by capitalist industrialization,[66] and, on the other hand, on object-relations theory of the mother-child relation.[67] This theoretical approach reduces family to a set of institutionalized relations of husband to wife and mother to child. Honneth sees the modern capitalist nuclear family as a private sphere separate from the rest of society and (at least ideally) independent of social and economic expectations. Honneth describes the family as having been "liberated" from the public sphere by changes in social and economic sphere starting in the 19th century.[68] Honneth's view of the family trends toward traditional gender roles. Honneth's typology theoretically takes an institutional view of family as child raising more than a view of family as relations of love.

Fraser has criticized Honneth for his view of family ideologically mystifying women's labor as "care."[69] Her point is well founded that what Honneth calls affective care in child-rearing is actually women's labor. Honneth constructs the family sphere as a private site of the marriage bond and child development,[70] which has the side effect of obscuring women's labor in the household. Honneth's views of the family sphere stem from the great emphasis he places on the importance of early childhood development, wherein young children develop from the continuity of parental care an understanding of their needs and their identity as a loved person. That loving relations help one develop a sense of self-confidence is uncontroversial, but Honneth adopts a version of psychoanalytic theory that all loving relationships are driven by the unconscious recollection of the first months of life and affectional bonds with one's mother or mother figure.[71] Honneth uses his interpretation of psychoanalytic theory to argue that the love relationship learned in childhood is a double recognition of mutual independence (self-assertion) and mutual care (symbiosis). He sees that double recognition as the genetically primary self-relation of self-

---

[66] Honneth, *Disrespect*, 144-146.
[67] Honneth, *The Struggle for Recognition*, 95-107.
[68] Honneth, *Disrespect*, 147.
[69] Fraser and Honneth, 220.
[70] Honneth, *The Struggle for Recognition*, 18. Honneth, *Disrespect,* 147.
[71] Honneth, *The Struggle for Recognition*, 98, 105.

confidence on which other practical relations-to-self and forms of recognition depend.[72] He further argues from this that the same logic of reciprocal recognition explains love relations and legal relations, claiming that the primary relations of love learned in early childhood form the basis of public ethical life,[73] which ties back to his Hegelian view of socialization in stages of recognition first learned within the family sphere.

However, and seemingly in contradiction, Honneth leaves love relations as separate from other human relations. Honneth sees the goals and desires of love relationships as "necessarily enclosed within the narrow boundaries of a primary relationship"[74] and thus unable to be extended to the wider social world. As we shall see later in chapter 2.4, this limitation on love creates problems for Honneth in viewing what motivates struggles for recognition. His attempts to place love relations within the Hegelian tripartite structure forces him to simplify the wide varieties of love theoretically to the primary bonds of the family, which he defends as a private sphere of affectionate bonds. This formulation sets up, as mentioned in his discussion of *Kramer vs. Kramer*, a moral conflict between the private family sphere and the public spheres of legal and esteem relations where two different sets of moral orientations collide.[75] If a legal moral orientation is imposed on a relationship of strong emotional attachments, it makes sense to describe those conflicts as being between the private family sphere and the public legal sphere; however, this is an external theoretical characterization that does not reflect how the individuals involved perceive and think about these conflicts. Through the rest of this book, I will discuss at length the importance of understanding the individual's perspectives and contributions to recognition relations.

Many conflicts within social interactions lie in tensions obscured by Honneth's separation of recognition relations into institutional spheres. We can reveal these other tensions through understanding that many interpersonal conflicts lie not in private versus public or family versus

---

[72] Honneth, *Disrespect*, 136. Honneth, *The Struggle for Recognition*, 98.
[73] Petherbridge, 109.
[74] Honneth, *The Struggle for Recognition*, 107, 162.
[75] Honneth, *Disrespect*, 152-157.

legal spheres, but in terms of two types of recognition relations: with norms and with individuals. Honneth's account of recognition as respect for others' moral autonomy helps explain the distinction I am making. Recognition requires that I respect others as having their own moral capabilities and accountabilities. If I only follow norms but do not see that these norms are important because of their connections with an individual, I am not fully respecting either the individual or the norms. I need to see the other person as a moral actor who is the reason why I am acting according to moral norms, and this respect for others' moral autonomy underlies an engagement with other individuals.

I can interact with others in terms of formalities and legalities, in terms of personal affectional bonds, or in terms of both. For example, I can assert my legal rights in a way that places me in a position better than a friend's, and perhaps to my friend's detriment, and in so doing I damage my relation of recognition with my friend. But if my friend is emotionally hurt by my exercising my legal rights, what is the root of the conflict between us? If my friend objects, it is not an objection against legal norms or a claim that I do not have legal rights but that I have placed priority in those rights over our friendship. Our conflict is not between a legal sphere and a friendship (love) sphere but between the practical choices of relations of recognition that are possible between my friend and me. I have engaged with the norms at the expense of my engagement with my friend, and this has caused hurt feelings. My prioritization of norms may be defensible, but my friend may want our relation of personal recognition to take priority over the recognition of norms.

Friendship is a relationship that has different expectations from workplace or economic relationships in which others will expect me to prioritize relating to the norms that guide our work and economic interactions. Nevertheless, the difference I am pointing out is not clear in Honneth's account because he places both economic transactions and solidarity (including friendship) in the public sphere of civil society, separate from the private sphere of family and love relations. Solidarity for Honneth occurs in a community of subjects sharing a value horizon of a collective conception of a good life and engaging as a community to realize it.[76] He also holds that self-esteem comes from solidarity with and approval from a community "organized along corporative lines."[77] I agree with Joel Anderson's assessment that

> Honneth's view is that one can properly speak of 'solidarity' only in cases where some shared concern, interest, or value is in play. What he is concerned with here is not so much the collective defence of interests or the political integration of individuals, but rather the presence of an open, pluralistic, evaluative framework within which social esteem is ascribed.[78]

My reading of Honneth, which may differ from Anderson's, is that Honneth assumes such an evaluative framework and shared concerns can occur only in communities of sufficiently large size that they can be organized along corporative lines. This precludes subcultures and small groups, an issue I will address more fully in chapter 2.4.

Honneth also associates self-esteem with the economic sphere because he sees social esteem as bound up with opportunities to pursue economically rewarding occupations.[79] An emblematic example of Honneth's conception of a community with which one has solidarity and from which one receives esteem is the working class sharing a collective interest and engaging as a community to realize their shared economic goals.[80] Meanwhile, Honneth distinguishes the recognition received in friendship from the recognition received in solidarity,[81] thus separating the love recognition of friendship from the esteem recognition of solidarity. Honneth's overly narrow definition of self-esteem as coming from mass communities in the economic sphere misses the reality that we gain our sense of self-esteem far more from friends than from strangers. It is from

---

[76] Honneth, *Disrespect*, 257. Honneth, *The Struggle for Recognition*, 91.

[77] Honneth, *The Struggle for Recognition*, 127-129; see also 62, 91, 134, 164.

[78] Joel Anderson, "Translator's Introduction," in Honneth, *The Struggle for Recognition*, xvii.

[79] Honneth, *Disrespect*, 75.

[80] See in particular, Honneth, *Disrespect*, 75-77.

[81] Honneth, *The Struggle for Recognition*, 94.

the particular and personal mutual recognition of friendship that much of our positive self-relations come.

Throughout my social interactions, I can behave formally and comport myself toward someone in a legalistic and impersonal manner. I can do this even to my spouse. Here, being formal differs from intimacy—I can, by my behavior, remove the intimacy from my relationship. This lack of intimacy is different from a violation of another's legal rights. Honneth is correct that within a family, individual subjects need to be able to claim principles of universal justice if their legal dignity is violated, such as in sexual or physical abuse, where obviously recognition is absent. But there is an area of misrecognition in our personal relationships that is not covered by Honneth's division between the legal and the family. To be inconsiderate to our spouse or friend is not a violation of their legal rights, but it is a violation of our affectional relationship. Respect is expected not just in legal terms but throughout personal relations. Lack of engagement with another individual I will explore in depth later in chapter 1.3.

Honneth's overinstitutionalization of the family sphere creates difficulties for him when he tries to address the affectional bonds of friendship, and a critique of his conceptions of friendship is necessary to correct its inadequacies. Friendship can be described in terms of recognition, but it does not map to Honneth's three spheres. Also, despite the fact that there are social norms for friendship, it does not qualify as a social institution because it is not as norm governed as Honneth assumes. Throughout his writings, Honneth groups friendship with marriage and parent-child relationships under the term "love relationships" in the family sphere.[82] In *Freedom's Right*, he groups family with friendship and intimate relationships under "personal relationships," a sphere that he continues to place alongside the civil sphere (now called "the we of the market economy") and the legal sphere (now called "the we of democratic will-formation"). His discussion of personal relationships in *Freedom's Right* amends his previous discussion of family and friendship, but in

---

[82] See for example, Honneth, *The Fragmented World of the Social*, 254. Honneth, *The Struggle for Recognition*, 25, 95.

Freedom's Right he is mostly concerned with how structural reforms of social institutions can ensure the socioeconomic conditions for the institutions of family and friendship that contribute to the development of a democratic ethical life.[83] This macrosocial view does not provide much insight into the intersubjective experiences of friendship.

Are friendships governed by social norms, or by the agreements of the individuals involved? There are social conventions to be sure, but individuals also bring distinct expectations to particular friendships. Any two individuals can make their own implicit or explicit agreements about their relationship, but as Honneth points out, we do consider that there is a difference between "true" friendship and "inauthentic" friendship. Although the norms of friendship may be vague, they can be drawn on as criteria to guide our relationships. Honneth considers the norm of friendship to be socially institutionalized as a shared body of knowledge about what practices constitute appropriate friendship.[84] His definition of friendship[85] considers "true" friendship to be similar to a legal contract with formal expectations and role obligations, which when violated allow a party to end the contract.

Honneth's idealized legalistic view of friendship may portray some instances (mostly in the past) of personal relationships but cannot be seen as a definition with broad application today. Honneth mentions that in the past personal relations were controlled with class distinctions that must be strictly obeyed and alliances that required a common interest but that since the economic prosperity and accompanying social class relaxation following World War II friendship has been transformed to include private relationships of friendship in which personal concerns and private matters could be shared. Although Honneth sees friendship now as being cultivated at all levels of society and gender barriers being at least partially broken, he still seems to see friendship in the character of a rule-governed transaction that individuals must learn to master. There is certainly truth in

---

[83] Honneth, *Freedom's Right*, 132-176.
[84] Honneth, *Freedom's Right*, 135.
[85] Honneth, *Freedom's Right*, 136-138.

this—one must learn how to become a good friend, learn how to trust a friend, care about a friend's well-being and concerns, and keep a friend's secrets. Each of these identifiable traits of "true" friendship is governed by normative expectations. Honneth takes this idea to a high level, saying that "friendship constitutes an institutionalized form of pre-reflexive commonalities marked by the implicit desire to reveal our own feelings and attitudes without reservation."[86] It is not an overly romantic sentiment to think that for most people in most situations, this does not fully describe the friendships lived by individuals. Individuals do practice friendships aware of unofficial rules that they violate at risk of disapproval, but the question remains as to what expectations individuals bring to their friendships beyond cultural normative expectations. Honneth seems to be aware of these complexities when he paraphrases Derrida's conception of friendship as having the two dimensions of moral responsibility: generality and particularity. A friend can appeal to the general moral norms that apply to all people, plus a friend can appeal to the bonds of sympathy and affection particular to him or her as an individual friend. Derrida finds that in this conception is a fundamental opposition in which the demand of affection is an asymmetrical obligation—one must give preferential affection to one's friends—whereas the normative moral demand is symmetrical—one is equally morally obligated to all individuals.[87] The legal obligations we have for another may be in opposition to our obligation to support our friends even if they violate legal norms. Honneth acknowledges this, but to my mind, he does not fully incorporate it.

It seems to me that there is much more to the phenomena of friendship than is being captured by Honneth's institutionalized discussion. What are the sources of these expectations for friendship? Surely, the norms of friendship are not legal authorizations but customs. Each culture, and subculture within a culture, would have particular customs attached to the concept of friendship that contain a loose set of normative expectations and complementary role obligations, yet the

[86] Honneth, *Freedom's Right*, 139.
[87] Honneth, *Disrespect*, 116.

practice of friendship is so variable and reflective of circumstances that cultural norms do not penetrate and regulate to a controlling degree. Individuals choose friendships for various reasons, and friendships serve the desires and involvements of the individuals involved. Instead of trying to provide formal definitions about what "true" friendship is, we would do better to consider friendship as consisting of varieties that fall under family resemblances to which particular friendships are similar to varying degrees. There are numerous different kinds of friendship, which vary according to the individuals, settings, and other circumstances involved. We see different types of friendships with different expectations that develop organically in the intersubjective dynamics between children, teenagers, businessmen, mothers of small children, smokers, sports fans, hobbyists, activists, and so on. We see that the norms for friendship differ when the individuals involved are acquaintances, companions, close friends, or best friends.

Understanding the complexity of friendship is important to understanding the vital importance of personal recognition to individuals. In intimate relationships, individuals have the potential for the strongest and most profound affirmations of (or harm to) their personal integrity and self-image. Mutual recognition is, Honneth says, the basis for a marriage,[88] and the recognition one receives as a child is internalized and becomes a disposition for one's future relationships. Throughout life, mutual recognition between significant others, between parents and children, and between friends provides the dispositions required for long-term attachments to other individuals.[89] To reflect the broad and complex importance of intimate relationships, we cannot limit the conception of love recognition and the self-confidence it engenders to the institution of the child-raising family. Love recognition is connected to numerous other aspects of intersubjective relations. Love in marriage, family, friendship, and solidarity is understood in everyday life to be a type of relationship in which one can freely express one's thoughts and desires with the

---

[88] Honneth, *Freedom's Right*, 143.
[89] Honneth, *Freedom's Right*, 154.

expectation one will be heard if not answered. Honneth is correct that love is a relation in which one can feel confidence that one's needs are valued and can be met. I add that this love relationship can be found in any area of social life whether or not it was first found within the institution of a family.

Wherever it occurs, a healthy love relationship is signified by emotional security within that relationship. Such emotional security can engender greater self-confidence in other personal relationships and social activities. The important point is that the love relationship is an interpersonal relationship of mutual care that can transcend the boundary of family. This has always been the case but has been brought into the open in recent years by the growth of nontraditional households. Marriage and childhood have been symbolic representations of love relationships, but individuals have always sought love recognition outside of these. Even the undeniably stilted bonding between men who are defined by patriarchal roles shows they are seeking recognition and solidarity in their friendships. These men can still feel free to express their thoughts and desires with the expectation they will be heard. That the range of thoughts and desires they are free to express is limited by patriarchal and misogynist recognition norms does not negate that such male friendships involve a kind of mutual affection. Women have arguably been freer to form friendships with other women with greater potential for intimacy because recognition norms allow that. Men and women have long found it more difficult to form friendships because societal expectations of male-female relations restrict them to superior-subordinate relations. Despite these norms, individual women and men can craft their own expectations in their friendships.

Honneth mentions the occurrence of friendships for instrumental reasons—what he calls "friendship-like relations," brought on by network capitalism and its pressure on employees to mobilize informal lifeworld skills in service of work-related goals.[90] Similar pressures on individuals occur from numerous sources beyond the workplace and "friendship-like

---

[90] Honneth, *The I in We*, 180.

relations" are quite common, perhaps even more common than "true" friendship. We all have a tendency to instrumentalize some of our friendships in order to make advantageous connections and outcomes. That we take advantage in a nonmanipulative way does not necessarily detract from the friendship. Here, too, the variety of relations and circumstances involved mean that normative expectations vary as to how much we can push the advantage of a friendship.

Friendship is not strictly a dynamic of mutual advantage. Love is a component of friendship—and it is similar to other relationships defined by love—but there are different kinds of love in different kinds of friendship. Friendship differs from marriage and parent-child relationships. One probably cannot fruitfully be friends with a large number of people, but one's circle of friendship can be larger than the tight circle of being a spouse or child, and this enables individuals to have a variety of types of friends. We care about our friends, and we will often act on their behalf out of love, perhaps with no expectations of receiving something in return. Each particular friendship will develop its own comfort level of reciprocal expectations. There are only some friends with whom you feel comfortable speaking about certain subjects and only some to whom you would feel comfortable lending money, and with each such friend, a certain difficult-to-define amount of money you are comfortable lending. This general overview of friendship indicates its complexity. We need not have a romantic ideal of relationships to see that what individuals expect in relationships goes beyond strict normative categories and reflects the individuals and circumstances involved. We recognize someone as a friend in a particular, not a universal, way and Honneth's tripartite structure does not adequately describe friendship.

When Honneth separates solidarity and love into different modes, he unnaturally separates recognition relations among individuals. Unless we were to take an uncharitable reading of Honneth that solidarity is possible only within a feeling of group pride—a reading Honneth distances himself from[91]—there is a strong connection between solidarity and care. In the

[91] Honneth, *The Struggle for Recognition*, 127-129.

normative terms of recognition relations, solidarity among friends and love among family members are both emotional bonds of devotion, and Honneth does not make a compelling argument for them being different modes of recognition. It seems more likely that familial love, friendship, and camaraderie are different varieties of affection rather than different forms of recognition. Shifting to misrecognition, how would betrayal of a friend be of a different normative mode than betrayal of a family member? The betrayal committed by the individual is at core the same violation of norms of trust and loyalty that transcends any formal boundary between social and familial relations. We could say truthfully that the likely expectations between friends and between family members are different, but then we should further say that the particular expectations in any relationship depend on the particular understandings of the individuals involved. There is, for example, a basic norm within a culture of what loyalty means, and perhaps more particular norms about the meaning of loyalty within a friendship and within a family, but still, the individuals involved need to interpret and apply their culture's norms to their particular situation. Whether the particular personal relationship we are looking at is between friends or between family members is relevant, but it is not definitive. This example of betrayal, and the larger discussion of friendship, love, and solidarity, suggests that Honneth's formal mapping of recognition and misrecognition to spheres of social levels is inadequate to portray everyday intersubjective relations. It would seem that particular recognition and misrecognition behaviors, rather than falling neatly into three modes, reflect a dynamic of combined engagement with norms and engagement with individuals.

1.1.1 - Seeing Recognition in Terms of Engagements Rather Than Social Spheres

What this brief discussion indicates is that recognition is not simply a matter of separate social spheres of family, state, and civil society. It is a matter of different types of intersubjective relations. Instead of thinking of recognition in terms of three social spheres, we can think of recognition as two modes of relations that nonabsolutely reflect two types of engagements—engagement with norms and engagement with individuals. Christopher Zurn observes that love is particularistic, whereas respect is universalistic.[92] I argue that this is the real distinction between love and legality and is a better description than linking differentiation with esteem recognition and universalizing with legal recognition. To love someone means to separate that person out from others in terms of our considerations and engage with that person as an individual. We care more about our loved one's needs and desires than we do for others', even though we do not willfully disregard the needs and desires of others. The distinction is better described by the type of recognition relation involved and what is being valued in that relationship.

Love is definitely a personal engagement. When there is no longer an engagement with the other individual, the love relationship is diminished and is in danger of fracturing. Seeing love as engagement with another individual fits with Honneth's concern about familial recognition becoming subordinated to the sphere of legal recognition, such as in his example of the couple in the film *Kramer vs. Kramer*. When two individuals in their interactions engage only in terms of norms and not with each other, then they definitely have blocked out their lifeworld of caring family communication and dependencies. We can better describe the recognition dynamic of a dysfunctional marriage in terms of engagements than in terms of spheres of recognition. Legal recognition requires a lack of personal recognition and, as Honneth's *Kramer vs. Kramer* example shows, personal recognition demands relations isolated from legal concerns. Honneth points to how appeals to reciprocal love are different from appeals to reciprocal legal justice—they are appeals not to rational insight but to the existence of commonly held affections between individuals. Appeals to love require the individuals involved to have a

[92] Christopher Zurn. *Axel Honneth: A Critical Theory of the Social* (Cambridge, MA: Polity, 2015), Kindle location 1123.

mutual preference for each other that corresponds to giving and receiving from each other to benefit their individual needs.[93]

This distinction based on type of recognitional engagement—engagement with norms and engagement with individuals—also describes the difference between love and esteem. Love is a personal relation of recognition in which there is mutual personal engagement. Esteem is an engagement with an individual but is not necessarily a personal engagement. Love has an unconditional character, whereas esteem depends on whether certain conditions are met. In love, what is valued is the other person, not what he or she does, whereas esteem values what another does as measured by social norms. What this distinction also shows is that there are two different esteem recognitions: We engage with norms in terms of deciding whether to esteem someone's accomplishments, and we engage with the other individual in loving him or her. We can esteem someone with whom we have no personal relationship; we can esteem a quality in someone even if we do not like him or her as a person. For example, we can esteem someone as intelligent but not want to be friends with him or her.

Using the two types of engagements, we can unpack what is going on in the recognition relations related to tenure and other social positions of status. With an office or position come certain rights and responsibilities that require certain responses from others, all of which are prescribed by norms. A head of a department is due a certain amount of respect, but that could be more a respect for the office than for the individual holding it. We have heard such sentiments when people say they respect the office of the president or prime minister but deeply dislike the individual holding that office. In such cases, one is engaging with norms but not fully engaging with the individual who holds the position. One can demand fair consideration for tenure based on having fulfilled the normative requirements. One can demand respect for one's position on the basis of an appeal to recognition norms, but one cannot demand to be liked. There is a difference between social esteem, as in an award, and personal esteem, as

[93] Honneth, *Disrespect*, 157.

in being held in high regard. If someone is given the institutional esteem of a promotion, it does not necessarily mean that other individuals will follow suit by feeling more personal esteem for that person. We respect our bosses whether we like them or not (certainly such respect also comes from self-interest to protect our own position), but whether we like them is different from their position as boss.

Similarly, supervisors can respect their subordinates in following the law and company policies, which is engaging with norms. Whether they are friendly and kind to their subordinates—engaging with them as individuals—is a different matter. Conversely, supervisors can show favoritism to subordinates and break rules in ways that benefit the subordinates. In this case, supervisors are engaging with those individuals but not engaging with norms. This is the case even if we can point to a cultural norm against nepotism. Such a prohibition against nepotism would be an attempt to stop excessive engagement with individuals that subverts engagement with norms. An important conclusion we can draw from this discussion is that we can recognize another in one way while at the same time misrecognizing him or her in another, a possibility I will pursue in chapter 1.3.

The operative questions in recognition are the recognition relations involved and the object of recognition behavior. When any individual or social institution is respecting someone's legal rights, the object of recognition must be the applicable legal norms. A human right does not exist separate from a human being, but a human right is not attached to a specific human individual. Legal rights are to be recognized and respected regardless of the specific person with whom you are interacting. A judge should recuse him- or herself from a case if he or she has a personal relationship with the plaintiff or defendant. The aphorism "justice is blind" hints at how applying legal norms properly means not seeing the individual—that is, not engaging with someone individually and not differentiating someone in the sense of favoritism, but universalizing the law to apply equally to all. Legal issues of all kinds are issues of engaging with legal norms universally without engaging with individuals and their circumstances. Laws against theft are universally applied and do not take into account individual needs. Laws banning women wearing the veil is an engagement with a general norm rather than with an individual's desire to wear one, subjugating that desire under the universal norm. Obviously, not all individual desires are of the same character, such as the desire to eat in order to survive versus the desire to wear an item of clothing, but the character of legal norms is the same.

The advantage of thinking of recognition in terms of engagements can be illustrated with a practical example. When I have the task of marking or grading a student's essay, I am engaging in two different forms of relations of recognition. One relation is with the rules of proper conduct for marking all student essays, which include standards on judging the essays and moral requirements such as impartiality. The other relation is with the achievement of the student—in this case, with the content and quality of the essay. To give students their due rights, I must engage in both relations: respecting the rules and standards by applying them impartially regardless of who has submitted the essay, and according proper esteem to the student on the basis of the particular student's achievements in the essay. I am engaging with the normative standards regulating the task, and I am engaging with the student through his or her essay. To do my task well and give proper recognition, I must involve myself in my task with both engagements. If I fail to involve with both engagements, I have not given proper respect and/or esteem recognition to the student.

To summarize this chapter, the shift I propose is to see recognition in terms of the relations between the individuals involved and what is being valued in that relationship rather than how the form of recognition can be mapped theoretically to a social sphere. Rather than viewing recognition in terms of the tripartite social structure, I propose viewing it in terms of relations with norms and relations with individuals. Seeing respect and esteem as different relations of recognition reveals that they are not tied to spheres of recognition as specified in Honneth's typology. An individual engages with norms and other individuals in all aspects of social life, and the varying degrees of those engagements tells us more about whether recognition is happening or not than does mapping the social situation to a social sphere. The example of marking or grading essays is one of many common tasks that do not map directly to Honneth's spheres. Marking essays is a task that has formal rules that must be respected, so is it in the legal sphere? It is not related to the state though, so must it be in the civil sphere? In a sense, yes, but the task is not strictly about esteem as Honneth implies with the civil sphere. A student can appeal to a just application of the rules that govern academic marking, and that appeal does not go to the state but to individuals within the nonstate academic institution, but this is not an appeal to esteem or solidarity.

Respect for norms and for their just application occurs throughout social interactions; they do not occur only in the legal sphere. Respect recognition is not simply legal recognition but is a behavior that is continually in the background of, and is a condition for, any recognition relationship. While marking essays, I have to treat students with respect (fairly); in working with others, I must observe the rules of the workplace; in loving my wife, I have to respect her rights, and so on. This shows that there is no distinct social sphere for respect recognition; at most, there could be a sphere that is only about respect (i.e., the political sphere), but even this is debatable. A lack of respect for rules leads to misrecognition of individuals. Similarly, a myopic, legalistic approach to norms runs the danger of injustice when the individuals involved and their circumstances are not engaged. The idea that gun ownership is a universal right has caused problems in the United States because the universal norm does not take into account different circumstances. Guns in an urban setting differ from guns in a rural setting, different types of guns pose different dangers, and so on. If the particularities of situations and individuals are not taken into account, legal recognition may not be achieved. Successful legal or esteem recognition requires engagement with both applicable norms and involved individuals. Honneth surely would not disagree with this. My argument is not that Honneth is incorrect in what he says but that an increased focus on the object of engagement in recognition behavior will improve our understanding of recognition relations and how they can go wrong.

1.2 - Rethinking Honneth's contrarian account of misrecognition

In this chapter, I take issue with Honneth's account of misrecognition, deeming it inadequate to describe individuals' experiences of misrecognition and, by extension, inadequate to be a basis for an account of struggles for recognition that are in response to misrecognition. In Honneth's theory, the significant importance of recognition for individual well-being and social cohesion is clear. Honneth holds that individuals can construct and maintain a positive self-relation only with the help of affirmative reactions from others.[94] This reliance on others is the reason why a violation of the principles of reciprocal recognition results in a moral injury to a subject.[95] If Honneth is correct, even to a degree, then a lack of recognition is a significant problem for society that critical theory must address.

It is easy to understand how oppressive laws and economic deprivation are harmful to individuals. Honneth expands the scope of injustice by arguing that subjects learn conceptions of justice through processes of socialization and come to expect that society will recognize them in accordance with social recognition norms. The disappointment of these normative expectations by actions contrary to recognition is experienced by subjects as violence to their identity claims.[96] In many cases, misrecognition is an active withholding of recognition such as denying rights or refusing social inclusion. Receiving exclusion, insult, or degradation violates and damages a subject's self-confidence, self-respect, and self-esteem. Because subjects rely on social recognition for their human identity, its denial is necessarily accompanied by the sense of a threatening loss of personality.[97] These injuries to one's integrity, honor, or dignity, Honneth argues, represent the normative core of the experience of injustice.[98] Individuals are vulnerable to misrecognition because of their

---

[94] Honneth, *Disrespect*, 134.
[95] Honneth, *Reification*, 153.
[96] Honneth, *The Fragmented World of the Social*, xiv.
[97] Honneth, *Disrespect*, 71-72.

need for recognition, and the experience of misrecognition is deeply important in an individual's life.

To describe behaviors that violate recognition norms, Honneth often uses the term "disrespect" rather than "misrecognition," but it is clear that by "disrespect" he means attitudes and actions that are the contrary of recognition. By "disrespect," Honneth means acts that deny subjects recognition for their particular claims to identity—disruptions or injuries to a subject's practical relation-to-self potentially severe enough to bring the subject's identity to the point of collapse.[99] Honneth also consistently links acts of recognition with social justice and acts of misrecognition or disrespect with social injustice. Although Honneth uses the term "disrespect" to refer to the denial of all types of recognition, because he uses the terms "respect" and "self-respect" to refer to a specific type of recognition (the legal), to avoid confusion I will use the term "misrecognition" to refer to all types of denial of recognition.

In "Recognition and Moral Obligation" and *Disrespect*, Honneth speaks of misrecognition in terms of moral injuries to affected subjects who are disregarded and denied recognition. He distinguishes between the experiences of a moral misdeed and of ill luck or constraint. In a moral misdeed, unlike in an amoral happening, one can easily show that an aspect of recognition was withheld by another person or persons. For Honneth, then, behaviors that transgress recognition norms are behaviors with moral significance. It is easy to understand that acts such as physical assault, fraud, theft, or humiliation are misrecognition behaviors that violate an individual's body or property. Honneth adds that in experiencing such misrecognition behaviors, the affected individual experiences not only a material injury to his or her body or property but also moral injury—"the accompanying consciousness of not being recognized in one's own self-understanding."[100] The affected individual's personal integrity is disregarded by acts of physical assault, fraud, theft, or

---

[98] Fraser and Honneth, 131.

[99] Honneth, *The Struggle for Recognition*, 131-132.

[100] Axel Honneth, "Recognition and Moral Obligation," *Social Research*, Vol. 64, No. 1, The Decent Society (Spring 1997), 23.

humiliation, and this has significant repercussions for an individual's positive relations-to-self. Misrecognition undermines the preconditions of individuals' self-realization. This follows logically from the insight that recognition is a precondition for individuals' self-realization, and, thus, recognition and misrecognition are contrary behaviors. Because recognition is so vital to an individual's well-being, a lack of adequate recognition effectively damages an individual.

In *The Fragmented World of the Social*, *The Struggle for Recognition*, and *Disrespect*, Honneth offers a systematic typology of three forms of misrecognition that parallel three levels of moral injuries and map directly to his three modes of recognition. The first form is forcibly depriving an individual of autonomous control over his or her own body; the second, structurally excluding an individual from certain legal rights; and the third, the denigration of individual or collective lifestyles.[101] Each of these forms of misrecognition excludes the individual from mutual recognition.

Honneth's examples for the first form of misrecognition are acts of physical humiliation such as physical abuse, rape, or torture.[102] These are examples of, Honneth says, the most fundamental type of human degradation because such acts of misrecognition strip an individual of physical autonomy. Being deprived of autonomous control of one's body is an injury far greater than the physical pain it causes; it also causes the individual to feel defenseless and violated. Individuals experiencing this physical humiliation form of misrecognition are deprived of that form of recognition that enables body-related self-confidence in their interactions with their environment. They are less capable of forming emotional attachments with others and maybe even with themselves—experiencing a form of psychological death. This type of misrecognition causes lasting damage to one's sense of self, rendering one less capable of expressing one's needs and feelings. Although Honneth does not specifically include it, we should add physical and verbal bullying as less severe, but still powerful, incidents of physical humiliation. The resulting feelings of

---

[101] Honneth, *The Fragmented World of the Social*, 250-256.
[102] Honneth, *Disrespect*, 136. Honneth, *The Struggle for Recognition*, 131-133.

violation and loss of body-related self-confidence are similar, albeit less severe than from rape or torture.

Honneth describes the second form of misrecognition as associated with one's awareness of being a morally accountable subject.[103] Honneth links this form of misrecognition with the legal sphere, though it seems apparent that legal discrimination is only one way in which one's self-responsibility is misrecognized. The second form's combination of the restriction of personal autonomy and the denial of equal moral rights fits with all forms of discrimination whether at the individual or macrosocial level and whether based on sex, race, religion, or something else. Being excluded not only has practical social consequences for an individual but also signifies to the individual that he or she is considered to be lacking full moral status in society and is deemed to be not on the same level as other individuals. This means that in practical and normative senses, the individual is socially ostracized as not being a worthy partner for mutual recognition. A woman or a member of a racial minority denigrated in this manner is not only denied full access to the society's institutional legal order but also denied full access to the society's normative moral expectations. This form of misrecognition will be witnessed by other individuals who will become disinclined to offer recognition to socially ostracized individuals and even may be encouraged actively to misrecognize those individuals. Individuals who experience this form of misrecognition are deprived of that form of recognition that enables self-respect for their own moral accountability. They are rendered less capable of considering themselves as persons worthy of receiving moral consideration and recognition. They lose their self-respect and their ability to relate to themselves as social partners on par with others—experiencing social incapacity or social death. As socially ostracized individuals, they are deprived of valuable socialization and become less capable of internalizing the moral norms of society and thus less capable of giving recognition to others.[104]

---

[103] Honneth, *Disrespect*, 136. Honneth, *The Struggle for Recognition*, 133-134.
[104] Honneth, *The Fragmented World of the Social*, 250-251.

Honneth places the third form of misrecognition, related to one's social value, along a spectrum—from being rude to someone in not greeting him or her to stigmatizing and denigrating individual or collective lifestyles.[105] From his comment that this form of misrecognition occurs when the hierarchy of social values "downgrade[s] individual forms of life and convictions as being inferior or deficient,"[106] we can guess that he is thinking that this form of misrecognition is directed toward people considered to be from the lower classes in a society. This would make sense in that working class people often experience their work and lives as being devalued. Honneth also links this form of misrecognition to "unconventional lifestyles,"[107] "individual forms of life,"[108] and conflicting lifestyles,[109] which seems to suggest not the working class but countercultures or people deemed by the majority to be deviant, such as homosexuals.[110] Honneth is unclear about what attributes of these "lifestyles" are being downgraded. Regardless, he states that these patterns of denigrative evaluation of individual or collective forms of life rob those misrecognized of being able to take a positive view of their abilities. Individuals experiencing this form of misrecognition are deprived of that form of recognition that enables an individual to feel positive toward him- or herself and to develop self-esteem. These individuals are rendered less capable of self-realization of themselves as individuals worthy of esteem.

> The self-descriptions of those who see themselves as having been wrongly treated by others, the moral categories that play a dominant role are those - such as 'insult' or 'humiliation' - that refer to forms of disrespect, that is, to the denial of recognition. Negative

---

[105] Honneth, *Disrespect*, 136. Honneth, *The Struggle for Recognition*, 134-135.

[106] Honneth, *The Fragmented World of the Social*, 251. Honneth, *The Struggle for Recognition*, 134.

[107] Honneth, *The Fragmented World of the Social*, 255.

[108] Honneth, *The Struggle for Recognition*, 134, 135, 143.

[109] Honneth, *Freedom's Right*, 175.

[110] This is especially true of his comment in *Freedom's Right*, 175, about the need within a family for tolerance of "lifestyles or preferences that fundamentally conflict with one's own."

> concepts of this kind are used to designate behaviour that represents an injustice not simply because it harms subjects or restricts their freedom to act, but because it injures them with regard to the positive understanding of themselves that they have acquired inter-subjectively.[111]

Such degradation disconnects individuals from the cultural traditions of their society, and they are cut off from group solidarity. The individual's identity and his or her place in society are diminished, resulting in a loss of self-esteem.

Honneth's typology shows how misrecognition has significant long-term consequences for individuals who experience it. Just as individuals can learn self-respect and self-confidence, they can also learn to have a lack of self-respect and self-confidence and even to develop self-loathing. Experiencing misrecognition, one lacks the confidence and security to express one's thoughts and desires. One becomes less able to make positive healthy connections with other people, further diminishing one's ability to receive recognition and affirmation from others. The individual learns to see his or her self as one without equal worth and rights. When mutual recognition is absent, Honneth says, individuals can fall into perceiving themselves and each other as objects and are indifferent to those aspects of individuals that are valuable.[112]

The importance of recognition means that misrecognition is an issue of major importance. However, although Honneth spends considerable effort discussing the concept of recognition and its usefulness for critical theory, his discussion of misrecognition is limited to brief descriptions of three kinds of misrecognition and the question of how those moral experiences motivate struggles for recognition. What explanations of misrecognition he provides, as summarized above, rest on seeing misrecognition as the contrary of a related form of recognition, mostly as its absence. I contend that Honneth's conception of misrecognition is

[111] Honneth, *The Struggle for Recognition*, 131.

[112] Axel Honneth, *Pathologies of Reason: On the Legacy of Critical Theory* (Columbia University Press, 2009), 34.

oversimplified, resulting in a serious deficit for his critical theory. If we are concerned about misrecognition, we want to know more about the forms of misrecognition.

One could argue that critical theory, including Honneth, has identified capitalism as a primary cause of misrecognition. Such a diagnosis, despite capitalism's pernicious influences on society and individuals, is insufficient at illuminating the moral experiences of individuals. Honneth is correct that critical theory needs to give attention to the moral experiences of individuals, but no critical theory to date, including his, gives us sufficient insights on misrecognition. I will take up the problems with Honneth's account of the motivations for struggles for recognition in Part Two. In the remainder of this chapter, I will discuss how Honneth's account of misrecognition is incomplete; then, in the following chapter, I will respond with an alternative account of misrecognition that answers the shortfalls in Honneth's account.

Honneth places misrecognition within the tripartite structure of recognition, classifying different aspects of socially caused injuries according to their recognition claims in the related sphere of recognition.[113] All individuals are morally vulnerable because their identity depends on affirmation from others. According to Honneth, because one's self-image and identity depends on the particular intersubjective relationships in which one receives love, respect, and esteem, experiencing misrecognition is a moral injury to particular relations-to-self that can be mapped directly to the tripartite structure that was diagrammed in Table 1. The three modes of recognition and three practical relations-to-self are love to self-confidence, respect/equal rights to self-respect, and esteem/solidarity to self-esteem. It logically proceeds, for Honneth, that a lack of recognition in one of the three modes results in an injury to a subject in that subject's related level of relation-to-self. Methodologically, "the number of modes of recognition is to correspond to the number of forms of moral injuries."[114] The more fundamental the level of self-relation that is misrecognized, the

---

[113] Fraser and Honneth, 114.
[114] Honneth, *Disrespect*, 138.

more serious is the individual's experience of a moral injury. Honneth distinguishes three levels of self-relation subject to moral injury: the genetically primary level of one's relation to one's physical and emotional needs, one's self-respect in being a morally accountable subject, and the awareness of having good or valuable capabilities.[115] One's physical self-relation is disregarded by acts of physical and emotional abuse and violence, one's moral self-relation is disregarded by acts of fraud or discrimination, and one's capability for self-relation is disregarded by acts of disdain and stigmatization.[116]

As with Honneth's typology of recognition in Table 1, we can demonstrate Honneth's typology of misrecognition in Table 2.

---

[115] Honneth, "Recognition and Moral Obligation," 25-26.
[116] Honneth, "Recognition and Moral Obligation," 26-27.

Table 2 - Honneth's topology of misrecognition

Spheres of Recognition (D 131-133)[117] **(RR 138-142)**	**Modes of Recognition (GR 501, 506) (RR 143) (SR 129)**	**Forms of Misrecognition (FWS 252-256) (SR 129, 131-134)**	**What Is Devalued (SR 129, 131-134)**	**Relation–to-Self That Is Injured (D 133-137) (RMO 23-27) (SR 129)**
Family - intimate relationships	Love	Physical and emotional humiliation, abuse, and neglect	Individual needs and bodily integrity	Self-confidence: Loss of trust and bodily related self-confidence
The state - legal	Respect/ equal rights	Denial of rights or moral status, social ostracism	Moral capacities and social integrity	Self-respect: Loss of fundamental self-respect as a member of a social community
Civil society - economic	Esteem/ solidarity	Downgrading of one's social value or the value of one's contributions	Productive capacities and social honor	Self-esteem: Loss of self-esteem

Honneth sees misrecognition in terms of the tripartite structure, and his account of misrecognition is fundamentally that it is the contrary of recognition, or, as Van Den Brink, calls it, an inverted image of the basic forms of recognition.[118]

Honneth's viewpoint is related to his institutional focus, and his discussion of misrecognition is focused on class structure and how theory

[117] Parenthetical references are to what I deem to be Honneth's clearest statements of the particular concepts, not the only place he references them. GR="Grounding Recognition," FWS=*Fragmented World of the Social*, RMO="Recognition and Moral Obligation," D=*Disrespect*, SR=*Struggle for Recognition,* RR=*Redistribution or Recognition?*

[118] Bert Van Den Brink, "Recognition, Pluralism, and the Expectation of Harmony," in *Axel Honneth: Critical Essays,* ed. Danielle Petherbridge (Leiden: Brill, 2011), 166.

can use individuals' moral experiences to overcome capitalism's façade of integration.[119] For example, Honneth speaks of the working class becoming aware of its role in the drama of class struggle. Honneth stresses that "the lower classes" do not reach this awareness through theory but through moral experiences—subjects do not experience the theory; they experience the misrecognition. This is a good insight, but Honneth does not adequately pursue this line of inquiry deeper than the level of social class.[120] Instead, Honneth keeps his inquiry into recognition and misrecognition focused on social groups. His brief mention of the problem that women's housework is unpaid is a functionalist description that does not delve into the moral experiences of individual women.[121] He argues instead that because the organization of societal labor ranks certain tasks as lower than others, determining the amount of social esteem possible for an individual, "the chances of forming an individual identity through the experience of recognition are directly related to the societal institutionalization and distribution of labor."[122] This is certainly true insofar as it goes, but the individual woman is as absent in Honneth's analysis as she is in the societal ranking of the value of labor. In addition to the necessary critique of the organization and evaluation of societal labor, we must consider a critique of the failure to evaluate and acknowledge the contributions of individuals. Honneth's analysis is not incorrect, but it is incomplete. By not giving more significance to the moral experiences of the individual in his analysis of the moral experiences of social class, he misses out on a fuller view of misrecognition and struggles against injustice.

To be fair, Honneth gives more consideration to individuals' moral experiences in his discussion of misrecognition in one sphere of recognition. Honneth associates the sphere of intimate relations with Hegel's social sphere of the family. When discussing misrecognition, Honneth refers to this as the "genetically primary level" of "physical needs

---

[119] Honneth, *Disrespect*, 90-91.
[120] Honneth, *Disrespect*, 71.
[121] Honneth, *Disrespect*, 76.
[122] Honneth, *Disrespect*, 76.

and desires"[123] and "the level of physical integrity"; his examples of misrecognition at this level are physical abuse such as rape and torture.[124] This association accentuates the problems with his tripartite structure of misrecognition. He wants to argue, on the one hand, that the family is the source of a subject's self-confidence, but, on the other hand, he discusses the moral injuries from physical abuse without tying that abuse to the family. I am trying to not oversimplify Honneth's position but merely point out that both his discussion of the morality of love[125] and his discussion of moral injuries show that misrecognition that damages self-confidence can occur outside of the Hegelian sphere of the family that Honneth has adopted. What this means is that the moral experiences of an individual and violations of an individual's physical integrity extend beyond the family sphere, and even the sphere of intimate relations if we expand the concept of the family sphere. Being raped violates not only one's bodily and psychological integrity but also harms one's capability to make decisions for oneself and lead a life of one's own choosing in all relations with the world, not just in family or intimate relations. Honneth is correct that physical abuse such as rape or torture damages feelings of self-confidence and trust in the reliability of the social world. This truth is not dependent on the theoretical conception of the tripartite structure but on individuals' experiences within the social lifeworld. Regardless of the source of the misrecognition and the social setting of its occurrence, it is the individual's distinct experience that informs us about the misrecognition and his or her response to it.

A significant problem in Honneth's account of misrecognition is his strictly positive account of recognition. Honneth sees that recognition norms affirm individuals' valuable properties and that if recognition norms are followed, other individuals will gain self-realization and autonomy through recognition. Jonathan Lear gives us two analogies that show us there is more going on in recognition beyond Honneth's positive account.

---

[123] Honneth, *Disrespect*, 136.
[124] Honneth, *The Struggle for Recognition*, 132-133.
[125] Honneth, *Disrespect*, 163-179.

Lear observes that the lion does not have a neutral stance toward a lamb but a recognitional stance that respects the lamb as a lamb. The lamb matters to the lion and the lion tracks the positive traits of the lamb, most notably the lamb's trait of being edible. Similarly, Lear says, a human narcissist cares about other individuals, taking an affirmative recognitional stance in which "the desires, intentions, motives, and projects of others really do matter to him ... It's just that they don't matter to him in the way we feel they ought to matter."[126] Lear's example of "respecting the lamb as a lamb"—that is, as food—is not a perfect analogy to Honneth's conception of recognition as mutual respect that leads to socialization into a shared lifeworld (clearly the lamb and lion are not socialized with each other). Still, Lear's point is sound that recognition is not necessarily a positive behavior that affirms the recipient—it may only affirm the one who is applying recognition norms. Lear's example of the narcissist illustrates the idea of tracking traits in a way that is contrary to moral sensibilities. Honneth would understandably reply that the narcissist is not engaging in proper recognition behavior that affirms and socializes the other. The reason that someone's desires should matter to us should not be because we want to exploit that individual. The question that Lear's example of the narcissist raises is to what extent recognition and other moral norms can be perverted or exploited. The narcissist is engaging with recognition norms, even if that engagement is perverted and results in a violation of our sense of moral standards and this dimension of recognition behavior needs to be considered.

Judith Butler claims Honneth oversimplifies the recognition relation, characterizing his view of recognition as a caring participation with others and his view of misrecognition as detached observations of them.[127] Participation, in Butler's reading of Honneth, means to take up the position of the other; failing to do so leaves the other reified, and we maintain a set of distant and reified relations to the other in which the other is merely an instrument of our own aims. Butler questions Honneth's limited position

---

[126] Jonathan Lear in Honneth, *Reification*, 136.
[127] Judith Butler in Honneth, *Reification*, 100-104.

of an either/or between taking up the position of the other or being in a reifying relation to the other. Butler's response is similar to Lear's in that it is possible that we can participate with others while still failing to take up the position of the other. Hateful or sadistic impulses toward others, she says, are not distanced and detached but are invested and involved; a view akin to Lear's comment about the narcissist. Butler points out the complexity of the recognition stance toward the other in which there are modes of engagement with the other that does not affirm the other, such as rage that seeks to eradicate the other.

Butler's response, like Lear's, speaks to the incompleteness of Honneth's account of misrecognition. Butler is correct that caring involvement is not a sign of recognition. Recognition for the victims of the lion, the narcissist, or the sadist is not mutual, but that does not mean that a kind of recognition-like behavior is not happening. The picture of recognition is more complex than Honneth's positive account that focuses on care and reciprocity. We also need to look at what a recognitional stance means and how it contributes to outcomes that we can call "recognition" and "misrecognition." The possible relations between recognitional stances that engage with recognition norms but result in injustice are what I will explore in the next chapter.

Given the account of recognition set down by Honneth, one is left to wonder why misrecognition occurs at all. Honneth is focused on the necessity of recognition for self-realization and, therefore, concentrates on the effects of recognition and misrecognition. As a result, Honneth has no substantive account of the phenomena of misrecognition or why misrecognition occurs. More problematic is that several aspects of his account of recognition make it difficult for him to construct any view of how misrecognition can arise. Given that recognition is so integral to human social life, and that we are socialized into recognition spheres, it is not surprising that Honneth considers recognition to be effortless: "[Recognition] means an *effortless* mutual acknowledgement of certain aspects of the other's personality, connected to the prevailing mode of social interaction."[128] The claim that recognition is effortless is a particularly interesting aspect of Honneth's conception of recognition that is pervasive, implicitly if not explicitly, throughout his work. In *Reification*, he proposes that there is a form of recognition that is a precognitive stance toward another individual, a comportment of being oriented toward another rather than an epistemic taking on of a perspective toward another. Honneth calls this precognitive, nonepistemic stance "antecedent" or "elementary" recognition that precedes the three modes of recognition—love, respect, and esteem. Elementary recognition, he says, is a necessary condition for our capacity to appropriate moral values in the light of which we orient ourselves toward others and recognize them in a normative manner.[129]

If recognition is elementary and precognitive, as Honneth claims, then that adds even more pressure for an explanation of how misrecognition can occur, especially given how pervasive misrecognition is. Honneth could respond that macrosocial structures such as capitalism suppress elementary recognition, as he argues in *Reification*. Certainly, macrosocial structures and institutional misrecognition can suppress and obscure individuals' intersubjective relations. The problem with that theory is that not only does it accord macrosocial structures tremendous power but it also implies an idyllic presocialization state in which individuals had mutual recognition before capitalist society interferes. What is more, if one conceives, like Honneth, of society as recognition orders, then we just move the question to the next level. How do macrosocial misrecognition orders like capitalism come about, and how are they able to entrench themselves?

If recognition is, as Honneth argues, effortless and precognitive, a vital part of being a human being, central to the normative fabric of society, part of the normative expectations held by all individuals, and so beneficially necessary to all individuals, why is mutual recognition not almost universally practiced? Recognition norms are, after all, norms—part of the normative tradition and practice of a culture loaded with the weight of expectations on individuals. Why would misrecognition ever

---

[128] Honneth, *Pathologies of Individual Freedom*, 50, emphasis mine.
[129] Honneth, *Reification*, 151-152.

occur if such attitudes and actions are so contrary to social norms and self-destructive to a society and its members? Any critical theory, especially one involving a theory of recognition, must provide an explanation for the widespread occurrence of misrecognition in human societies.

Honneth's theory of recognition picks up the story at social reactions to misrecognition, not what contributes to the occurrences of misrecognitions. For example, Honneth stresses that his theoretical interest is the conceptual understanding of the normative and motivational sources of social discontent.[130] What he provides is a thought-provoking account of the core of normative expectations that individuals have of the social order, the value of which I in no way question. My contention is that we would do well to add to Honneth's "theory of recognition that locates the core of all experiences of injustice in the withdrawal of social recognition"[131] a robust theory of what the withdrawal of social recognition is and how it could occur. I share Honneth's program of seeking access to everyday experiences of injustice and the pathologies of social life, but my concern is that his analysis of social injustice focuses more on the symptoms than on the disease. My intention is to push Honneth's theory of recognition further into the question of what misrecognition is and how it is experienced by both individuals who receive and inflict misrecognition. My hope is that a fuller picture of misrecognition will lead to insights into how it arises and persists in society despite the harm it creates and into what brings individuals to deny others social recognition.

Returning to Honneth's characterization of misrecognition, his principal definition of misrecognition is that it is the contrary of recognition and, as my tables illustrate, his typology of misrecognition maps directly onto recognition.[132] Honneth often describes misrecognition in terms of a deprivation or denial of recognition rather than a behavior of its own kind. His characterization in *Disrespect* is one of a denial of recognition—the denying of one's social value and contributions or the

---

[130] Fraser and Honneth, 125, 128.

[131] Fraser and Honneth, 128-133.

[132] I am setting aside for now other elements involved in recognition, for example, as discussed in his "Grounding Recognition" essay.

denying of one's bodily and psychological integrity. His characterization in *Reification*, similarly, is one of a denial of recognition—specifically, a forgetfulness of recognition that he terms "reification," a cognitive mistake in which we perceive other individuals "as mere insensate objects."[133] Honneth considers the norms of recognition to be the basis of community, in which children are socialized and through which they become socially accepted members of the community.[134] Honneth considers mutual recognition to be already affirmed prior to interpersonal interaction through the internalization of the norms of recognition.[135] This consideration commits him to the position that within any social community a violation of the norms of recognition would be an instance of misrecognition; therefore, misrecognition is contrary to recognition.

Honneth's view of misrecognition as the contrary of recognition leaves a binary picture in which, if an individual is engaging with recognition norms in his or her actions, then recognition is happening, whereas the lack of such engagement means misrecognition—as a lack of recognition—is happening. This reasoning is internally consistent, but does it adequately explain misrecognition behavior? Honneth's picture of recognition norms invites two questions: one, does the engagement with and application of recognition norms always mean that recognition is occurring; and two, is misrecognition only a lack of the engagement with and application of recognition norms? I answer in the negative to both questions because some forms of misrecognition occur in which an individual is engaging in the tracking and application of recognition norms in such a manner that misrecognition rather than recognition results. The difference between recognition and misrecognition cannot be simplified to a question of engagement with recognition norms, as I will demonstrate in the next chapter.

---

[133] Honneth, *Reification,* 56-57.
[134] Honneth, *The Struggle for Recognition*, 78.
[135] Honneth, *The Struggle for Recognition*, 45-46.

To close this chapter, Honneth's spheres and related modes of recognition are formal distinctions that do not do justice to the dynamics of intersubjective relations. Honneth's formal distinctions are valuable in helping us understand recognition and misrecognition, but the complexity of intersubjective experiences and identity formation calls for a more robust picture that reflects the complex and dynamic experiences of individuals in their social relations. Honneth's philosophy remains trapped in the Hegelian model of an institutional ethical life. Honneth's philosophy is a detailed analysis of the external structure of the house but without the needed analysis of the occupants of the house.

An individual experiences recognition and misrecognition not in terms of theoretical categories but as specific instances of behavior in which he or she is involved. An individual's experiences of recognition and misrecognition are not general but specific to that individual and his or her specific life. Our theory needs to reflect that though the intersubjective relations of recognition and misrecognition occur according to social norms, these relations have an essential individual-centered nature. I do not suggest that Honneth denies the individual-centered nature of recognition but that more needs to be said about it to understand recognition and misrecognition. More fruitful than Honneth's typological strategy of mapping recognition onto Hegel's formal social spheres is to approach interpersonal recognition relations as they are experienced by the individuals involved. With such a phenomenological methodology, I will explore recognition relations and how they go wrong, and this approach will identify types of misrecognition that are left unrevealed by the formal divisions of state, civil society, and family. This phenomenological approach also calls into question Honneth's account of struggles for recognition, a question I will explore in Part Two after a clearer picture of misrecognition has been gained.

1.3 - A Multidimensional Account of Misrecognition

This chapter will sketch the basic parameters of a view of misrecognition that replaces Honneth's binary account of misrecognition by looking at how individuals act within the normative structure of their social environment. My approach is first to show how Nancy Fraser's critique of Honneth and Honneth's reply in *Redistribution or Recognition?* shows how discussions of justice and recognition are intertwined and related to social status and intersubjective relations. I argue that Honneth's actual and possible responses to Fraser's criticisms point to the importance of intersubjective relations in questions of recognition and misrecognition. The distinction uncovered in the previous chapter between engaging with norms and engaging with individuals points to the need for both engagements to satisfy the demands of justice in recognition relations. The remainder of this chapter explores the various ways that lack of engagement with either norms or individuals leads to injustices of misrecognition and how understanding behaviors in terms of the engagement with norms, engagement with individuals, and engagement with action illuminates misrecognition behaviors.

I agree with Nancy Fraser's argument[136] that recognition should be conceived of as a matter of justice and treated as an issue of social status—a position, however, that I think is valuable in a different way than she uses it. Fraser's objection to Honneth is not that recognition is not an issue but that the recognition order is an issue separate from and secondary to the distributive mechanisms of society. Fraser proposes a perspectival dualism whereby class and status (cultural identity) are analytic, but not substantive, distinctions, and maldistribution that is rooted in the economic structure is a substantive distinction; thus, there are two analytically distinct types of injustice—economic (maldistribution) and cultural (misrecognition). The problem with her proposal is that there is no way to disentangle the links between recognition and distribution and no good theoretical reason for attempting to do so. Individuals' actions and social

---

[136] Fraser and Honneth, 17-29.

relations are shaped by recognition norms, and Honneth's conception of a recognition order is relevant. Inherent in the distribution of labor is the distribution of social status. Whatever the technological developments that contributed to the emergence of capitalism, the social structure of capitalism was going to reflect the established recognition order, including the hierarchies of class, race, and gender.[137] The division of labor and recognition are inextricably linked. Issues of distribution are deeply influenced by, if not dependent on, issues of recognition. A social group is denied its just share of economic distribution because its members are denied equal status, and that denial of social status is a matter of recognition. For Fraser to try to create separate issues of economic class and social status is to miss the fundamental issue of what status means—a value judgment about a person's worth that informs other substantive judgments. Maldistribution is a question of misrecognition, and misrecognition is a matter of injustice.

Fraser also denounces Honneth's position that the hurt feelings of misrecognition are the motivation for struggles for recognition. She wants to decouple the normativity of recognition from the psychological effects of misrecognition in order to strengthen the analysis of injustice. To this end, she argues that misrecognition is not a psychical deformation but an institutionalized relation of subordination that is morally indefensible whether the subjectivity of the oppressed is impaired or not.[138] In this, she seems to misunderstand what Honneth is doing in his project, something Honneth alludes to in *Redistribution or Recognition?*[139] Honneth's purpose is to understand social conflicts by uncovering the motivations for struggles for recognition; he is not engaging in an analysis of injustice. Honneth is focused on the effects of institutionalized patterns of cultural values and subordination that create in their victims the moral injuries of distorted identity and impaired subjectivity that he believes motivate struggles for recognition. That he focuses on this to the neglect of the

---

[137] See, for example, C. Leeb, "Marx and the Gendered Structure of Capitalism," *Philosophy and Social Criticism*, Vol. 33, No. 8 (2007), 833-859.

[138] Fraser and Honneth, 32.

[139] Fraser and Honneth, cf. 237.

question of what misrecognition is opens his theory up to misunderstandings such as Fraser's. Nevertheless, Honneth is correct to place impaired subjectivity alongside economic maldistribution as injustices and as motivations for social conflict. As Nicholas Smith observes, the psychical injuries from misrecognition "are not even notionally separable from the sufferer's place in the economic order."[140]

Related to the maldistribution issue, in the essay "The Fabric of Justice,"[141] Honneth argues that justice is not to be equated with the just distribution of basic goods but is instead a matter of intersubjective relations. His argument can be briefly summarized as follows. What we call social justice is measured in terms of individual autonomy, but the distribution of goods cannot on their own enable individuals to achieve autonomy. This can be seen, Honneth says, when we consider that we cannot understand goods such as financial resources as chances for freedom by considering the meaning of these goods themselves, but only by understanding our relation to them. To be able to perceive their relation to financial resources, individuals must already have a conception of what life aims are worth pursuing and realizing by using financial resources. Conceptions of life aims are not "things" that can be distributed like a material good—individuals acquire them through their own efforts within their interpersonal relationships. Honneth is correct that instead of speaking strictly about the distribution of goods we should speak of relations of recognition and patterns of granting justice (though distribution of goods is strongly related to relations of recognition).[142] Honneth considers the material of justice to be a "special class of intersubjective relations in which citizens accord to each other normative worth."[143] To "accord to each other normative worth" is a description of reciprocal recognition, and Honneth's conception of justice is that it results

---

[140] Nicholas H. Smith, "Recognition, Culture, and Economy: Honneth's Debate with Fraser," *Axel Honneth: Critical Essays*, ed. Danielle Petherbridge (Leiden: Brill, 2011), 336.

[141] Honneth, *The I in We*, 35-50.

[142] Honneth, *The I in We*, 42.

[143] Honneth, *The I in We*, 46.

from the intersubjective relations of reciprocal recognition. The importance of recognition to an individual's well-being means that recognition is a moral issue: The presence of reciprocal recognition is justice, and its absence is injustice.

Honneth's insight that justice requires mutual recognition has a lacuna that needs to be addressed. Honneth's emphasis is on the role of social institutions to defend recognition norms, and one could infer from Honneth's account that recognition is a system of norms that informs us what conduct is proper when we encounter certain types of people in certain types of situations. This gives the impression, intended or not, that if recognition norms are in place and engaged with, then there is justice in recognition relations. For two reasons, I think there is more to recognition. First is that the norms themselves may be unjust, so following them would lead to injustice. Second is that engaging with the norms themselves is not always sufficient to achieve justice. We need to take these two aspects of recognition into account and extend Honneth's insights into the importance of recognition in justice by clearly indicating all that is required in recognition relations to achieve justice.

The idea that justice has varied demands and applications is mentioned by Honneth,[144] but he does not adequately develop this idea. More recently, Honneth said, embedded within a discussion of individuals' socialization into their society's recognition order, that

> subjects acquire the capacity to move about within the normative structures of their social network by treating each other in accordance with the specific kind of recognitional relationship they maintain with each other.[145]

I think this points to a core aspect of recognition—that it is a behavior within the constellation of relationships between individuals that must be

[144] "There is not just one demand of justice, rather there are as many demands as there are specific applications of the one, all-encompassing value of freedom." Honneth, *The I in We*, 64.

[145] Honneth, "Rejoinder," 396.

constantly maintained by the individuals involved. I do not think that this is a radically new thought for Honneth but that it opens up a new emphasis on recognition relations that I wish to expand. Unlike Honneth, I do not think that "a just society requires no more than that subjects learn the various patterns of mutual recognition 'well enough.'"[146] I certainly understand his point—that we need not place a moral burden on individuals to excel at the "art" of recognition. However, injustice occurs when recognition relations are dysfunctional, and recognition relations can be dysfunctional in ways beyond individuals not learning the patterns of mutual recognition—in other words, misrecognition is more than recognition norms not being applied.

To recognize another is to see him or her as deserving of moral consideration and to acknowledge his or her experiences as real and worthy of consideration. As Zurn observes, only other recognizing agents can engage in the mutual interactions of recognition and participate in our claims of normative behavior expectations.[147] We can have expectations of nonhuman entities, but we cannot make normative claims on those entities, nor can we recognize them or expect recognition from them. Mutual recognition and normative behavior require intersubjective involvement with other human beings as human beings. Because recognition is related to certain aspects of another individual, it is a specific response to a specific individual. Because recognition is *by* someone *of* someone, recognition is a relation between individuals. It is reasonable then to consider misrecognition as a dimension of social interaction in which recognition relations between individuals lack appropriate reciprocity. Recognition relations are complex, and we need to delve into what is involved in occurrences of misrecognition to craft a more expanded and finer-grained account than Honneth's underdeveloped account of misrecognition as the contrary of recognition. We need to clarify the relations of recognition norms to injustice and identify which norms

[146] Honneth, "Rejoinder," 395.
[147] Zurn, *Axel Honneth,* Kindle locations 1696-1697.

contribute to injustice, and we also need to clarify the nature of our relations with individuals who are the recipients of our recognition.

Heikki Ikäheimo provides a helpful way of conceiving of differences in recognition relations.[148] He first distinguishes between vertical and horizontal recognition. Vertical recognition occurs between persons and norms and institutions. Social norms and institutions exist if and only if individuals recognize them as authoritative (upward vertical recognition), and social institutions such as governmental bodies recognize persons as possessing rights (downwards vertical recognition). Horizontal recognition occurs between individuals, with Ikäheimo distinguishing between two forms: normatively mediated and purely intersubjective. The normatively mediated form of horizontal recognition is one individual recognizing another individual as a bearer of rights or entitlements stipulated by norms for which the recognition is obligatory. The second, purely intersubjective, is a recognitional response to another as an individual person independently of his or her rights and entitlements. Ikäheimo further identifies two modes of purely intersubjective horizontal recognition: conditional, in which concern for the other individual is instrumentally calculated in terms of one's own interests, and unconditional, in which concern for the other individual is not conditioned by prudential considerations. Ikäheimo's reason for making these distinctions is to argue that only unconditional purely intersubjective horizontal recognition—recognition that is not of another individual as a bearer of a normative status but as an individual irreducible to functional significance—can be called "love" and "respect."[149]

Ikäheimo's discussion makes clear the real-world benefits of mutual recognition and the harm that comes from misrecognition. Humans are

---

[148] Heikki Ikäheimo, "Conceptualizing Causes for Lack of Recognition: Capacities, Costs and Understanding," *Studies in Social & Political Thought*, SSPT 25 – Special Issue: Pathologies of Recognition (2015), accessed November 11, 2016, http://journals.sussex.ac.uk/index.php/sspt/article/view/45.

[149] I acknowledge the usefulness of Ikäheimo's three dimensions of horizontal recognition—the deontological, the axiological, and the contributive—but elect not to add that layer of complexity in this current discussion.

autonomous beings, but one of the essential features of the human life-form distinguishing it from animal life-forms is that humans are governed by social norms authorized by humans themselves. This means, Ikäheimo says, that to live a human life, human individuals must recognize "vertically upwards" some norms as governing their lives, and it also means that they must recognize some others horizontally both in the normatively mediated sense as bearers of the rights, duties, entitlements, and responsibilities prescribed by the norms, and in the purely intersubjective sense as having or sharing authority on those norms.[150] Human freedom, then, is not a general independence from others (which is impossible) or freedom from being determined by anything other than oneself. Concrete freedom is finding oneself affirmed as having authority by other individuals whom we affirm as having authority in the unconditional mode of respect. This mutual affirmation is the goodness of mutual recognition. Genuine freedom is therefore a practical question of the real-life capacity and propensity for individuals to have genuine respect recognition for each other.[151]

How I interpret and apply Ikäheimo's conceptions is to understand that though we must vertically recognize that norms govern our social lives, there is more to applying a recognition norm than an awareness that applying it in one's interaction with another individual is the appropriate thing to do. Recognition requires a set of norms and social institutions to guide recognition, but it also requires that we actively engage in intersubjective recognition relations. In many circumstances, only a particular way of engagement with the individual in his or her distinct circumstances is proper recognition of that individual. In any particular human interaction, I need to tailor my response to the individual in front of me; my recognizing a particular individual is conditioned by his or her individuality. Justice demands that we consider what norms apply to the current situation, plus it demands that the application of those norms be tailored to suit the individuals involved.

---

[150] Ikäheimo, 32-33.
[151] Ikäheimo, 35-36.

Justice requires engagements with recognition in two dimensions, one vertical with recognition norms, and one horizontal with individuals, meaning that nonengagement with either norms or individuals is misrecognition that can lead to injustice. This horizontal or personal demand on recognition relations is not articulated by Honneth, whose theory provides an insufficient structure of recognition. The demands of recognition, aside from a narrow set of legal relations, go beyond the conventionality of applying norms to groups of people. Justice requires that some forms of legal recognition apply equally to all individuals and, therefore, requires nonengagement with other individuals in their particularities. Basic human rights are invariant, but nearly everything else in social interactions is variant. Even a judge needs to apply the norms according to the individual circumstances. We need to modulate norms according to individual circumstances and a range of interpretations dependent on the individual. Within the need for engagement with other individuals, there are public interactions in which engaging with the individual is necessary but in which we do not need to engage the person *as* an individual. For example, in commercial transactions, we are polite to those who serve us or to the individuals we serve, but we do not always need to know them personally. We can engage with individuals in ways that do not take into account their individuality, though we are still recognizing them as human beings deserving of moral consideration. There are other interactions in which recognition requires engaging with another individual in a way that recognizes the individual as an individual. In personal relations such as between family and friends, and in mentoring or other care relationships, only unconditional personal engagement meets the needs of recognition and justice. Unconditional purely intersubjective horizontal recognition should appear in more than only the most intimate relationships, however. This is because intersubjective recognition relations that are based on sincere care for others are sincere expressions of our humanity and are what, more than any other social activity, cultivates self-realization and autonomy, and, thus, justice. As Ikäheimo concludes, "social relations imbued with mutual unconditional or 'genuinely personifying' recognition are the ideally free relations for norm-governed beings like us."[152]

The importance of horizontal or personifying recognition raises the question of whether recognition is a behavior of perceiving positive qualities within another individual or an attribution of those positive qualities to the individual. Honneth identifies two possible models that try to characterize the nature of recognition:

> the model of attributions as a result of which the other subject acquires a new, positive property, or ... the model of perception, according to which an already-present property of a person is, as a secondary matter, merely strengthened or publicly manifested. In the first case, what we call 'recognition' would award or supplement the affected subject with something she had not had before; in the second case, by contrast, it would be a matter of a certain kind of perception of an already independently existing status.[153]

Honneth reasons that if we adopt the attributive model, then that means recognition behavior would not be in response to the individual and his or her internal properties but would be creating those properties in the individual. If this is the case, we must hold that recognition does not assist an individual toward autonomy but is actually creating autonomy in the individual. If instead we adopt the response model (Honneth's other term for the perception model, which I think is the more descriptive term in that recognition is more than just passive perception), then we can hold that we are indeed recognizing potentials and properties in an individual that are independent of the act of recognition and that recognition is not wishful or mistaken thinking unrelated to actual properties that are the object of recognition.[154] The response model of recognition shows us how

[152] Ikäheimo, 38.

[153] Honneth, "Grounding Recognition," 506-507.

[154] Terry Pinkard, "Recognition, the Right and the Good," in *The Philosophy of Recognition: Historical and Contemporary Perspectives*, ed. Hans-Christoph Schmidt am Busch and Christopher F. Zurn (Lanham, MD: Lexington Books, 2010), 129-151.

recognition happens when individuals identify positive potentialities present in others.[155] This meshes with McBride's interactive account of recognition that links social norms, individual agency, and our sensitivity to recognition of others.[156] In McBride's account, recognition relations are the mechanism of orienting ourselves to the social world, and our sensitivity to recognition is an essential part of our individual agency. We respond to the normative demands of our culture and to the properties of others while we struggle for recognition from others. It stands to reason that to identify, reinforce, and make manifest the positive potentialities in others requires an engagement with other individuals.

The response model leads to a problem identified by Honneth. If we are perceiving and responding to something within others, then they must possess the qualities we are recognizing. But if they already possess those qualities, then why do they need affirmation from others to develop a healthy relation-to-self? Honneth's answer is to forge a middle ground between the attributive and perceptual/response models:

> although we make manifest, in our acts of recognition, only those evaluative qualities that are already present in the relevant individual, it is only as a result of our reactions that he comes to be in a position to be truly autonomous, because he is then able to identify with his capabilities.[157]

---

[155] Honneth, "Grounding Recognition," 510. Patchen Markell's rejection of the response model unfairly links its acknowledgment of potential with traditional patterns of dominance. Markell places too much weight on his interpretation of how dominance is justified in terms of potentiality and actuality and does not, in my opinion, succeed in establishing that the response model "risks importing this fundamental inequality into the logic of recognition." Patchen Markell, "The Potential and the Actual: Mead, Honneth, and the 'I,'" in *Recognition and Power: Axel Honneth and the Tradition of Critical Social Theory*, ed. Bert van den Brink and David Owen (New York: Cambridge University Press, 2007), 106. I also find unconvincing Markell's argument that Honneth's theory of recognition, by focusing on individual potential, is blind to actualized forms of injustice.

[156] McBride, 5.

[157] Honneth, "Grounding Recognition," 510.

Or, as Arto Laitinen puts it, there must be both adequate insight on the part of the recognizer and mutual insight on the part of the recognized to acknowledge and internalize the recognition.[158] Thus, both the recognizer and the recognized have crucial roles to play in recognition, and neither can do it alone. This means that recognition is a relation between individuals in which both must be engaged with the recognition norms of their culture and with each other for recognition to be successful. When both the recognizer and the recognized are engaged with the norms and with each other, recognition enables the properties or qualities internal to the individual to be made intersubjective and public. The individual is affirmed as a valued part of the community, which lets others know something about the individual and lets the individual know his or her qualities are publicly valued. Prior to recognition, an individual may feel she has positive qualities—for example, she could feel she is a good artist—but it is only in the act of being recognized that positive qualities become affirmed for both the individual and others. Without recognition, any positive feelings the individual has about herself are precarious because they are internal and unaffirmed.[159] This is why individuals desire and need recognition—to solidify their feelings about themselves and to learn about new qualities they did not realize they had.

Engagement is at the heart of recognition because recognition always takes an object. This is because recognition is an intersubjective relation between individuals and is not detached from individuals. The recognition norms are universal within a culture, but to be operative, the norms must be applied to an individual. Because recognition is related to "certain aspects" of another individual, it is a specific response to the way a

---

[158] Arto Laitinen, "On the Scope of 'Recognition': The Role of Adequate Regard and Mutuality," in *The Philosophy of Recognition: Historical and Contemporary Perspectives*, ed. Hans-Christoph Schmidt am Busch and Christopher F. Zurn (Lanham, MD: Lexington Books, 2010), 319-342.

[159] There is also the possibility that someone is personally happy with her artistic creations, for example, and feels good about her achievements without need for the assessments of others. This real possibility does not easily fit into the discussion of social recognition and calls for further consideration.

specific individual is. Recognition is recognition only if it has intention in it. As Honneth says,

> [Recognition is] not to be understood as a side-effect of an other-directed action but rather as the expression of a free-standing intention; whether we are talking of gestures, speech acts, or institutional measures, these expressions and procedures are cases of 'recognition' only if their primary purpose is directed in some positive manner towards the existence of another person or group.[160]

Recognition is a relation that is the expression of a purposeful intention, not incidental or accidental, but directed and specific. As Honneth says, reciprocally granted entitlement to a certain level of consideration provides the background against which subjects learn to experience themselves as deserving respect, promoting their self-determination.[161] The norms that make up this background must be brought to bear on an individual, the process of which Honneth did not delve into but is critical for understanding recognition and misrecognition. Recognition norms are nonspecific and need to be made specific through an expression of intention. General recognition norms point to possible recognition behaviors, but this potential behavior must be made manifest through an individual's intention directed at another individual.

To describe the intentional linking of recognition norms to a specific individual, I will borrow the concept of de-severance. An act of de-severance is an act of bringing something into salience[162] or making it significant to one's actions. De-severance is mostly thought of in terms of objects in regions of space,[163] but the practice of engaging with the region of social norms and bringing particular norms close and relevant allows us

---

[160] Honneth, "Grounding Recognition," 506.

[161] Honneth, *The I in We*, 46.

[162] Jeff Malpas, *Heidegger's Topology* (Cambridge, MA: Massachusetts Institute of Technology, 2007), 76.

[163] John Russon and Kirsten Jacobson, in *Bloomsbury Companion to Heidegger*, eds. Francois Raffoul and Eric Nelson, (London: Bloomsbury, 2013), 345-352.

to apply them to our social situations. Social norms are present in the cultural background. Norms exert a constant influence on individuals, and the following of norms can be a nonreflective and unconscious action. Recognition is different because it requires an intention—an unconscious following of the norms is not a recognition of another. Therefore, recognition norms, though also present in the cultural background, become active and part of recognition only when an individual de-severs a norm from the cultural background and brings it into salience in his or her interaction with another—bringing it from the background of possibilities into the foreground of action. Without this de-severance, following a recognition norm is accidental and is not recognition, and it is less likely to be beneficial to the other individual. An engagement with the recognition norms is required.

Similarly, to respect another individual is to de-server that individual from the background and give him or her our attention. As Honneth says, "We care only about those events and are affected only by those occurrences that are of direct and unmediated relevance for the way we understand our lives."[164] This may sound harsh, but I think he is correct to say that this is what we mean by "sympathy" and "care"—that something affects us. For example, when we hear of a natural disaster on other side of the world, we understand that people have suffered, but we understand in an abstract way. If we are aware that someone we know was at the location of the natural disaster, our perception significantly changes. If someone with whom we are on intimate terms is involved, then our reaction to the disaster changes even more significantly. Only if we are involved with the area or an individual who is involved will we respond to a natural disaster with intersubjective recognition. A more general recognition is still possible, but it will be different in character—general and not intersubjective, though still laudable, and perhaps even more laudable if we value acting beyond self-interest. As an expression of our humanity, we care in the abstract about the suffering of others, and can take tangible action such as donating to a relief cause helping those affected by the

---

[164] Honneth, *Reification*, 151.

disaster, but it will lack the same care and engagement we feel from being directly involved with those affected. We will usually care much more and do much more when we are directly involved with other individuals who are involved in events. Going beyond personal involvements into political action is another dimension of recognition that I will discuss in chapter 2.4.

Recognition is a matter of caring about others in terms of significance, if not fondness. Human interaction that is without care for another's needs and well-being is itself a kind of misrecognition. The mutual nature of recognition calls for an intersubjective engagement between individuals of mutual valuing if not mutual affection. Because recognition is a relation, recognition comes more easily within a personal relationship. The more relations of recognition one has, the easier it is to add more relations of recognition. According to Stanley Cavell, maintaining social relations requires engaging with another individual such that one is existentially involved in the emotional world of the other individual. The involvement Cavell describes need not be intimate but does need to be a "stance of acknowledgement" of the other individual that is emotional rather than cognitive. This involvement is a recognitional stance of mutual sympathy through which we come to understand that we have a moral responsibility to react to the other individual in specific ways.[165]

Honneth's interpretation of Cavell focuses on Cavell's prioritization of empathetic over cognitive engagement, which Honneth uses in service of his argument for what he calls "antecedent acts of recognition."[166] Honneth's question of how it is possible for us to lose sight of our recognitional practices is predicated on his assumption that recognition is antecedent to our social practices. The problems with Honneth's concept of antecedent or elementary recognition are discussed elsewhere by other scholars.[167] I will leave that aside and turn instead to how Honneth seems

---

[165] Stanley Cavell, "Knowing and Acknowledging," in *Must We Mean What We Say?* (Cambridge, UK: Cambridge University Press, 1976), 238-266.

[166] Honneth, *Reification*, 51-56.

[167] See for example, Zurn, *Axel Honneth*, Kindle locations 1285-1370.

to miss the implications of Cavell's position that a stance of acknowledgment is an existential involvement in interpersonal communication. Honneth tries to force Cavell's idea into his own concept of antecedent recognition.[168] Rather than argue that a forgotten antecedent recognition of others is the cornerstone of reification of others, I will explore possible reasons why an individual would not engage with other individuals in their interactions with them. Honneth offers some good insights on this, but these insights bear more fruit by moving the discussion from Honneth's cognitive considerations into the intersubjective engagement to which Cavell refers.

The conscious intention of recognition within an intersubjective engagement needs to be defined in more detail than saying it is a caring participation with others. I define the intersubjective engagement necessary for recognition as a comportment toward others of sincere and concrete openness and responsiveness to others as being individuals with their own capabilities and desires. Intersubjective engagement is a manner of interpersonal relations that is both considerate of the needs and status of the other individual and requires awareness that one has effects on other individuals. It does not seek to define, reduce, control, or dominate others. Intersubjective engagement is a recognition that "supposes that I cannot see right through you"[169] and that it is my responsibility to see you and listen to you. I can recognize the positive properties of another individual only if I have the freestanding conscious intention of perceiving that person and interacting with him or her in a positive manner.

In the rest of this chapter, I will explore ways in which recognition relations have gone wrong and lead to misrecognition. First I will discuss misrecognitions in which the problem is in vertical recognition, either disengagement from norms or engagement with problematic norms, and then I will discuss misrecognitions in which the problem is in horizontal

[168] Honneth, *Reification*, 57-59.

[169] Luce Irigaray, *I Love to You*, trans. A. Martin (New York: Routledge, 1996), 104.

recognition in which there is insufficient or improper engagement with other individuals.

1.3.1 - Disengagement from Norms

Engaging with recognition norms is part of our acceptance of our moral responsibility, and lack of a sense of moral responsibility is a significant factor in misrecognition. By Honneth's definition, recognition behavior is a tracking of specific positive properties in others as measured by means of social recognition norms. For example, my society's recognition norms teach me that I should respect honesty and that when I know someone who is honest in his dealings, I recognize that individual as honest and treat him accordingly. Given Honneth's picture of misrecognition as the contrary of recognition, it would seem that misrecognition behavior can be defined as occurrences in which recognition norms are not engaged, not applied, or both. If, to continue the example, I meet someone who is honest, but I either do not care about honesty or do not recognize the other's honesty, I am not valuing the other appropriately. This type of misrecognition is most easily seen in legal areas such that if I do not consider a right to be important or do not acknowledge an individual's entitlement to that right, I will not behave as required by that right toward the individual, and that is misrecognition.

But is it always the case that engagement with norms means recognition is happening, or is the connection between recognition norms and misrecognition not a binary one? A closer analysis of that relationship of recognition norms and misrecognition behavior reveals a complex relationship. First, I will look at the ways that individuals do not engage with norms (a lack of vertical recognition), and then I will explore ways in which individuals can engage with norms that, in practice, perpetrate misrecognition on others. It is counterintuitive to think that misrecognition behavior could maintain engagement with recognition norms, much less possess a sense of moral responsibility toward those misrecognized, but it is the case in some misrecognition behaviors.

If an individual or social institution is not engaging with norms, then misrecognition is a likely consequence. Individuals are socialized into social norms and learn their value, so broad general disregard for recognition norms would be, or at least should be, rare. It is possible that someone can consciously and willfully disregard all norms, taking herself out of mutual recognition relations despite the cost of becoming a pariah in her community. However, given the essentialness of recognition for social functioning, it is far more likely that nonengagement with norms is a specific disregard within a specific situation. Such a specific disregard can be related to a specific other individual, but I will take up that possibility later. Here, I speak of a nonengagement with norms within a specific but temporary situation in which moral responsibility for recognition norms is forgotten or obscured but not entirely abandoned. At times, we become oblivious to others in our everyday tasks and morally injure others in our inattention, but we can be prodded into awareness at any moment by seeing how we are not treating another appropriately. The mistake in this type of misrecognition is procedural, not in the sense of a formal procedure but in that we are, within a specific timeframe, caught up in processes in which norms are forgotten and recognition behavior thus becomes absent. An example would be being so focused on one's current activity, such as driving or walking in a crowded area, that one forgets the rules regarding behavior, being either rude or otherwise negligent in our moral obligations to others. This type of misrecognition is not a cognitive mistake because its behavior is prereflective and is resolvable by reflection on our actions.

There can also be a more deliberate nonengagement with norms when individuals believe that certain norms are not appealing or convenient within a specific social environment. Disengagement from norms is compartmentalized to suit one's own interests without a rejection of moral responsibility in general. Individuals can rationalize away their responsibility to follow specific norms in specific situations, such as in their workplace. Business owners, for example, can neglect the health and safety of their employees to preserve profits while at the same time being honest in their accounting practices. A supervisor could think that recognizing his employees' needs is unimportant because they are his subordinates but still treat friends and family justly. Workers, perhaps in response to their employers' actions, could believe that norms do not apply, or apply differently, in specific situations on the job. A worker could see dishonesty on the job as acceptable if it increases her productivity. Another could rationalize that his theft of company property is acceptable. Another could feel that she does not owe politeness or camaraderie to fellow workers because it is "just a job." Security and police forces who do not consider respect for civilians a part of their job is another example. By suspending the application of recognition norms in particular aspects of one's life, one is perpetrating misrecognition by cutting off recognition within that aspect of life.

The compartmentalizing of recognition relations is common in modern life. In various areas of our lives, we neglect norms to varying degrees, such as when the pressures of social demands encourage one to take expedient ways out of the burdens of responsibilities. This dereliction of responsibility to act in accordance with recognition norms is similar in form to, but is normatively different from, a responsible restriction of recognition. An example of the responsible form is when teachers close off options of friendship with students out of responsibility to their students not out of disregard for them. Recognizing another's role as a student includes avoiding crossing boundaries of intimacy that potentially would harm the student. However, a teacher who thinks he does not owe any students basic courtesies such as timely responses to their e-mails is deliberately not engaging with recognition norms concerning students, and this disregarding of the moral responsibilities of being a teacher is misrecognizing students. Understanding an individual's level of awareness of and engagement with recognition norms will help us to understand what may be going on in misrecognition behavior.

We must also acknowledge that misrecognition can occur when the recognition norms are engaged with but misapplied. Instances of misapplied recognition norms are when an individual is aware of the recognition norms and intends to apply them properly but is, for whatever reason, not succeeding. This could result from an individual not understanding the recognition norms or how to apply them or not understanding that his or her current situation calls for recognition. This inadequate application of recognition norms is a cognitive mistake on the part of an individual that is most likely an unintentional mistake and free of antagonism. Young individuals are especially prone to not understand how to act in certain situations because of their lack of life experience, and, despite good intentions, they can fail to recognize others properly. Misapplied recognition also describes any breach of customary protocol because of inexperience rather than malice.

In the above examples of nonengagement, the norms themselves are not causing misrecognition and injustice—it is the lack of engagement with the norms that leads to misrecognitions. It is also possible that engagement with norms leads to misrecognition if the norms themselves are misrecognitions. I identify two types of recognition norms that are misrecognitions, differentiated by whether the norms are tracking putative negatives, which I call "normative discrimination," or putative positives, which I call "pathological recognition." I will discuss each in turn.

1.3.2 - Normative Discrimination

What I call "normative discrimination" is the use of recognition-like norms that designate particular social groups as having negative traits that characterize those groups as deficient and inferior. These norms are a form of negative recognition that mediates our interactions with certain groups, dictating that the appropriate response is to deny these groups positive recognition and moral consideration. Because the discrimination is guided by reçognition-like norms, individuals perpetrate it believing they are behaving properly. Normative discrimination is the authoritative core of hierarchical oppression that separates a social group for exclusion from the benefits accorded to "proper" social groups.

The negative recognition of normative discrimination differs from a negative response to violations of norms such as disapproving of dishonesty or theft. There, the negative response recognizes the rights of those who have been wronged, and a negative response to wrongdoers is an appropriate upholding of norms. When we punish someone who has been convicted of a crime with imprisonment or fines, we are upholding general norms that recognize the rights of victims of the crime, even if we are denying recognition to the convicted individual's freedom and desire to not be punished. In contrast, a normative discrimination is when a trait that should be neutral to moral norms, such as skin color, ethnicity, or religion, is taken as a negative and all who hold that trait are regarded as less worthy than others. Bader's "criteria of ascription," by which he categorizes structural asymmetries of power and practices of discrimination, oppression, and exclusion as being socially defined and ascribed characteristics of targeted groups, are examples of normative discrimination.[170]

Normative discrimination is directed predominantly at social groups separated by race, gender, class, and so on. Additional illusionary negatives are often attributed to a social group, such as labeling all Muslims as violent, all Jews as dishonest, all gays as promiscuous, all who live in poverty deserving their poverty because they are lazy or ignorant, and so on. Normative discrimination disregards and often actively denies the consideration of individuals and their particular traits and contributions. How the targets of normative discrimination actually are is irrelevant to the negative stereotypes because the illusionary negatives attributed to the group dominate social perception of all members of the group. Perpetrators unreflectively follow the norms that dictate behavior toward the targeted groups. The normative character of normative discrimination discourages questioning whether the traits it attributes to targeted groups are actually present in individual members of that group.

---

[170] Veit Bader, "Misrecognition, Power, and Democracy," in *Recognition and Power: Axel Honneth and the Tradition of Critical Social Theory*, ed. Bert van den Brink and David Owen (New York: Cambridge University Press, 2007), 244-246. The wealth of detail in Bader's table of ascriptive criteria is impressive, though at points problematic, the full analysis of which is beyond the scope of the current study. Suffice for now to say that Bader's central idea of socially defined characteristics being used to discriminate against targeted groups is essentially what I call normative discrimination.

Normative discrimination can be taken to the extreme of a group being considered to be undeserving of any moral consideration. This misrecognition is beyond a lack of awareness of the moral standing of others and is a conscious antagonism toward others. An individual engaged in this comportment considers the appropriate response to other groups of human beings is to deprive the other actively of recognition as a human being. The extreme hostility toward a number of historically marginalized groups such as Gypsies and Jews in Europe, Dalits in India, and Burakumin in Japan are examples of this extreme normative discrimination. Someone born into one of these groups is condemned for life to misrecognition. The stigma attached to certain diseases or conditions also fits into normative discrimination. Those afflicted with leprosy were outcast from society as unclean.[171] More recently, those afflicted with AIDS have suffered similar pariah status. In both cases, the ostracizing was accompanied by moral rebuke, the victims condemned as immoral simply for having a disease. One could say these people are rendered invisible, but it is more accurate to say they are condemned as unfit to be included and are dispossessed of rights and status.

Slavery, in particular the institution of slavery in the United States, is a historical example of how normative discrimination is a distinct form of engagement with recognition norms that leads to misrecognition and injustice. Slavery shows that normative discrimination precedes a denial of recognition relations—the criterion of ascription in this case rendering African people as beings to enslave because they are inferior. Slavery is a relationship defined by a malicious use of power, but slavery in the Americas did not result from taking away an existing recognition relation from members of a community and enslaving them. Indentured servitude and debtors' prisons are a destruction of an existing recognition relation. An impoverished European (already suffering from normative discrimination because of his or her class) was condemned to a debtors'

[171] A good study of this is Ricardo Fabrino Mendonça, "Recognition and Esteem: A Case Study of the Struggles of People Affected by Leprosy," in *The Politics of Misrecognition*, ed. Simon Thompson and Majid Yar (Farnham, UK: Ashgate Publishing, 2011), 145-168.

prison because he or she allegedly violated his or her responsibilities as a member of society. The social institution of debtors' prisons operates as a social relation that can be used properly or improperly. However barbaric we would consider the practice today, the social institution of debtors' prison was part of society's structure of legal recognition norms. An individual could be rightfully condemned to debtors' prison and an individual wrongly condemned to debtors' prison would be suffering an injustice according to society's norms. Distinctions between just and unjust imprisonment were possible because inmates were, at least to a point, considered members of society with whom recognition relations were possible.

Slavery operates under a very different set of assumptions because the normative discrimination based on race denied the possibility of recognition relations. Rather than a rupture of a recognition relation of social inclusion, the slave is, as Orlando Patterson observes, natally alienated: denied *a priori* the possibility of recognition relations.[172] As Frantz Fanon observed, racism reduces others to nothing more than skin, a skin to which they are chained and determined. The recognition norms of the dominant culture are imposed onto the oppressed who are represented through normative discrimination as mere animal bodies unable to think, reason, or speak properly.[173] The Native Americans and Africans enslaved by Europeans were always outsiders to the European slavers and had never been afforded recognition other than normative discrimination. The recognition order of European culture negatively recognized non-Europeans as inferior and uncivilized, and this normative assumption framed European encounters with indigenous people throughout the world. Africans and Native Americans had never been included, so enslaving them was ethically possible in a way that enslaving Europeans was not.

Slavery was fundamentally different from being excluded from the community and denied rights because the enslaved human beings were

---

[172] Orlando Patterson, *Slavery and Social Death: A Comparative Study* (Cambridge, MA: Harvard University Press, 1982), 13.

[173] Frantz Fanon, *Black Skin, White Masks*, trans. Charles Lam Markmann (New York: Grove Press, 1967), 110-113.

considered property. Indentured servants were also treated as a kind of property to be bought, used, and sold. What is different between slaves and indentured servants is the type of recognition relations involved. The indentured servants' status as property was defined by contracts for set terms, and their recognition as free beings was held in abeyance, under the assumption that the servant willingly entered into the contract. Similarly, the prisoner, whether debtor or criminal, has a status with a limited time frame. Indentured servants were subordinated, deprived of freedom, and often exploited, yet they retained a recognition relation to society with the hope of improvement of their social standing, however limited that potential may have been. Slaves, being natally alienated, had a very different recognition relation. Questions about slaves' integrity, honor, autonomy, or self-respect were nonsensical to anyone who engaged with the norms that specified what the slaves were—property. Slaves were, as Patterson observes, annulled of rights and identity, without ties to past or future, unrecognizable as human beings, at best shadow members of society.[174]

Slavery was not an act like flogging, rape, torture, or social ostracizing. Slavery was enforced through violence, but the violence stemmed from a systemic misrecognition attitude of normative discrimination. The attitude of impossibility of the slaves' social inclusion preceded the enslavement because the normative discrimination framed the recognition relations with the slave whether the slave was captured or born into slavery. Before the violent act of enslavement occurred, the target, reduced to skin as Fanon said, had been deemed to be compatible with enslavement. Whether the assessment was that the slaves were undeserving of freedom or deserving of enslavement, the misrecognition was a normative discrimination against those who possessed the trait of dark skin and, therefore, lacked humanity, dignity, and rationality. It is not so much that the slave was objectified as a tool as much as it was that the slave was tracked as being of no value beyond menial labor. The slave master did not seek recognition from the slaves—the slave master sought

[174] Patterson, 263.

work and obedience from them no different than from his other beasts of burden. The normative discrimination against those of dark skin precluded the possibility of human recognition in any direction. Here, I say "human recognition" because a slave could be prized and praised in the same way a good horse could be.

Our contemporary society does not have slavery per se, though a Marxist theorist could point to low wages as a form of slavery. Our society retains the normative discrimination of what Andrew Sayer calls "contributive injustice"—the social misrecognition that restricts what members of social classes are allowed to contribute, particularly in terms of occupations.[175] The lottery of birth restricts most individuals to an inheritance of class distinction that limits their economic opportunities, whereas members of the lucky sperm club[176] inherit wealth either directly or through privileged opportunities for education, jobs, and careers. As Sayer observes,[177] public attitudes support the idea that greater contributions to society deserve greater compensation, but the public attributes the value of contributions on the basis of class and an unequal distribution of labor. The social structure produces unequal opportunities, with jobs with higher social status and compensation going to a privileged class. Most of the problems of distributive injustice stem from this contributive injustice because low-value jobs are given low-value compensation. Sayer correctly observes that what individuals are allowed to contribute is at least as important as what they receive in terms of resources.[178] This misrecognition is centered on jobs and occupations, but it extends to educational and cultural opportunities, the health hazards and health care one encounters, where one can afford to live, and all of the lifestyle opportunities that go with these. Contributive injustice is a

---

[175] Andrew Sayer, "Contributive Justice and Meaningful Work," *Res Publica* 15 (1), 2009, 1-16.

[176] My term, not Sayer's.

[177] Andrew Sayer, "Misrecognition: The Unequal Division of Labour and Contributive Justice," in *Politics of Misrecognition* (Farnham, UK: Ashgate Publishing, 2011), 87-103.

[178] Sayer, "Misrecognition: The Unequal Division of Labour and Contributive Justice," 92.

normative discrimination against others who are not allowed to contribute and not allowed to use their talents and explore their possibilities. A wide range of social groups are negatively tracked and restricted as to the occupations they can enter. Women being occupationally restricted is connected to pathological recognition, as I will discuss next, but the normative discrimination against women as weaker and less rational also restricts their occupational opportunities and leads to the glass ceiling within occupations. Minorities of race, ethnicity, and religion are also negatively discriminated against and restricted to low-value occupations. Mostly though, contributive injustice is tied to class, with labor divided between blue-collar and white-collar, and individual workers are subsumed under the norms that designate as inferior their social contributions and status.

Despite the fact that contributive injustice damages not only the afflicted individuals but also the whole of society that misses out on the potential contributions of so many, its injustice persists because the normative discrimination is seen as a proper response to how things are. Sayer observes that one of the most common contemporary misrecognitions is underestimating the extent to which structural inequalities give only some individuals preferential access to practices that are socially recognized.[179] Sayer argues that the cause of this unequal distribution of occupations—society's structural inequalities—is likely to be misrecognized as being the deserved product of effort and intelligence. Furthermore, specific individuals' contributions are evaluated according to the unequal distribution of labor, misrecognizing their contributions and qualities. The combination of these two misrecognitions means that regardless of individual traits and efforts, the economically privileged are seen as having earned their wealth, and the economically disadvantaged are seen as deserving of their lack of wealth. This denial of recognition for the economically disadvantaged is a normative discrimination that sees them as inferior: The poor deserve to be poor because they are lazy and

[179] Sayer, "Misrecognition: The Unequal Division of Labour and Contributive Justice," 87.

incompetent. The companion misrecognition is assuming that any wealthy person, especially white men, has wealth because of earning it through hard work and superior ability. These misrecognitions hide and reinforce contemporary society's structures that created class inequality, contributive and distributional injustices, and their accompanying pathological recognition and normative discrimination norms.

All forms of normative discrimination reduce individuals to a negative preconception without individuality and perhaps without humanity. The negative preconception, not the other individual, is being seen, and the other is being viewed through the negative preconception and treated with hostility on the basis of it. The mistake in normative discrimination is that the perpetrator is guided by his or her own preconceptions (though these preconceptions are usually learned from the culture's recognition norms) rather than the attributes actually possessed of the other individual. The perpetrator assumes, if not insists, that the oppressed others conform to those preconceptions, and the perpetrator is resistant to contrary information. Negative recognition norms are a denial, often with malice, of the positive values and contributions of others who hold particular traits and, thus, are misrecognition. Oppressed individuals are reduced to objects and rendered without voice or will, and their experiences, words, and actions are suspected and delegitimized. Today, for example, Muslims are tracked (literally and figuratively) as terrorists; their every word and action is treated as suspect, and their claims for recognition as human beings are delegitimized.

In today's pluralistic society, malice in normative discrimination often reflects social insecurity by dominant groups against minority groups. Racists, sexists, homophobes, jingoists, and antireligious bigots of all stripes imagine themselves harmed by the social inclusion of hated and feared groups. To see others one thinks inferior being treated equally by society is perceived as a moral insult. Normative discrimination also arises in the midst of ethnic and sectarian conflicts. When tensions exist between social groups, all sides can become paranoid and overly sensitive to what the other groups are doing. Actions by the other groups are negatively tracked and perceived as threatening, and the success and well-being of other groups may be perceived as a matter of the others receiving greater and unfair advantages, thus diminishing one's own perceived social position. In the eyes of a Capulet, there is no good in a Montague.

Common targets of negative stereotyping are subcultures and countercultural movements, such as religious sects and youth movements. As Stanley Cohen observed, the behavior of subcultures, such as the violence between mods and rockers in the United Kingdom in the 1960s, is exaggerated by the mainstream culture to hysterical proportions, generating unwarranted hostility against those subcultures.[180] Members of the subculture are stigmatized as moral outsiders or, as Cohen calls them, "folk devils," who are defined as a threat to the mainstream social order, values, and interests. The perceived threat becomes a moral panic,[181] rousing normative discrimination against the members of the subculture. Members of a subculture are labeled as deviants, and "once a person is thus type cast, his acts are interpreted in terms of the status to which he has been assigned."[182] I will explore ways that members of subcultures respond to misrecognition in chapter 2.4.5.

The morality of normative discrimination is easily compartmentalized by perpetrators. Those who deny equal rights to women, minorities, immigrants, or other groups often do not see themselves as being against rights and equality. They would see their exclusion of particular groups not as a double standard but as consistent with and upholding of moral norms. They would justify their disparate treatment with an interpretive narrative of why targeted groups are deserving of exclusion. Superficially rational arguments are used to justify the misrecognition as a case of the victims deserving it and even that there is an ethical demand to misrecognize these individuals because of their traits. The presence of normative discrimination reinforces an environment in which mistreatment of others is defensible. Normative discrimination is essentially what Honneth describes as social ostracizing. Instances of normative discrimination will

---

180 Stanley Cohen, *Folk Devils and Moral Panics: The Creation of the Mods and Rockers* (London: Grenada Publishing, 1972).
181 Cohen, *Folk Devils and Moral Panics*, 9.
182 Cohen, *Folk Devils and Moral Panics*, 12.

be witnessed by other individuals who will become disinclined to offer recognition to socially ostracized individuals and will even be encouraged actively to misrecognize those individuals. Powerful individuals and institutions can use arguments and persuasion to convince others to engage in normative discrimination against targeted groups or individuals. Similarly, individuals can appeal to interpretive narratives to provide post hoc validity for misrecognition motivated by personal reasons. Often, rational arguments are not needed to tap into fear and hatred of others who are different.

The misrecognitions discussed above are behaviors in which individuals believe they are acting appropriately. Even the victims of misrecognition may come to believe their treatment is appropriate. Individuals in groups targeted by normative discrimination can identify with the definitions ascribed to them but at the cost of their social and personal value without receiving any compensatory positive self-affirmation. Pierre Bourdieu's concept of a social field can help us understand this.[183] A culture generates a social field of objective structures and relations within which individuals perceive, interpret, and act. The rules of the field that structure intersubjective relations include recognition norms, which, through socialization, become part of individuals' habitus—their dispositions and embodied agency within the social field. How individuals perceive, assess, and interact with each other is structured by their position within the social field and the recognition norms that structure interactions. When recognition norms are discriminatory, they distort individuals' conceptions of what appropriate recognition behaviors are. These distortions can become engrained in individuals' habitus and thus part of their daily attitudes and behaviors beneath reflective awareness. Such a psychological adaptation is a self- misrecognition in which the misrecognition received from others is internalized into one's habitus. The distortions are part of

[183] Pierre Bourdieu, *The Field of Cultural Production* (Cambridge, UK: Polity Press, 1993).

> the set of fundamental, pre-reflexive assumptions that social agents engage by … accepting the world as it is, and of finding it natural because their mind is constructed according to cognitive structures that are issued out of the very structures of the world.[184]

Normative discrimination is the foundation and structure for social prejudices and discrimination.

Conversely, McBride argues that the socially disadvantaged can still maintain a sense of subjective well-being. One can opt to identify with one's lowly social position by seeing one's status as part of a larger purpose and can boost one's self-esteem through taking this perspective.[185] The structures of the social field and the interactions between individuals mediate but do not determine the exact behaviors of individuals. Despite the pressures of misrecognition, individuals can resist the messages of normative discrimination. As we will see in chapter 2.2, the concept of habitus also helps describe how individuals can reject misrecognition and struggle for recognition.

Normative discrimination is the foundation of prejudice, and its hierarchical structure is so common it pervades human society. Within normative discrimination, the engagement is with the preconceived notions of others, prompting disengagement from and obliviousness to how the situation and other individuals actually are. This oblivious disengagement behavior hinders communication and intersubjective recognition. McBride describes an occurrence of this disengagement by the British government in 1931:

> The Indian delegates had been organized into *religious* groups by the colonial power. Gandhi objected vehemently but colonial officials were immovable in their determination to view Indians primarily through the lens of sectarian division.[186]

---

[184] Pierre Bourdieu and Loïc J.D. Wacquant, *An Invitation to Reflexive Sociology* (Chicago: University of Chicago Press, 1992), 168.

[185] McBride, 117-118.

[186] McBride, 37, emphasis his.

The British disengagement that saw Indians only in terms of British categorization had its most disastrous consequences in the shortsighted partition of the land into Hindu India and Muslim Pakistan. McBride also quotes Patricia Williams on the attitudes of white tourists to local black churches, saying that for the whites, "no one existed for them who could not be governed by their intensions."[187] These condescending and patronizing attitudes are not seen by perpetrators as disrespectful, and it might not even occur to them that they are misrecognitions. We could count some of this as the manifestation of privilege, but in a broader sense it reveals a common human laziness to engage with others and be open to perceiving them as they are.

Both of these examples show how normative discrimination engenders an oblivious disengagement that takes the form of a dichotomy between oneself as subject and the other as object. Kelly Oliver observes that in this dichotomy, one imagines oneself as self-sovereign and imagines the others as unable to govern themselves.[188] Oliver argues that the subject-object dichotomy results from the pathology of oppression, which explains the British colonial example, though in Williams's example, the white tourists are not actively oppressing the black worshippers but are treating them as objects to be used by their self-sovereign selves. The subject-object attitude and its behaviors of condescension are choices individuals make, and individuals maintain the ability to engage with other individuals despite social norms. It seems easier to see that the subject-object attitude leads to disengagement,

---

[187] McBride, 37, quoting Patricia Williams, *The Alchemy of Race and Rights* (Cambridge, MA: Harvard University Press, 1991), 72. Her full quote: "As well-intentioned as they were, I was left with the impression that no one existed for them who could not be governed by their intentions. While acknowledging the lack of apparent malice in this behavior, I can't help thinking that it is a liability as much as a luxury to live without interaction. To live so completely impervious to one's own impact on others is a fragile privilege, which over time relies not simply on the willingness but on the inability of others—in this case blacks— to make their displeasure heard."

[188] Kelly Oliver, *Witnessing: Beyond Recognition* (Minneapolis, MN: University of Minnesota Press, 2001), 3.

oppression, and various kinds of social ostracizing, shunning, and disregard and that these general social environments of oppression maintain, but do not create, the subject-object dichotomy.

1.3.3 - Pathological Recognition

Recognition norms that purport to recognize groups of individuals positively but in practice misrecognize them I label "pathological recognition." The term "pathology" refers to the study of disease not the disease itself,[189] so the term "pathology" is used incorrectly if it designates a social structure of a system a "social pathology" despite its widespread adoption in critical theory. The term "pathological" means related to or caused by a disease.[190] It is in this sense that I mean pathological recognition—recognition norms that cause injustice.

In pathological recognition, social relations are structured by a recognition order that designates social groups, such as women, as having particular traits that should be positively recognized. Within this recognition order, individuals recognize others by engaging with and applying their culture's seemingly positive recognition norms. This type of misrecognition behavior conforms to a recognition-like structure that socializes individuals into behaviors that emulate recognition, but the norms are pathological in that the cultural recognition norms are concealed misrecognitions, the application of which does not support others' self-realization and autonomy. Pathological recognition norms erode others' autonomy by subsuming them under recognition norms that define them and limit their possibility for recognition—for example, the traditional characterization of the traits and contributions of women. Unlike

[189] "pathology, n.". OED Online. December 2016. Oxford University Press, accessed January 06, 2017,
http://0-www.oed.com.serlib0.essex.ac.uk/view/Entry/138805?.

[190] "pathological, adj. and n.". OED Online. December 2016. Oxford University Press, accessed January 06, 2017, http://0-www.oed.com.serlib0.essex.ac.uk/view/Entry/138800.

normative discrimination, the recognition norms of pathological recognition provide an affirmation of the value of targeted individuals. Both forms normatively restrict individuals and their possibilities, but pathological recognition deals with norms that focus on alleged positives that exclude other positives, whereas normative discrimination focuses on alleged negatives.

What I am calling "pathological recognition" encompasses portrayals of negative recognition as domination, as advanced by, for example, Althusser,[191] Butler,[192] Markell,[193] and McNay.[194] These theorists address how recognition is used to maintain social domination by motivating subjects to serve the interests of power. Individuals are recognized for adhering to their responsibilities and duties to society, and their recognized compliance gives them a social identity. These theorists tend to reject recognition as irredeemable. Althusser rejects recognition because he sees it as the central mechanism of ideology, and McNay rejects recognition as a possible model for emancipatory critique, á la Honneth. Butler sees recognition as intertwined with domination and enforced conformism and considers the idea that freedom can be realized through recognition as part of an ideology that contributes to the dominant recognition order. Similarly, Markell sees the pursuit of recognition of our identity from social institutions as unobtainable, contributing to injustice rather than emancipating us from it.

What these negative conceptions of recognition tend to overlook is the fact that the forces of domination succeed because they are exploiting a positive social mechanism. Recognition can be and is distorted and used to dominate people because recognition can also have a positive influence on

---

[191] Louis Althusser, "Ideology and Ideological State Apparatuses," reprinted in *Lenin and*
Philosophy and Other Essays, trans. B. Brewster (New York: Monthly Press Review, 1971).

[192] Judith Butler, "Eine Welt, in der Antigone am Leben geblieben wäre," *Deutsche Zeitschrift für*
Philosophie, 49, 2001, 587599.

[193] Markell, *Bound by Recognition*.

[194] McNay, *Against Recognition*.

individuals. The problem is that these differences can be difficult for individuals to discern. As Honneth says, we need to distinguish the false forms of recognition from its correct morally positive forms, even though identifying "correct and morally required" recognition is even more difficult than Honneth assumes.[195]

Honneth's concept of ideological forms of recognition is similar to pathological recognition in that it acknowledges the positive aspect of a false form of recognition. I argue that Honneth's ideological recognition is a subset of pathological recognition, and the features of ideological recognition will appear in my phenomenologically fuller account of pathological recognition. Honneth characterizes social recognition as ideological when it merely evokes a self-conception that motivates a subject to accept tasks and obligations willingly and conform to a social role despite there being no prospect of positive material change that lives up to its evaluative promise.[196] There are three problems with that definition, a definition that seems to be contradicted by Honneth himself throughout his paper. First, recognition's normative character means that it always motivates individuals to conform to a social role and accept tasks and obligations willingly, so this cannot be a feature of what distinguishes ideological recognition from healthy recognition. Second, the evaluative promises of any form of recognition are not easily materially measured, and this is especially the case with pathological recognition that promises a sense of meaning and belonging more than material progress. Looking at fulfillment only in material terms misses that ideological recognition could, and often does, provide an identity benefit. Third, these negative forms of recognition actually promise very little material change—they offer only promises of inferior recognition that are largely kept because what is promised is only a milder experience of subordination. An example Honneth gives of ideological recognition is the promise to employees of

---

[195] Axel Honneth, "Recognition as Ideology," 325, in *Recognition and Power: Axel Honneth and the Tradition of Critical Social Theory*, ed. Bert van den Brink and David Owen (Cambridge, UK: Cambridge University Press, 2007), 323-347.

[196] Honneth, "Recognition as Ideology," 328, 346-347.

their greater freedom, individuality, and self-fulfillment if they become "entrepreneurs" of their own labor power and skills. This vague promise encourages employees to adopt a certain set of attitudes and actions; however, the employer's promise is not recognition at all but a ploy that shifts responsibility for inadequate compensation for labor away from employers and onto employees, which is a type of selective misrecognition I will describe later. Honneth's definition of ideological recognition is limited to a critique of some aspects of capitalism, so he misses the larger picture of pathological recognition.

We need to broaden Honneth's conception of ideological recognition while focusing on the idea of a process that socializes individuals into particular self-conceptions. By doing so, we can see that pathological recognition is less about material promises than it is about appealing to individuals' sense of practical identity, even though the identity that is being affirmed limits those individuals. Elsewhere in his paper, Honneth refers to the repeated praise of the fictional Uncle Tom's submissive virtues as an example of ideological recognition,[197] but the master who praises Tom never promises much to Tom, and certainly there is never any real improvement in Tom's material circumstances. What Tom does receive is affirmation of his identity as a good compliant servant. That the putative identities of pathological recognition give individuals a sense of meaning and value is why it is appealing to those being limited by it, despite its limiting assessments.

Pathological recognition can exploit two positive aspects of recognition: its normative role as a guide for proper conduct and its importance for individual development and relations-to-self. Pathological recognition can make people believe they are affirming themselves be applying the pathological recognition norms, and in doing so they are affirmed by others as behaving properly. Pathological recognition remains influential as long as the targeted recipients do not come to realize fully both that they are not receiving equal recognition and that this inequity is unfair. This is why pathological recognition is accompanied by narratives

---

[197] Honneth, "Recognition as Ideology," 325.

that justify and maintain the recognition order and its norms. Social norms provide objective criteria for knowing what is expected of us and for assessing our own actions.[198] We are socialized into the habit of relying on norms to guide our behavior. By distorting recognition norms to give the appearance that following the norms either affirms individuals and/or exemplifies proper conduct, the recognition order can influence people into misrecognition behavior that could advance a conformist ideological agenda. Critique of this ideological structure is necessary to reveal its assumptions and influences in order to open the possibility of individuals' awareness of the structure and its ideological manifestations and to motivate them to struggle against misrecognition.

What I argue separates false forms of recognition from positive ones is that the former attribute to individuals stereotypical traits and value judgments that are used to subsume individuals under a group definition. These attributed recognition norms hinder those individuals' possibilities for self-realization and receiving recognition for their actual qualities and contributions. Because pathological recognition norms appear to be positive recognition but in practice perpetrate misrecognition, they are false, dis-ease-causing forms of recognition. Pathological recognition is not purely negative in that at the same time that it misrecognizes and harms people, it socially affirms them. This is the case even though the positive affirmations are deceptions that mislead individuals into accepting affirmations that limits them.

Honneth gives the example of the idea of the heroic soldier, which grants to men who suffer social insignificance and a lack of prospects a type of recognition by becoming part of the military subculture.[199] This example is well worth exploring to illustrate one way that pathological recognition works. In the military subculture, individuals gain a measure of prestige and honor while at the same time being treated as nonautonomous servants of the state, if not used as canon fodder to achieve aims in which they have little or no involvement or from which

[198] By "objective" here I mean in terms of one's culture.
[199] Honneth, "Recognition as Ideology," 326-327.

they do not benefit. It is, at its core, a pathological recognition that lionizes war and honors "Our Glorious Dead" while downplaying the reality that they are, indeed, now dead.

We should not doubt that many served honorably, and whether they acted for king and country, for their families, or for their comrades in arms, they did their jobs properly and are worthy of our esteem. We also should not doubt that the esteem many individuals give to military veterans is sincere and with cause. Many of those who adopt the pathological recognition norms are not deliberately misrecognizing others but are following social norms, so they believe they are behaving properly. Individual soldiers accept the pathological recognition of military glory because for many who served, it provided them with a place to belong, a role to fulfill, and a sense of purpose, even if it denied them other options for self-relation and social affirmation. Maybe they had no better options, because of their social position and society's contributive injustice, to achieve social status.

This is why pathological recognition cannot be reduced to ideological machinations of the power structure. Instead, we need to see how recognition relations develop a life of their own, becoming part of the social fabric of normative expectations. Pathological recognition works because there is reason for individuals to accept the narrative that distorts individuals and their possibilities, and with time this distortion becomes the accepted normal. Often, we find pathological recognition in cultural traditions, largely unthought and unseen, part of a culture's system of beliefs. Our theoretical approach to pathological recognition is best served by understanding it as a largely prereflective form of recognition whose normative conceptions of individuals appears to value their traits and status positively but has lost touch with its tangible effects on individuals.

A prime example of pathological recognition is the traditional classification of women as caregivers—the normative evaluation of a "good" woman as a wife and mother. The traditional social definition of womanhood tracks positive qualities, such as being caring and nurturing. Such a classification of women has the appearance of recognizing women, but it does so in a limiting way. This pathological recognition does not empower women or engender their self-realization. In practice, it limits women's autonomy and self-image by socializing them into accepting a seemingly positive self-image as a caregiver.[200] The norms assigning women caregiver roles place women into restrictive gender roles that, among other effects, define women's care work as part of a woman's natural disposition and thus not real labor warranting compensation.[201] The pathological recognition norms defining women's nature as being caring and nurturing beings assumes that women should pursue caregiving as their life's work—either as a wife and mother or in caregiving professions such as nursing or teaching.

The pathological norms defining women in this way preclude other possibilities for recognition—if one is recognized as being a caregiver, then one cannot easily also be recognized as powerful, creative, or intellectually gifted. Also, women's caregiver role is recognized as a less valuable contribution compared with the contributions made by men. No matter how good a wife and mother a woman is, she still would not be esteemed highly compared with men. She does "women's work" while men do real work. What is recognized and honored excludes women as individuals with particular traits or behaviors but is instead an impersonal, stereotypical perception of women, and this identity is attributed to women as a group. The effect of this pathological recognition is that other possible roles for women that do not include the recognized traits are discouraged if not outright denied to women. The pathological recognition of women directly hinders women. Betty Friedan argues in her work, *The Feminine Mystique*, that it is the ideal of femininity, which she calls the "The Happy Housewife," that most damages the self-determination of women by ideologically restricting them to the norm of being a housewife and mother, neglecting education and work.[202]

---

[200] Honneth, "Recognition as Ideology," 326.

[201] See discussion of this by Fraser in *Redistribution or Recognition?* See also Honneth's brief discussion of this in *Disrespect*, 76.

[202] Friedan, Betty. *The Feminine Mystique: Contexts, The Scholarship on The Feminine Mystique*, eds. Kirsten Fermaglich and Lisa Fine, (New York: W.W. Norton & Co, 2013).

This suppression of women's choices is not necessarily practiced by individuals maliciously—even though it often can be—and may actually be considered by its practitioners as a form of compassion toward women by keeping them "safe" within the boundaries of their presumed nature. They may, with sincerity, believe that they are being benevolent toward women by recognizing their putatively positive character. They would be affirmed in that assessment by society, which is telling them they are honoring and supporting others, while at the same time hiding the damage that is being inflicted by the pathological recognition norms and associated behaviors. The traditional characterization of women recognizes them through a biased filter. Traditional paternalistic and misogynistic attitudes toward women misrecognize women as the weaker sex while at the same time instituting as a norm the moral need to protect supposedly weak women from potential dangers. This pathological recognition erodes women's autonomy under the pretext of taking moral responsibility for women. That the norm of "protecting" women from physically demanding activities and occupations is restrictive, sexist misrecognition does not negate the fact that those engaging with the recognition norms could consider themselves as acting with moral responsibility toward women. This does not excuse the sexism and ignorance involved, but acknowledging the moral element of the misrecognition allows us to understand better the persistence of such pathological cultural norms.

The positive character of pathological recognition explains why women (and men) do not realize how deeply women are harmed by misogynistic gender roles and attitudes. Recognition obscures this damage by positively reinforcing the imaginary unity of gender and social attitudes about gender and helps constitute women's and men's identities. Women receive positive public recognition beneficial to their practical relations-to-self when they conform to the behaviors set down by the recognition order. Men also receive beneficial recognition when they conform to the recognition order and enforce gender roles and give or withhold recognition to women according to women's conformity to the pathological norms. The point here is that there are positive recognition benefits received by both men and women for conforming to gender roles.

The presence of recognition teaches women that subordinate behavior is good, and it teaches men that subordinating women is good. Importantly, men who reinforce gender roles are recognized as benefiting women. For example, a man is esteemed for supporting his wife and kids—but it is worth noting that this sentiment puts the wife and children on the same level of dependence on the man. McNay has observed that "the family perpetuates systemic relations of oppression as much as it reproduces values and cultural norms."[203] The recognition norm of the heterosexual nuclear family is inherently structured by asymmetrical relations of power and enforced by pathological recognition norms.

Misogyny is a systemically generated subordination that is maintained by recognition. That gender roles are propagated in terms of recognition helps explain their persistence. By objective, external criteria, women are being subordinated and harmed by this "recognition," yet women and men find it difficult to overcome misogyny because its pathological recognition norms are embedded within society's other, healthy recognition norms and, thus, are part of the fabric of cultural attitudes (i.e., women as subordinate caregivers is a recognition norm). Men and women are socialized into a society's set of recognition norms, and they are reacting rationally to the recognition norms that are dominant in their culture. The pervasiveness of a culture's pathological recognition norms gives individuals reason to believe that the norms are true and proper. Because men and women need mutual recognition and social acceptance, it is in their self-interest to adopt recognition norms concerning women and behave accordingly in their interpersonal relationships. Thus, through recognition, women have a stake in their subordination. As John Stuart Mill said more than a century ago,[204] it is rational for woman to serve the system as best she can. What is more, the normative content of recognition normalizes the expectation of the

[203] Lois McNay, "Having It Both Ways: The Incompatibility of Narrative Identity and Communicative Ethics in Feminist Thought," *Theory, Culture and Society* 20 (6), 2003, 17.

[204] John Stuart Mill, *The Subjection of Women* (Indianapolis, IN: Hackett Publishing, 1988).

subordination of women. For men, women's inferiority is naturalized, and their place as superior to women is affirmed. For women, their subordination feels natural in that it is familiar even when it feels wrong somehow. As McNay says, the objective structures of subordination are taken in by individuals and naturalized as subjective dispositions, undermining their capacity to do more than endure the current state of affairs.[205] Both men and women are colonized by misogyny, and recognition is a key mechanism of this colonization. Understanding that recognition perpetuates misogyny also explains why there is a backlash against women's liberation and feminism. Western men have lost their symbolic status as heads of the family. Some, lacking socialized roles to accept these changes, react by clinging to the previous gender role distribution more fiercely.[206] Social changes that disrupt recognition relations create tension and conflict to which not everyone has the inner strength to respond positively.

Pathological recognition is the link between ideological structures and practices of subordination. Ideological forms of subordination cannot prevail without an adequate level of buy-in from all concerned. As Amy Allen says,

> Regulatory regimes cannot maintain and reproduce themselves; instead, they must be maintained and upheld by the individuals whom they regulate. The cultivation of an attachment to those regimes is an extremely effective and economical tool for getting individuals to maintain and uphold such regimes; in that sense, the regime needs the attachment of the individuals it regulates in order to persist.[207]

---

[205] Lois McNay, *The Misguided Search for the Political* (Cambridge, UK: Polity Press, 2014), 16, 29.

[206] Honneth, *Freedom's Right*, 160.

[207] Amy Allen, *The Politics of Our Selves: Power, Autonomy, and Gender in Contemporary Critical Theory* (New York, NY: Columbia University Press, 2008), 77.

The way that power structures can achieve buy-in and attachment from individuals is through recognition norms. Recognition norms provide a moral grammar that individuals can use to gauge their own and others' behavior. Recognition norms of all types are authoritative and normalizing—those following them see them as the basis for judging themselves and others. Generally, individuals want to do what is considered proper and help maintain social order, and they are given reason to believe that by complying with traditional gender attitudes they are doing good for themselves and others. When individuals respond to their socialization by adopting pathological recognition norms within their lives, those subordinating recognition norms persist and propagate through the generations.

The pathological recognition model offers us an advantage in our efforts toward emancipation of individuals from the oppressions of misrecognition and injustice. We could argue that the individual *should* understand the negative consequences on others of pathological recognition norms, but that is asking the individual to rise above the socialization of his or her culture and act in a way that is contrary to how social institutions tell them to act—a perhaps necessary effort, but difficult for any individual to attempt much less achieve. An example of this is the practice of female genital mutilation (FGM) in some African, Middle Eastern, and Southeast Asian cultures. Within those cultures, the practice is considered normal and morally right as part of the norms that recognize girls in that culture. Those who carry out the practice probably believe the procedure will benefit the girl in the long term, including preserving her virginity, making her more desirable for marriage, and affirming her as a member of their culture. The practice has been viewed by other cultures as barbaric, misogynistic, and a form of child abuse that harms the girls being "recognized" in that it forces girls to undergo a painful and enduringly debilitating procedure. Those outsiders, recognizing girls' right to bodily integrity, have pressured cultures practicing FGM to ban it, meeting with varying degrees of success. Condemning these cultures as backward or irrational will not be as productive in stopping this social practice as will understanding FGM as a pathological recognition norm that those who practice it have reason to believe is proper conduct on their part. Understanding that FGM is sustained by being seen as a positive recognition norm moves the conflict about the practice to a question of recognition. More than simply criticizing FGM in moral terms, which comes off as paternalistic condescension, discussing the social practice of FGM as pathological recognition frames the discussion of FGM in terms of how best to value women. In so doing, we can appeal to cultures practicing FGM to change what they value and from that change their recognition norms and recognition relations with women. In this case, it would mean valuing women by recognizing the integrity of a woman's body and her right to control her own body rather than pathologically recognizing the value of a woman's body as a thing to be controlled and manipulated to serve male ideas of beauty and worth.

Pathological recognition is widely prevalent, and the traditional view of women is only one example. The basic structure of pathological recognition—recognition norms that ascribe putative positive traits to individuals but that actually hinder the autonomy of those individuals—can be applied to any group. What unites all instances of pathological recognition are norms that designate only some attributes of a group as valuable while overlooking others. We can see that both pathological recognition and normative discrimination encourage a lack of engagement with other individuals because those individuals are subsumed under group identities and general norms, which limits recognition relations and the possibilities for individuals. The classification of women as caregivers recognizes women who are quiet, nurturing, and long-suffering, but it does not honor, perhaps does not even see, women who are bold, intelligent, and creative. Pathological recognition and normative discrimination limit individuals' expression of talents and ideas and often actively silences targeted groups. If, for example, one has a limited view of East Asians as excelling in math and science, one can easily fail to recognize that they have talents and interests in the arts and humanities. If one has a limited view of blacks as physically talented in entertainment and athletics, one can easily not recognize their cognitive talents in academia or leadership roles. These stereotypes limit possibilities for recognition relations and opportunities for the individuals being stereotyped, failing to recognize them as human individuals who possess unique talents and personalities. Such stereotyping is common in human societies across race, ethnicity, gender, religion, and other group traits.

Pathological recognition can target a whole culture. For example, in a culture dominated by patriotic zeal, expressions of loyalty to the state and the state's preferred narrative are recognized, allegedly for the good of all citizens, whether the citizens actually benefit or not. A political regime can establish one version of the state's history and image under the guise of patriotic loyalty, demanding and imposing one exclusive recognition of people and events while misrecognizing and silencing all other perspectives and voices. Patriotic loyalty mandates that certain recognition norms be maintained, and those who differ or dissent are denied recognition. This form of discrimination against free expression also targets members of subcultures, who are seen through a biased filter—the issue of subcultures I will take up in chapter 2.4.5.

There is a tension between engaging with recognition norms and engaging with individuals that is reflected in the tension between egalitarianism and multiculturalism. I cannot hope to discuss the politics of recognition fully, but some brief comments are in order to show how these ideas match with the discussion of recognition norms of pathological recognition. Charles Taylor's conception of the politics of recognition is the multicultural demand for recognition of the identity of subaltern groups, such as indigenous peoples, and distinct cultural groups, such as francophone Quebecers.[208]

An opposing view is offered by Iris Young who has criticized the ideal of egalitarianism that has denied marginalized groups their particular identities, and she sees the antidote to it as particular recognition of those groups.[209] The norms of egalitarian inclusion are molded by the dominant group, subsuming subcultures under universal norms that in practice

---

[208] Charles Taylor, "The Politics of Recognition," in *Multiculturalism*, ed. Amy Gutmann (Princeton, NJ: Princeton University Press, 1994), 25-74.

[209] Iris Young, *Justice and the Politics of Difference* (Princeton, NJ: Princeton University Press, 1990).

control and oppress individuals. Subcultures have long been assimilated into the dominant culture, prime recent examples being the treatment of North and South American and Australian First Nations peoples who were stripped of their heritage, language, and culture to fit into an ersatz idea of equality.

Going further is Kwame Appiah who remarks on the confining nature of particular recognition—that demanding recognition as an African-American or homosexual may win recognition, but with it comes a set of particular normative expectations and demands that can be a tightly scripted identity that is as burdensome as being denied one's identity.[210] In such recognition, one is being seen only as a member of a particular group separate from the general populace. Being seen as a member of a group can impose ideological prejudices, either pathological recognition and normative discrimination or both, subsuming individuals under a group identity blind to individual differences.

The concepts of normative discrimination and pathological recognition do not in themselves explain how they emerge (which is a much larger discussion beyond the current scope), but they can help explain why ideologies persist despite the damage they inflict on society. The mistake in pathological recognition cannot be blamed on individual perpetrators because the mistake resides in traditional social norms or attitudes that permeate a culture, usually unseen in the fabric of cultural attitudes. The concept of a pathological recognition norm is significant for critical theory and could be more useful theoretically than the traditional concept of a social pathology. It adds depth to theories such as those of Zurn, who argues that inegalitarian social structures persist because they naturalize the artificial way social power has structured society, which distorts second-order processes of belief formation and the comprehension of them.[211] Individuals fail to understand that social conditions are not

---

[210] Kwame Anthony Appiah, "Identity, Authenticity, Survival: Multicultural Societies and Social Reproduction," in *Multiculturalism*, ed. Amy Gutmann (Princeton, NJ: Princeton University Press, 1994), 149-163.

[211] Christopher F. Zurn, "Social Pathologies as Second-Order Disorders," in *Axel*

natural but are the results of socially determined relations of power that contribute to deleterious social outcomes, leading them to conform their beliefs and behaviors voluntarily to contribute materially to their oppression. Zurn is essentially correct, but he does not sufficiently factor in the social reality that normative discrimination and pathological recognition provide the normative evaluation of individuals' meaning and value and that these are appealing and even rewarding to men and women.

1.3.4 - Forgetting the Other Individual

So far, we have discussed misrecognition behaviors that are shaped by engagements with problematic norms and seen briefly how they discourage engagements with individuals. Now, we begin to move to misrecognition behaviors that more directly stem from a disengagement from other individuals. The moral aspect of human interaction is that recognition is possible only at a level of engagement in which other individuals are seen as having a moral value. Intersubjective engagement means interaction with and awareness of other individuals as individual human beings with thoughts and desires similar to one's own who deserve moral consideration. Recognition that is a rigid normalization of traits and contributions absent intersubjective horizontal recognition does not affirm individual self-realization or freedom. Likewise, a racist could follow the letter of the legal norms against discrimination, perhaps only to avoid losing his job, but actually have no intention to recognize another individual when it is possible to do so without repercussions. Horizontal intersubjective engagement is a necessary, though not sufficient, condition for recognition behavior, and ambivalence about others is at the root of misrecognition. Given the importance of recognition relations in an individual's development of self-realization, breakdowns in the intersubjective engagements that cultivate recognition can easily lead to moral injuries. I will describe four ways in which the other individual is forgotten and intersubjective engagement breaks down.

Honneth: Critical Essays, ed. Danielle Petherbridge (Leiden: Brill, 2011).

Withdrawal from moral relations

Withdrawal from moral relations is not a rejection of norms as much as a broad disinterest in recognition relations with others resulting in nonsocial or antisocial behavior. This withdrawal from meaningful interpersonal relations most likely occurs within certain social interactions rather than across an individual's entire life. This type of misrecognition is not seeing others either positively or negatively because engagement is absent. The individual does not perceive his or her connections with the world and other individuals in it. In this type of misrecognition, one is possibly self-absorbed in anxiety, insecurity, or poor self-esteem, perhaps as a result of psychological trauma, with a diminished capacity for engagement with others; thus, what interaction there is is nonintersubjective and devoid of moral engagement. Ethical responsibility to others according to recognition norms is forsaken in the face of insecurities and alienation. One is no longer responsive to others, and one no longer considers them in one's behavior. Individuals who engage in this type of misrecognition behavior may not be at ethical fault because the mistake is often not a conscious, rational choice. The behavior of sociopaths would probably be placed in this category, but few individuals who engage in this type of recognition are sociopaths and are more likely victims of depression, trauma, or social oppression. In such behaviors, the withdrawal from intersubjective relations precludes possibilities for recognition relations.

Structural lack of intersubjective engagement

An unconscious unawareness of the moral standing of others could be the result of social forces that may predispose individuals to disregard the moral standing of others and thus be blind to recognizing their particular contributions. This kind of reduced attentiveness causes recognition to fall into the background and slip out of sight—what Honneth calls reification. In reification, we "lose sight of the recognitional prerequisites of social practices while carrying out these very practices."[212] Recognition is precluded because an individual is not engaging with others intersubjectively. Reification, Honneth says, is an annulment of recognition caused by cultural practices independent of individuals: "Subjects can forget or learn later to deny the elementary recognition that they generally grant to every other human being, if they continuously contribute to a highly one-sided form of praxis that necessitates abstraction from the 'qualitative' characteristics of human beings."[213] An individual's unconscious diminished moral responsibility is not the fault of the individual because the misrecognition behavior is an unreflective comportment caused by social forces, in particular, the forces of capitalism. The individual is subsumed in social processes in which recognition relations are forgotten and recognition behavior is absent.

Temporary lack of intersubjective engagement

Depending on how powerful the processes are that diminish a sense of moral responsibility, the misrecognition could be structurally entrenched in interpersonal interactions or could be a by-product of a temporal forgetfulness from which an individual can recover. If it is the former, misrecognition behavior is entrenched and difficult for an individual to perceive, much less overcome. If it is the latter, then perhaps moral responsibility to others is only forgotten or obscured but not entirely abandoned. Not engaging with others intersubjectively precludes the possibility of adequately recognizing others, resulting in misrecognition such that we are unaware and inconsiderate. These are behaviors in which we are no longer responsive to the other and we no longer recognize the other for who he or she is and how he or she is behaving. Within this type of misrecognition, the perpetrator would not see the other individual, resulting in blindness to the positive contributions and capacities of others, forestalling recognition. However, this is not to say that the individual who is not engaging intersubjectively is deliberately engaging in misrecognition behavior or is even aware of misrecognizing others. A perpetrator could be

---

[212] Honneth, *Reification*, 58.
[213] Honneth, *Reification*, 155.

so engrossed in his or her activities, even while conducting them in a moral way, that he or she loses awareness of dealing with another human being. We go about our activities aware that others are present but not recognizing them as individuals, and this misrecognition is part of the self-absorption of everyday life. Honneth gives the example of a tennis player who is so focused on winning that she forgets her opponent is her best friend. Her goal has become independent of the context in which it originated, and "any attentiveness for the cooperating partner vanishes completely."[214] The tennis player has not forgotten the rules of the game but has forgotten her opponent's humanness and is no longer engaging intersubjectively with her friend. Winning the match has become a single purpose independent of her other relations to the world. Such a forgetfulness of others is commonplace in everyday life when we are caught up in everyday tasks and fail to notice and appreciate others as individuals like ourselves—such as Honneth's example of not greeting someone because we are unaware of him or her.[215] In such forgetful behavior, we reify other individuals—not seeing them as agents whose contributions and personal well-being should be taken into account. We perhaps remain polite, giving the appropriate gestures of civil behavior, but because we are forgetting the other, our courtesy is cursory and cold. This unintentional disengagement from others is temporary and does not necessarily lead to the elimination of all intersubjective engagements.

Important questions concerning this dimension of misrecognition include the nature and extent of the lack of intersubjective engagement and whether it is the result of a deliberate withdrawal from intersubjective engagements or an involuntary loss of the capacity for intersubjective engagements. Deliberate withdrawal from intersubjective relations is not a forgetting but a denial or defensiveness resulting in not considering the

---

[214] Honneth, *Reification*, 59, 155. Honneth, in response to criticism, admits his example does not illustrate reification as he originally hoped, but he retains the example as one of forgetting antecedent recognition. I believe the example better illustrates a temporary lack of intersubjective engagement as I describe it here.

[215] Honneth, *Disrespect*, 136.

possibility of others' contributions and personal well-being. A deliberate withdrawal is most likely isolated within certain social interactions rather than across an individual's entire life—for example, an individual being inconsiderate of others while posting comments online—engaging in thoughtless or aggressive behaviors he or she would not engage in within other interpersonal interactions.

Disengagement may also result from general insecurity and anxiety. We are, as McBride says, recognition-sensitive beings[216] because our well-being depends on receiving recognition, as Honneth says. We need recognition from others, and the potential lack of it is a threat. It is no surprise that with our social life comes anxiety about how others will judge us and our actions. Such anxiety can easily limit how much we are willing to risk exposure to negative judgments from others, resulting in our deliberately holding back from engaging with others. Tension in recognition relations explains a great deal of the social anxiety we all have, and it explains why some individuals protect a positive self-image by telling themselves they do not need others' approval, which is another way intersubjective engagement can be cut off. Within our relationships, changes in circumstances or in other individuals change our recognition relations with them. We are creatures of habit, and we tend to resist change. The threat of changes in relations can be wearisome and troublesome, and the temptation to withdraw from intersubjective engagement is there.

Involuntary disengagement from others may result from psychological trauma or deep anxiety. Survivors of abuse or trauma and children who did not receive sufficient emotional bonding may be less capable of intersubjective engagement as a result of their abuse or neglect. We would be wrong to hold this emotional incapacity against them as a moral failing, but such individuals are prone to misrecognizing others. The mistake in this dimension is less cognitive than existential or psychological, by which I mean that though rational reflection can bring

---

[216] McBride, 136-137.

one to awareness of one's lack of intersubjective engagement, it cannot compel one to engage with others in a personal manner.

Objectification of others

One could engage with specific other individuals but nonetheless take them to be the same as others who seem to possess similar traits and capacities. This generalization neglects the distinct traits and needs of the individual, objectifying or commoditizing him or her. In more benign forms, objectification is a general depersonalization, akin to the temporary lack of intersubjective engagement, in which only a general recognition of that individual is possible. We may be recognizing that individual as a human with rights and moral consideration, but because we are not engaging with that person as a specific individual, we are less open to recognition relations beyond acknowledging him or her as a human being. The other individual is perceived as only a member of a type and is objectified or commoditized.

Objectification is often a more malevolent action engrained in the prevailing recognition order. Normative discrimination against groups easily leads to objectification of individuals whose particular traits and capacities are erased by an identity attributed to them, a status that opens up the objectified to abuse. Within patriarchy, women not only are treated in terms of pathological recognition but also are objectified as beings in service of male desires. Sexual objectification of women has multiple forms and degrees, but the common denominator is that women are the proper objects of male sexual desire, the proper purpose of women being that they are used in order to satisfy that desire. As Timo Jütten has argued, sexual objectification of women is more than instrumentalization of them; it is a social meaning imposed on them that undermines their autonomy and equal social standing even at times when they are not being used as an instrument to gratify male desire.[217] Sexual objectification is a complexly pernicious issue, but what I find important for the current topic is the link between objectification and oppression. To objectify another

---

[217] Timo Jütten, "Sexual Objectification," *Ethics* 127 (1), 2016, 27-49.

individual is to see that person as not worth engaging with intersubjectively. We know that we have more latitude in how we treat objects than in how we treat other human beings, and we can use objects as we see fit. When individuals are objectified, they are objects for our use. In sexual objectification, the woman is excluded from intersubjective engagement because her normative status is as a sexual object, and not even a particular sexual object, but a fungible one. She is a commodity to be bought, sold, and used. This, I argue, is because objectification, unlike pathological recognition or normative discrimination, sees the victim as having use value but not as an individual. The companion to pathological recognition's putative positives of women's gender roles is that women are portrayed as subordinate objects whose value is lessened by intersubjective engagement (and, of course, any intersubjective engagement reveals the woman is not an object). This normative status of women as sexual objects not to be engaged with as individuals enables human trafficking and sexual slavery. Attempts by women to exercise their autonomy in opposition to their imposed social meaning are met with stern and perhaps violent attempts to reassert their objectification.

Misplaced care

It would seem that if a lack of care is misrecognition, then recognition includes care. That is true, but the presence of care does not mean recognition. Care about another can be misguided and not intersubjective and, thus, a form of misrecognition. Recognition is an intersubjective relation, and we expect it to be so. We expect other humans to care about our rights and well-being, if not for us personally, at least in that they expect the same from us in return. A stance of normative expectations is involved in all of our everyday activities. Socialization teaches us normative expectations about how humans should act, but socialization is just one way that we learn to have normative expectations about our world. Objects behave with some degree of regularity, and we learn to have normative expectations about the behavior of objects. In dealing with both human beings and nonhuman objects, our expectations shape our intentional stances and behaviors, our experiences, and our interpretations.

The significant difference between humans and nonhuman objects lies in our normative expectations that other individuals should consider us in their behaviors that may affect us. If a tree branch breaks our window, we do not feel misrecognized that the tree did not take our property rights into account; but if a child of an appropriate age throws a ball through our window, we feel anger that the child did not recognize our expectation that our property be respected. We do not hold the tree morally responsible as we do the child because we expect recognition from other humans (i.e., we expect them to care about our rights), but we do not expect the same from nonhuman objects.[218]

However, care and expectations can be separate from recognition, and it is possible to have normative expectations for other humans that are normally associated with nonhuman objects. This confusion is possible because nonhuman objects can be personified, with care becoming objectified, skewing normative expectations. A man could "love" his sports car and take time and effort to care for it, giving it everything it needs, but we would not say the man recognizes his car in the sense that we mean recognizing other people. When we care for a car, the car does seem to respond to our care for it with events or states that match our expectations—its paint gleams from polishing, the engine runs smoothly after a tune-up, and so on. It is incorrect to say that the car itself responded in the way a person would respond to our care, but our normative expectations about the effects of care are met. We learn to have expectations of objects, and those expectations are often confirmed, and this becomes part of our everyday understanding of the world and our orientation to it. The point I am trying to make is that we can interact with others in terms of the orientation we have toward nonhuman objects and treat other individuals like nonhuman objects in the way we care and have expectations about their responses to our actions but fail to care about them as human individuals. We are going through the motions of providing care and consideration, but in a detached way. In so doing, we

[218] The behavior of animals presents a gray area as to how much intention and responsiveness we expect different animals to have for us.

are showing care but not engaging with them intersubjectively. We think we are being kind and considerate, but because we are not intersubjectively engaging with them we are misrecognizing them. If other people seem to respond in ways we expect, then we think recognition relations with them are fine, and we do not look deeper into the relationship or our actions. An intersubjective engagement with the other individual is forgotten. Any relationship could fall into this pattern of a lack of intersubjective engagement.

1.3.5 - Self-absorbed Disengagement from Others

Self-absorbed disengagement is a set of behaviors of misrecognition of obliviousness toward certain other people. Earlier, we saw how normative discrimination created an oblivious disengagement from members of another social group. There is a similar misrecognition in which the disengagement is driven not by social norms but by individuals' choices. In myriad situations, individuals misrecognize others by failing to acknowledge another individual or judging that the other individual is not worth engaging with as an equal. Perhaps the other is considered to have no qualities of value or not having wants or needs worth considering. A line is drawn between those who are "us" and those who are "them," and we engage with "us" but not with "them." These considerations that another individual is one of "them" structures assumptions about how those other individuals are.

Obviously, many assessments of those who are "them" are informed by normative discrimination, but we must also acknowledge that similar discriminatory behaviors are not based on macrosocial-level characterizations of large social groups like race and gender but on microsocial-level characterizations of individuals. For this reason, the causes of and corrections needed for these misrecognitions are to be found in interpersonal relations rather than social structures. This is why I term it "self-absorbed" disengagement because the misrecognition is driven by an individual or small group's certainty in their self-assessments about the worth of another person. Their own self-certainty makes them resistant to contrary information. Therefore, the injustices caused by self-absorbed disengagement must be understood at the microsocial level. Self-absorbed disengagement is misrecognition in its denial of the other individual's value.

Instances of this misrecognition behavior involve restricting the granting of recognition to a select few, while disregarding or denying recognition to others. It is characterized mostly by its drawing of a line between "us" and "them" on the basis of considerations outside of normative discrimination assessments. Various kinds of social ostracizing, shunning, and disregard at the microsocial level are examples of self-absorbed disengagement. Honneth gives the example of a robber recognizing his companions while misrecognizing his victims.[219] Similar divisions are drawn by almost all individuals who, wittingly or not, engage more with individuals within their group but less with those outside their group. This explains the tendency that all individuals have of according more recognition to those within their social circle than to those outside it. Many people will see their own family or social group as more important than those outside of it. We each have our own lives and our own involvements and relationships, and it is no surprise that we tend to place more importance on individuals and relationships close to us.

The human tendency to view those outside our own group through a lens of our own preconceptions is perhaps the most common form of misrecognition. This disengagement happens at all levels of society, from ignoring other individuals who are not our friends or family, to governments not seeing members of groups for who they are. Unlike normative discrimination and pathological recognition, this type of misrecognition is not driven by social norms as much as by individuals' decision of inclusion and exclusion. It tends not to have the entrenched power of normative discrimination. However, because the misrecognition is informed by self-absorbed characterizations and is played out within personal lives, the level of hostility can be very high.

---

[219] Honneth, *Disrespect*, 227.

So far, I have discussed the dimension of personal engagement only in its positive aspect—that because acknowledging another individual's positive traits is recognition, the absence of this acknowledgment is misrecognition. There is another aspect in which the personal engagement is perverse. This form of misrecognition is also caused by self-absorbed considerations, but there is intersubjective engagement rather than disengagement. Intersubjective engagement is perverse when it is perpetrated with intentions contrary to affirming the other person positively. Perverse engagement with another differs from a lack of individual engagement such that the other individual is engaged with but the perpetrator is self-absorbed and thus the desires of the other individual are ignored and this perverse engagement is itself misrecognition behavior. Instead, in regard to the individual engaged with, recognition norms are willfully neglected because the needs and desires of the other are subsumed under the perpetrator's desires. Unlike normative discrimination that targets a social group, in perverse engagement the perpetrator targets a specific individual, believing either that this specific individual does not deserve to be treated well or that this individual's deservedness is unimportant in the context of the perpetrator's larger concerns. Perverse engagement would range from selfish neglect to active manipulation of another to sadistic behavior. Examples of perverse engagement would be a bully who targets a specific individual to abuse or a boss who harasses a particular employee. Most bullying and harassment are targeted antagonism that can be understood as perverse engagement. Another example is a con artist who is engaging with an individual expressly to swindle him or her. The con artist may have selected a target on the basis of the target's perceived vulnerability or gullibility, and the con artist ignores the norms against theft and dishonesty, specifically in terms of that individual, even if the con artist is honest with others. The con artist is engaging with the other, recognizing and acting in response to the individual's qualities, only in the service of his or her involvement in the successful swindle, but there is not necessarily a specific antagonism toward the target.

The complexity of the negative aspect of personal engagement can be unpacked further. The misrecognition behavior of perverse individual engagement is characterized by the focus of the self-absorbed perpetrator being on a personal relation but not on recognition or moral norms. In other words, the character of perverse individual engagement is not "these norms are irrelevant" but "for this specific individual these norms are irrelevant." A stalker is obsessed with a specific individual to the extent that norms of appropriate conduct are subsumed under the stalker's fantastic desires and that disregards how the other individual actually is. Stalkers often falsely believe the objects of their obsession return their interest and do not take in information to the contrary. If the stalker was engaging intersubjectively with the other individual, he or she would take into account the expressions of noninterest from the other person. But because the stalker is engaging not with the other but with his or her own attributed identity of the other, there is no intersubjective engagement. An individual seeking revenge on another is engaged with that individual but seeks to harm him or her, so the engagement is not intersubjective. The perpetrator considers that the other deserves to be harmed, not affirmed. A sociopath could be considered as an individual whose nonengagement is nearly universal—a depraved lack of concern for all other human beings and moral responsibility to others according to recognition norms is abandoned.[220]

1.3.6 - Selective Disengagement from Others

There is yet another consideration of engagement with others that illustrates the complexity of recognition relations. Withholding recognition can be a positive behavior that upholds moral norms. Our engagement with norms leads us to withhold recognition from someone who has failed to live up to those norms. Those who fall short of normative demands—from those who commit criminal acts to students who do poorly on an

---

[220] Martha Stout, *The Sociopath Next Door: The Ruthless Versus the Rest of Us* (New York: Broadway Books, 2005).

assignment—are not deserving of recognition in regard to particular norms. In response to this, we are morally obligated to withhold recognition from these individuals within the specific realm of their subnormative behavior. Their actions do not, of course, require or entitle us to withhold recognition in areas beyond that specific instance of subnormative behavior. This means that criminals do not entirely forfeit their membership in the moral community—they retain other rights even when they have forfeited their right to freedom if the legal norms call for that. Likewise, a teacher is required to award a low mark to a student for the one assignment the student has done poorly on, but the teacher cannot justifiably withhold recognition to the student outside of that one assignment. If we are still engaged with the individual, then we will not commit any extracurricular withholding of recognition because our continued engagement with that person as an individual means that we continue to hold him or her as generally worthy of recognition. Individuals who capriciously misrecognize another beyond the specific normative wrongdoing are no longer engaging with the other individual even though they think they are still engaging with norms. It is common though for negative judgments to bleed into other areas in such cases. An individual deemed to be unworthy in one area can see that judgment extend into all areas of his or her life such that that person is no longer respected or trusted in any area and he or she becomes ostracized.

The misrecognition of social ostracizing can be a case of engagement with norms but a lack of engagement with individuals. For example, an individual has committed a moral transgression and is held in contempt by others as a person rather than merely being reprimanded for the particular transgression. In some societies, the sins of the father are held against the children. This would be an engagement with norms but a lack of engagement with individuals because the moral stigma that may be justifiable for the father should not be transferred to the children who are separate individuals. If we remain engaged with both norms and individuals, then we treat others justly by both doing justice to our social norms through withholding recognition in deserved instances and also doing justice to individuals by not going beyond letting the punishment fit the crime.

This raises the question of how we should think about the damage done to an individual's self-esteem when recognition is withheld from him or her with just cause. We could consider that such withholding is in the best interests of the individual. For example, we are not helping a student to learn and grow as a person if we are so protective of his or her self-esteem that we are unwilling to award deserved low marks. In this, we can see that withholding recognition is benevolent and that, in fact, we are actually recognizing the student as a student and responding to him or her as worthy of appropriate instruction, which includes awarding a low mark when warranted. Punishment by withholding of recognition may also occur for reasons that could be considered unjust. A parent could withhold recognition from a child over the child's choice of career or friends or if the child was homosexual. A father can insist that his child can be a daughter but not a student or physician. Such familial conflicts are struggles over recognition, a topic I will engage with in depth in Part Two.

1.3.7 - The Dimension of Engaging in Action

Any misrecognition behavior will manifest in some degree of action. Some misrecognition behaviors are passive, such as a forgetful disengagement with norms or individuals. Other misrecognition behaviors are active in that the individual is consciously and deliberately engaging in the behavior. We can gauge this dimension of action in terms of the time and intensity of the behavior. In terms of time, a misrecognition behavior could be temporary or enduring. In terms of intensity, misrecognition behaviors can range from mild, passive behaviors to strong antagonism. Looking at the combination of time and intensity, we can gauge a misrecognition behavior on the dimension of engagement with action. Not all misrecognitions have the same intensity and breadth of effect, and this dimension reflects that. Another aspect of the dimension of action is the scale of misrecognition behavior—it could occur at individual, community, or societal levels—one individual engaged in a behavior up to a widespread social practice. The dimension of engaging with action is a secondary dimension in that it does not occur independently of one or both of the other two dimensions of engagement with norms and engagement with other individuals

Actions include decisions about which engagements to include within a particular situation. In a Kantian perspective of the type Honneth endorses, we must be capable of putting aside our personal interests and abstract from existing social norms a view of moral conduct within our particular situation. Such a view does not work when applied to Honneth's example of a professor who notices an act of plagiarism on the part of a close colleague.[221] Surely, Honneth suggests, the professor should not put aside moral demands for the sake of a close colleague. Is this a case in which the professor needs to decide between engagement with a friend and engagement with the norms of academic integrity? On which side of the dilemma will the professor act? Such questions can be asked about a wide range of human moral decisions.

Another aspect of the dimension of action is how misrecognition can be internalized. Misrecognition behaviors such as a lack of engagement usually are directed at others, but an individual's disengagement may extend to her disengaging from herself, resulting in her misrecognizing herself. The focus of action is herself, and this is significant. Any of the aforementioned types of misrecognition can apply to one's attitude and actions toward oneself, including not engaging with oneself or engaging with or disengaging from social norms related to oneself. To continue with our example of the traditional attitudes toward women, if a woman applies those social norms to herself, she is engaging in misrecognition of herself as much as any other individual who applied those same norms to her. By engaging with the social norms about women, the woman disengages from herself as an autonomous individual. This relates directly to Honneth's insight that recognition and self-realization are related—the woman "colonized" by the social norms is less capable of recognizing herself and developing her own self-realization, which would empower her to see the

[221] Honneth, *The I in We*, 110.

misrecognition of women present in the social norms. Misrecognition traps women in this way—misogynistic social forces using the power of recognition against women.

1.3.8 - How the Multidimensional View Helps Critical Theory

The change in approach I advocate is to replace a macrosocial top-down picture of misrecognition, such as Honneth's typology, with a fine-grained phenomenological picture of multiple dimensions in misrecognition behaviors that offers greater explanatory power. The multidimensional view replaces Honneth's binary view of misrecognition as the contrary to recognition without replacing Honneth's conceptions of the value of recognition. The multidimensional view can also replace Renault's institutional approach.[222] In Renault's analysis of the role of institutions in recognition, he touches on misrecognition, but his typology, though slightly different from Honneth's, remains top-down and adds a complicated categorization that still lacks a direct view of the importance of relations between individuals. Renault's typology of vertical recognition and misrecognition follows Honneth's and is put forth largely in service of other arguments, for example, against ideal theory. Suffice to say that any theory of recognition is lacking if it does not include consideration of the fine-grained multidimensional aspects of misrecognition. I will pick up Renault's discussion of struggles for recognition in Part 2.

The multidimensional view illustrates how misrecognition can occur in multiple spheres of recognition—legal, economic, and personal—and across sphere boundaries. For example, rather than lump all physical humiliation and violence into one type of misrecognition as Honneth does, the new typology can better distinguish two types of physical abuse—malicious acts that express personal reasons (starting a fight) and

---

[222] Emmanuel Renault, "The Theory of Recognition and Critique of Institutions," in *Axel Honneth: Critical Essays,* ed. Danielle Petherbridge (Leiden: Brill, 2011), 207-232.

pathological recognitions that express social norms of behavior that justify physical degradation (violence against women and children).

We can also use the multidimensional view to understand better the layers of comportment that structure misrecognition behaviors. For example, is an act of torture a product of a cultural environment that justifies torture of certain individuals? Or is it more accurate to see an act of torture as an individual lacking moral responsibility for another? Or is it some combination of both? Only by using a fine-grained analysis of the particular behavior and the comportments of the torturer can we fully understand it. Perhaps the torturer's behavior can be explained simply by social forces or perhaps not. Only by means of a fine-grained approach that looks at the specific misrecognition behavior can we know. One criticism that can be raised to my description of analyzing an act of torture is that a full fine-grained phenomenological analysis of every single misrecognition behavior is impossible and that an extensive analysis of individuals and their behaviors would, in some instances, be more time-consuming than it would be worth in results. I acknowledge this, but I do not suggest that every misrecognition behavior be analyzed, only that we use the multidimensional view to examine exemplar cases that illuminate what may lead individuals to engage in misrecognition behaviors and how misrecognition is experienced by individuals. I think it is important to acknowledge that human behavior is complex and that a methodological approach must reflect that complexity. The dimensions of misrecognition are not binary either-ors but are present in varying degrees and with varying degrees of awareness within the individual engaging in the behavior. By looking at misrecognition through multiple dimensions, we can give individuals and their particular behaviors due consideration.

Analyzing misrecognition behaviors through the multidimensional view reveals that individuals encounter conflicts among recognition demands and that these conflicts must be resolved on the individual level. The structural recognition order alone cannot adequately explain what happens in recognition conflicts. There are two reasons for this. First, as Nancy Fraser has observed,[223] the recognition order interacts with other modes of social order, and this interaction affects all aspects of interpersonal relations; thus, any interpersonal relationship is structured by multiple social forces in addition to the recognition order. Second, personal relationships are varied, reflecting differences in the people involved and the circumstances in which they find themselves; thus, the recognition order is applied differently in different relationships and even within relationships when circumstances change. A binary view of recognition and misrecognition also cannot adequately explain recognition conflict. Perhaps some interpersonal situations can be easily delineated into a simple either-or decision whether to recognize another or not, but more likely, interpersonal situations are more complicated and so are the processes of finding the proper course of action. Within Honneth's three spheres of recognition, we would have to try to understand recognition conflict in terms of a conflict between the spheres. For example, to understand why a man would or would not forbid his wife or daughter to work outside the home, we would have to postulate his conflict as being between his family sphere and the civil society sphere. This is not an unreasonable approach, and may describe some particular relationships, but a more fine-grained picture of recognition and misrecognition, which the multidimensional view provides, reveals other possibilities and yields deeper understanding.

We can delve deeper into this with the example of the fictional Tevye in *Fiddler on the Roof.* Tevye is a man deeply engaged with the norms—the tradition—of his culture. His personal struggle is between his engagement with his culture's norms and his engagement with his daughters. For his oldest two daughters, Tzeitel and Hodel, he chooses to recognize their autonomy to decide whom to marry and blesses their marriages despite their behavior going against tradition. But for his daughter Chava, he withholds his recognition and his blessing of her choice of fiancé, choosing instead to engage with his culture's tradition. For each daughter, his choices are deeply personal, reflecting his conflicting engagement with his culture's recognition norms, his

---

[223] Fraser and Honneth, 214.

engagement with his daughters, and his personal conscience. What, if any, misrecognition behavior Tevye is engaging in is a matter of interpretation. Was he misrecognizing Chava by not accepting her autonomous choice? But here he was following the recognition norms of his culture, so could we say that he was recognizing his culture's tradition against mixed-faith marriage, which "should" take precedence over his young and inexperienced daughter's autonomy? By that reasoning, was he actually misrecognizing Tzeitel and Hodel by not enforcing the wisdom of their culture against their personal choices? If we were to look at Tevye's behavior only through Honneth's typology of misrecognition, we would not be able easily to understand his actions or answer these questions about him. One could reply that the proper recognition norm for Tevye to follow is the autonomy of other individuals and that he was, therefore, correct to choose that recognition behavior with Tzeitel and Hodel and incorrect not to choose it with Chava. Although this answer sounds right to liberal minds, it creates a problem with the concept of social norms and the recognition order. If it is the institutions of culture that inform Tevye and other individuals about what qualities in others should be recognized, then why would they—indeed, how could they—choose to recognize another's autonomy when the social institutions tell them not to recognize it? Only if we look at recognition and misrecognition beyond a recognition order maintained by social intuitions can we make sense of behaviors like Tevye's and the very real issues raised by his fictional story. Most importantly, for Tevye and real-life individuals, recognition and misrecognition behaviors are intersubjective happenings in their daily lives in which they are involved. Misrecognition behaviors are informed and structured by, but not wholly determined by, social institutions and norms.

The multidimensional view shows that misrecognition includes not only a structure of social institutions but also the expressions of individuals. Not all misrecognition can be blamed on institutional recognition norms because some forms of misrecognition stem from individuals' disengagement from others. Whether quotidian forgetfulness or self-absorbed disengagement, when our care about others and how our behaviors affect them is lacking, misrecognition and injustice are inevitable, and we cannot evade our personal responsibility, yet engagement with norms and with others is no guarantee of just behavior. Recognition and justice mean recognizing individuals as individuals who have personal attributes and desires. Engagement requires listening to the testimony of others and valuing them and their experiences—seeing them as active agents, not objects.

An example of the advantages of the multidimensional approach is the analysis of racism, which is usually thought of in terms of institutional racism, in which social institutions are structured to privilege one racial group over others. The power of institutional racism and its recognition norms based on racial preference is undeniable. Race is a cultural construct (as, of course, are gender and class), and cultures create social hierarchies and power relations between racial groups that are often unjust. All individuals are situated within these unjust power relations, living under a racially tagged group identity and social hierarchy. Racial group identities serve political and ideological functions by reducing individuals to a group-based identity. It is therefore sensible to focus, as philosophers have, on culturally constituted racial group identities situated within group power relations. As important and useful as is a macrosocial focus on interactions between racial groups, such a focus does not exhaustively explain the dynamics of racism. Also crucial to understanding racism is a view of how racial discrimination is perpetuated through individual misrecognition behaviors and the experiences of individuals both on the giving and receiving end of racist misrecognition behaviors. Methodologically, if we reduce our view of racism to group-on-group dynamics, then we run the risk of deindividualizing others similar to the way in which racism itself strips human beings of personal identity.

The multidimensional view of misrecognition enhances our understanding of racism by providing a fine-grained view of racial discrimination as it is lived by individuals on both sides of racial oppression, which is particularly important when considering the post–civil rights world. Critical race theorists argue that Western social institutions still function to maintain white privilege even though racial discrimination is outlawed. Charles Mills argues that despite advances in civil rights legislation, white supremacy has changed only from de jure to de facto.[224] This change is described only partially by an analysis of social institutions. Mills is correct that the concept of race, though a social construct, is nevertheless real in that it materializes in social practices of its perpetrators and the "felt phenomenologies" of its victims.[225] Mills sees whites as being socialized into ethical codes of conduct that are structured by race. The pervasiveness of white supremacy, Mills argues, extends beyond the legal and political into the economic, cultural, cognitive, and bodily spheres of individuals' lives, putting individuals into a certain relationship with social reality that almost metaphysically determines their being and consciousness.[226] If there is merit to this conception of white supremacy, then an individual's experience of social reality is highly racialized, but does that mean that one's experience is determined wholly by the social structures of white supremacy? It is undeniable that the pathological recognition norms of racial stratification create an environment that encourages racism. If social norms specify racism as the proper structure for society, then does that mean that everyone in society is acting in a racist manner? Or is something beyond engagement with social norms going on in an individual's racial misrecognition behavior? If so, and we need to find only one instance of an individual behaving without racism to prove it, then pathological norms are not determinative of racist behavior. A macrosocial view of structural racism will reveal only group-on-group dynamics, whereas the multidimensional view, incorporating a microsocial view, will show us both group and individual dynamics of racism.

Despite the pressure of pathological norms that promote racism, we can also conceive of someone who is fully aware of the social norm of unequal power relations in his or her culture but chooses not to act on it. It would be incorrect to suggest that an individual could never disbelieve or

---

[224] Charles Mills, "White Supremacy," *Companion to African-American Philosophy*, ed. Tommy L. Lott and John Pittman (Oxford, UK: Blackwell Publishing, 2003), 269-283.

[225] Mills, 273.

[226] Mills, 274.

act contrary to prevailing racist social norms, and we must ask what makes it possible for individuals to resist social pressures. An individual could believe that nonwhites are equal to whites and have a general comportment toward nonwhites of being open to them as individuals possessing moral agency and deserving of equal treatment, opening up the possibility for recognition. Recognition is specific to an individual, not to a race, and every individual retains the capability of recognizing another individual despite the power relations of his or her society. If racism is the reduction of an individual to a racial group identity, then the counterweight to the social norm of racial discrimination is engagement with another as an individual—to see him or her as possessing his or her own distinct qualities and contributions. Engagement with another individual discloses him or her as a person in his or her own right beyond a mere member of a group.

The multidimensional view of misrecognition can also reveal levels or varieties of misrecognition within racism. If we look at slavery, there is no question that the institution of slavery in any era is a structural injustice that misrecognizes groups and individuals. Within the structural misrecognition of slavery, however, are complex interpersonal relations, collaborations, and rebellions that can be revealed with the multidimensional view of misrecognition. Anyone involved in a plantation that exploits the labor of slaves is undeniably actively and knowingly participating in the oppression of the slaves, misrecognizing their moral rights. Further to this though, we can ask how a particular white person working at the plantation is treating the slaves. One could be more cruel or less cruel to the slaves, and this would be a different level of misrecognition or recognition within the overarching injustice of slavery. Being a relatively kind master would not erase the injustice of slavery, but clearly a distinction must be made between levels of cruelty within the institution of slavery. It could be the case that a plantation foreman engages with individual slaves and believes they are human beings who should be treated well. Lacking the legal power to free the slaves, he tries to better their lives how he can. Also consider the example of a white person living in the American South during segregation. This person has engaged with individual blacks and does not agree with the laws and social norms that racially discriminate against blacks. The white individual lacks the power to change the laws and social attitudes of misrecognition against blacks, but in personal dealings with blacks, this individual recognizes their moral agency, qualities, and needs. If this individual takes no political action to change the unjust laws and power relations of society, are we right to condemn this individual as perpetrating misrecognition? If we were to make such judgments only in terms of institutional actions, then we would have to condemn this inaction. However, not all action furthering justice is political action, and a simple act of recognizing another's human dignity and according that individual kindness and respect is a move toward justice. It is through such individual engagements and actions that institutional injustices can be fought, as I will describe in Part Two.

Looking at individual interactions, we can uncover intersubjective engagements and recognitions within structural misrecognition. Within structures of misrecognition, recognition does not come effortlessly, but it can happen. In the other direction, we can identify some individuals who went beyond the prevailing norms of normative discrimination to greater action of misrecognition against nonwhites. Individuals in the Ku Klux Klan took misrecognition behavior beyond what the racist power structure society had set down; though oppression of blacks was a social norm, only a few individuals lynched blacks. The point of these examples is that within institutional racism are varieties of misrecognition behavior that are revealed by applying the multidimensional view to individual behaviors. The multidimensional view can be used similarly to explicate any of the other isms of any society.

The preceding portrayal of the dimensions of misrecognition replaces Honneth's typology as a better description of the diversity of individuals' misrecognition behavior. The misrecognitions perpetrated by and experienced by individuals do not map onto Honneth's typology of misrecognition that is essentially the contrary of his typology of recognition—a typology that is too narrowly construed to encompass the diversity of misrecognition behaviors. Rather than seeing misrecognition as simply a violation of recognition norms, the multidimensional view sees misrecognition as a complex response to everyday circumstances that involves engagements with various norms and with other individuals. A multidimensional view of misrecognition reflects the complexity and diversity of particular misrecognition behaviors. The multidimensional view illuminates that, though social institutions set the stage, misrecognition behaviors occur at the microsocial level of individual and small group interactions. Recognition is best viewed not in terms of spheres but in terms of a web of interpersonal relations. This realization adds complexity to our task of understanding misrecognition, but it gives our critical theory greater explanatory power.

Part Two: Rethinking Struggles for Recognition

All the reflections I have so far presented converge in the thesis that the multifarious efforts of a struggle for recognition are what will enable critical theory to justify its normative claims.
- Axel Honneth[227]

2.1 - The Importance of Struggles for Recognition

Part One's discussion on improving Honneth's inadequate account of misrecognition is a precursor to a discussion of the possible responses to misrecognition—struggles for recognition. Honneth calls for the struggle for recognition to be "the guiding thread of a critical theory" and sees struggles for recognition as setting the pace of historical transformations because they are responsible for development and historical progress.[228] I will reconstruct Honneth's motives for going beyond the first and second generations of critical theorists, despite his sharing their aims. Then, I will outline my concerns about Honneth's theories on struggles for recognition while agreeing with him about the importance of struggles for recognition in critical theory.

Honneth resolves to move away from what he sees as an overemphasis within social theory, going back to Machiavelli, on the social struggles for self-preservation and material resources. Honneth sees that social struggles over resources or political power are at their heart struggles based on the moral concern that a society's norms are not reflected in actual social relations. His emphasis within social theory is that social struggles are about the establishment of relations of mutual recognition—struggles that arise when normative expectations have been violated. By struggles for recognition, Honneth does not mean struggles for honor as Hobbes and Machiavelli theorized, but the struggles for the

---

[227] Honneth, *Disrespect*, 77.
[228] Honneth, *The Struggle for Recognition*, 144.

normative approval of others that Honneth considers to be the precondition for personal identity formation and human flourishing.

Honneth sees his project as continuing the tradition of critical theory, and he adopts critical theory's idea that historically effective rationality has been distorted, that the cause of the negative state of society is capitalism's deficit in social rationality, and that the pathology of capitalism can be overcome only through a process of enlightenment among those involved. Honneth's reasons for adding recognition and struggles for recognition to critical theory can be seen in his critique of earlier critical theorists. Horkheimer stated that the goal of critical theory "is to liberate human beings from the circumstances that enslave them."[229] Critical theory's aims have been to seek what will transform structures of social domination and bring about social emancipation from injustice. That includes explaining what motivates social protest movements and what is lacking when protest against injustices does not happen. However, Honneth criticizes the founders of the Frankfurt School, Max Horkheimer and Theodor Adorno. Honneth states:

> Horkheimer's early writings remained trapped within a Marxist philosophy of history that could tolerate a pre-theoretical interest in social emancipation only in one class, the proletariat. Early on, Adorno had founded the point of departure for his critique of society so decisively on Marx's critique of fetishism that he could no longer find any trace of an intramundane transcendence in the culture of everyday life.[230]

On Adorno's later work, Honneth is even harsher, saying that:

> critical theory's turn to Adorno's historico-philosophical negativism finally marked the historical point at which the endeavor to link critique back to social history failed completely.[231]

---

[229] Max Horkheimer, *Critical Theory* (New York: Seabury Press, 1982), 244.
[230] Honneth, *Disrespect*, 65.
[231] Honneth, *Disrespect*, 65.

Furthermore, Honneth said that Horkheimer and Adorno's "one-sided and exaggerated" analysis of historical development only managed to replace nature with the large-scale purposive-rational organization of totalitarian systems.[232] They saw totalitarianism as the culmination of a pathological process of rationalization—the pathological process of civilization. Horkheimer and Adorno's approach

> excludes any factors that do not stand in a more or less direct relation to the process of technical rationalization in the historical process in which totalitarianism emerges. Thus as much as Horkheimer and Adorno take account of developments such as the mass media, and as much as they take pains to account for psychic dispositions, their analysis of these events is always limited to discovering only further forms of a totalitarian form of reason.[233]

There is, Honneth argues, little or no room in such a historical view to identify, much less solve, social misdevelopments that disrupt communication and reason. Theory that is too far removed from everyday experience and practice is not useful. Similarly, Honneth criticizes Foucault for conceiving of social change at the level of systems, presenting a one-dimensional society in which social domination comes from a systematic disciplinary regime. This negative and totalizing theory, Honneth argues, leaves no room for the identities of social groups and their social struggles outside the institutionalization of disciplinary power.[234]

Honneth is more accepting of Jürgen Habermas's project, which located in communicative activity the instrumental activity that is suppressed by social pathologies. Habermas's idea is that linguistic rules govern communication and serve as a normative structure that defines what humans need to understand each other and be socially successful. When communicative activity is suppressed by domination, it impedes

---

[232] Honneth, *Disrespect*, 29.

[233] Honneth, *Disrespect*, 29-30.

[234] Axel Honneth, *The Critique of Power: Reflective Stages in a Critical Social Theory*, trans. Kenneth Baynes (Cambridge, MA: MIT Press, 1991), 195.

humans from applying those linguistic rules to understanding each other. The communicative paradigm has the potential to illuminate the effects of social pathology and the emancipation from it; however, Honneth sees the paradigm's claim to universalizability as abstracted away from social reality and the willingness of subjects to adopt the goals of communicative rationalization. For this reason, he believes that Habermas's theory creates a gap between normativity and the pretheoretical resources that can anchor critique in everyday intersubjective relations. Therefore, Honneth says, "The emancipatory process in which Habermas socially anchors the normative perspective of his Critical Theory in no way appears as an emancipatory process in the moral experiences of the subjects involved."[235] Honneth accepts the intersubjective, sociological presuppositions of Habermas's theory but finds its linguistic, theoretic framework too limited to the structures of symmetry and reciprocity in language.

Honneth extends Habermas's communication paradigm beyond the structures of language into the structures of everyday intersubjective relations. Honneth calls for a realistic concept of emancipatory interest not in terms of linguistic conditions but centered on the idea of a core rational responsiveness by subjects to defects in social rationality.[236] The expansion of morality depends on the struggles by subjects to have their identity claims recognized within everyday relations of mutual recognition.[237] Honneth says that resistance to social injustice is not motivated by positively formulated moral principles but by subjects' experiences of having their intuitive notions of justice violated.[238] To reflect the moral experiences present in social life, he moves the focus of his inquiry from theoretic rationality to the moral experiences of subjects to uncover the normative perspective in which the emancipatory process appears. Honneth advances an intersubjective paradigm in terms of a theory of reciprocal recognition rather than a theory of communicative understanding, believing "that social recognition constitutes the normative

---

[235] Honneth, *Disrespect*, 70.
[236] Honneth, *Pathologies of Reason*, 42.
[237] Petherbridge, 16-17.
[238] Honneth, *Disrespect*, 71.

expectations connected with our entering into communicative relationships."[239] Feelings of injustice in response to misrecognition are "pre-theoretical facts," meaning that a critique of relations of recognition identifies its own theoretical perspective in social reality.[240] Honneth believes that through an intersubjective paradigm framed not as a conception of rational understanding, but as a conception of the conditions of recognition, we can indicate the degree of harm to the normative presuppositions of personal interaction that is directly reflected in the moral feelings of those involved.

A theme in Hegel's thought is the struggle of the individual toward joining with the social order, and Honneth adopts Hegel's idea that recognition brings about an increase in social integration. Honneth agrees with Hegel that there must be some kind of basic mutual affirmation between subjects for any form of social cohesion to come into existence.[241] Honneth follows Hegel in seeing the striving of subjects for recognition as a productive force for social change and the development of legal relations. These relations, Honneth believes, are won through social struggles driven by moral indignation over rejection of claims to recognition. Honneth thus sees struggles for recognition as morally motivated conflicts over the expansion of recognition relations, which can and should become a structuring force in the moral development of society.[242]

Honneth believes that social theory needs to start from the concept that every collective act of social resistance against injustice can be traced to a set of moral experiences that can be interpreted in terms of recognition and misrecognition rather than pregiven interests.[243] Rather than seeing social movements against injustice as conflicts of interests, high-minded ideals, or class struggle, Honneth says that "the collective interest behind a conflict [can be seen as being] constituted within a horizon of moral

[239] Honneth, *Disrespect*, 71.
[240] Honneth, *Disrespect*, 72.
[241] Honneth, *The Struggle for Recognition*, 43.
[242] Honneth, *The Struggle for Recognition*, 49, 93.
[243] Honneth, *The Struggle for Recognition*, 161, 164-165.

experience that admits of normative claims to recognition and respect."[244] Human actions cannot be reduced to the purposive, rational pursuit of material interests. Instead, the moral feelings of having been treated unjustly can lead to collective actions. Because that struggle is universal, it can motivate social action whenever the desire for recognition is thwarted.[245] The feelings of hurt and violation are reactions to what subjects consider to be morally indefensible circumstances, which includes struggles over the just distribution material goods. It is difficult to discern how many struggles for material goods are in actuality struggles for recognition, but as alluded to earlier in the discussion of Nancy Fraser's criticism of Honneth, it would be incorrect to leave out the importance of recognition relations in the discussion of maldistribution and the resistance to it. For critical theory, Honneth's conception moves social conflict and development beyond conflict over material resources into struggles for morally justified social relations and structures, though he collapses struggles for recognition into political struggles. Honneth believes that academic theories have rarely considered the collective feelings of being misrecognized and, thus, have not understood social structures of domination as pathologies of recognition relations.[246]

For Honneth, struggles over distribution of resources are, in essence, struggles over recognition, aimed at changing the cultural interpretations of whose contributions are valued. Thus, Honneth is concerned about the "lasting inequality in the distribution of chances for social recognition."[247] Fraser, with some merit, accuses Honneth of viewing all social processes, including subordination, through the single lens of interpersonal recognition relations, reducing society to a recognition order that illegitimately totalizes society and social processes into a single mode of integration. Fraser acknowledges that some struggles do challenge the prevailing cultural interpretations of the value of contributions (recognition) but says that Honneth's focus on recognition misses the

[244] Honneth, *The Struggle for Recognition*, 166.
[245] Honneth, *Reification*, 9.
[246] Honneth, *The Struggle for Recognition*, 159.
[247] Honneth, *Disrespect*, 93.

operation of impersonal system mechanisms unconnected to normative ideas of who is valued. Fraser calls for seeing struggles for recognition as struggles for egalitarian redistribution.[248]

Honneth believes that Fraser has been unfair to his position[249] and insists on the importance of critical theory considering that social reality is guided by normative criteria that give rise to moral experiences, moral injuries, and moral claims to justice. Honneth's rejoinder to Fraser makes several valid points. It makes sense that resistance to injustice is an emotional reaction, not just a rational one. It also makes sense that unjust distribution occurs within processes laden with normative significance. Honneth rightly points out that Fraser's concept of participatory parity is a particular idea of the good that, like recognition, seeks to increase individual autonomy[250] and that arguably can be seen as a struggle for recognition. It is also the case that, if systemic distribution injustices are to be solved long term, the cultural norms and application of those norms must be transformed. Forcible material remedies for an unjust distribution of goods are unsatisfactory measures compared with a cultural paradigm that values fairness in distribution. Even if we were to say that an issue of injustice was solely a matter of material distribution, the struggle against it still requires the consideration of recognition. This is because Honneth is correct that social integration requires mutual recognition; in other words, others are not integrated if they are not first recognized as worthy of integration. Honneth's view of recognition is overly simplistic at times, and Fraser is correct that Honneth reduces society to a recognition order, but his insight that people fight for recognition is an important and necessary addition to critical theory.

Honneth correctly emphasizes the importance of struggles for recognition in social life and social change. I do not disagree at all with the importance of struggles for recognition. My contention, though, is that similar to Honneth's incomplete account of misrecognition, his account of

---

[248] Fraser and Honneth, 213-216.
[249] Fraser and Honneth, 237.
[250] Fraser and Honneth, 259.

struggles for recognition is also incomplete and needs to be amended. Honneth's account bases struggles for recognition on the moral experiences of individuals whose identity claims have been denied, and he states that they are further motivated by collective social movements of political resistance. However, his account remains functionalist and does not fully capture the experiences and actions of individuals, and his account thus falls short of the goals he sets out for critical theory. Given the theoretical importance he places on struggles for recognition, a clear and robust account of struggles for recognition is very important, and this includes the questions of what brings an individual to engage actively in a struggle for recognition and what actions he or she takes.

Honneth's narrative of what motivates struggles for recognition can be summarized as follows. Subjects are socialized into their society's recognition norms, which subjects internalize and thereby develop normative expectations about how they should be treated. If these normative expectations are disappointed, subjects' relations-to-self are injured, and subjects feel the hurt of these moral injuries in a way similar to that of physical injuries, and subjects realize they are being illegitimately denied recognition. We could react with hurt, shame, or rage as a result of our normative expectations being disregarded. Anger is an informed response to the dissonance between the current situation and how we have learned things "should" be, and feelings of injustice are experiences of disappointments of well-founded claims of recognition. When we see others receiving rights that are denied to us, our resentment is a response informed by our having learned to believe that we also deserve to receive those rights. In these emotional experiences, Honneth says, we come to realize that we depend on the recognition of others, and this motivates us to claim that recognition.[251] The hurt feelings of anger and resentment in response to experiences of misrecognition can motivate an individual to struggle against those perceived to be the source of the misrecognition.

---

[251] Honneth, *The Struggle for Recognition*, 131-139.

Struggles for recognition are motivated not by just any emotional hurt but by those moral injuries to relations-to-self that damage an individual's sense of well-being that is developed through recognition and socialization. Subjects learn to have normative expectations of social recognition that positively regard their well-being. When those expectations are disappointed, Honneth says, we experience a moral crisis. Misrecognition strikes at our sense of self; it devalues us and brings with it a loss of personal self-esteem and self-confidence, resulting in the suffering of distortions of our sense of identity. Maintaining our positive relations–to-self depends on receiving recognition of the same from other subjects. When our positive self-relation is disregarded by others, we are injured by the misrecognition.[252] Subjects engage in confrontation with others not purely over self-preservation but because they believe their identity claims are being insufficiently recognized. Such confrontations are ethical moments within a collective social life that challenge an individual to defend his or her positive relations-to-self. The purpose of a struggle for recognition is to repair the damage done to one's positive relations-to-self by moral injuries, and Honneth believes this damage can be repaired only by recognition. Struggles for recognition, then, seek to either restore previous recognition relations or find new recognition relations that will soothe the hurt feelings and establish positive ones.

The experiences of hurt feelings from misrecognition make sense as a necessary prerequisite for struggles for recognition. Perhaps one could be aware of being treated unjustly without being affected by it, but it makes sense that one is motivated to struggle for recognition only if one has become aware that one is not receiving recognition. But Honneth stresses that subjects will not know they are being treated unjustly unless they have some knowledge of a moral norm that is being violated in their case and that subjects will not be able to articulate their feelings of being misrecognized unless they have access to a moral language by which they can express their feelings.[253] This narrative is plausible within Honneth's

---

[252] Honneth, *Disrespect*, 134.
[253] Honneth, *The Struggle for Recognition*, 170.

theory of recognition. The socialization process leads us to have normative expectations of our community and others. The social norms of our community give us reason to believe that others will be and should be willing to respect us and treat us justly, and these social norms provide us with the moral language by which to interpret our feelings in response to how we are treated. This characterization of Honneth answers Bader's criticism that feelings of being exploited, oppressed, excluded, or marginalized do not have to be linked to misrecognition to have motivational force.[254] Bader's criticism is based on his association of misrecognition with prestige hierarchies of social esteem, and he counters that the exploitation of being forced to deliver surplus labor is not about social esteem and would not be interpreted by workers as misrecognition. I say, to the contrary, that workers' awareness of their exploitation comes from the violation of their normative expectations that they should be treated justly and compensated fairly for their labor. Therefore, their feelings of being exploited come from an awareness that moral norms have been violated in their case and that they are not being recognized. The workers may then feel motivated to struggle for the recognition that they should not be exploited. Exploitation, oppression, exclusion, and marginalization are misrecognition whether or not one's self-esteem is damaged.

As compelling as is Honneth's story behind struggles for recognition, it is not without significant problems and inconsistencies. An important difficulty in Honneth's account of struggles for recognition is a lack of clarity about how an individual moves from a damaged relation-to-self to engaging in a struggle for recognition. Honneth seems content to state that the negative emotional reactions to misrecognition and humiliation constitute the psychological basis for realizing one is being misrecognized and that these moral experiences are the motivation for struggles for recognition.[255] Honneth does not assume that every experience of

---

[254] Bader, 254.
[255] Honneth, *The Struggle for Recognition*, 131-139.

misrecognition leads to a struggle for recognition, but his account is not fine grained as to the phenomena of struggles for recognition.

Also problematic is the link Honneth makes between the moral crisis of experiencing misrecognition and political resistance. Honneth attempts to show how social struggles can be explained on the basis of the dynamics of subjects' moral experiences.[256] Basing social movements of political resistance on individuals' moral experiences is good, but remaining in the tradition of critical theory, he focuses on macrosocial movements, and in so doing he leaves out a large area of phenomena of struggles for recognition. I agree with Honneth's contention that there is a connection between moral injuries and political resistance movements but think that this important insight is underdeveloped. Honneth does not preclude the possibility of an individual struggling for recognition outside of political resistance by a social movement, but he says very little about this possibility. Also problematic is Honneth's apparent position that an individual will not be motivated to political resistance without a preexisting social movement. This position calls into question how a social movement can begin if individuals engage in acts of political resistance only when they are motivated to do so by an existing social movement.

Honneth's account of struggles for recognition is incomplete. Left unanswered are two central questions. The first is this: How does one move from the realization that one is misrecognized to a motivation to struggle for recognition? The second is this: How do individuals express their motivation to struggle for recognition? To the first question, I argue that Honneth is missing something crucial from his account. I explore this in what I call the "agency problem," which investigates the question of why not all individuals who experience misrecognition attempt to struggle for recognition. I argue that something more than the presence of hurt feelings is needed to explain individuals' undertaking struggles for recognition—also needed is a sense of individual agency that an individual draws on to move beyond moral injuries into struggles for recognition. This sense of agency in the context of struggles for recognition informs my

---

[256] Honneth, *The Struggle for Recognition*, 139.

analysis of the second question, the discussion of which I term Honneth's "political movements problem," in which I will address several related issues regarding the weak connection Honneth makes between individuals and political movements. I will discuss each "problem" in turn and then show the relation of these two problems and how an account of struggles for recognition can be expanded to give it greater explanatory power of individuals' experiences.

2.2 - Honneth's Agency Problem

Honneth places considerable importance on understanding struggles for recognition, seeing them as "the guiding thread of a critical theory."[257] I agree with the importance of those struggles and agree with much of Honneth's account of struggles for recognition. My contention, though, is that there is a dilemma in Honneth's account of what motivates struggles for recognition. According to Honneth, to act autonomously, an individual first needs to receive recognition; however, he does not adequately explain how individuals can undertake a struggle for recognition without autonomy. I argue that to resolve Honneth's dilemma, we need to, in addition to hurt feelings from misrecognition, include some form of agency in the individual who, lacking the recognition necessary to be autonomous, and being damaged by misrecognition, nevertheless has some capacity actively to seek recognition.

Honneth says that the negative emotional reactions to being misrecognized are the necessary psychological link to move an individual from mere suffering to action.[258] Honneth says that being treated unjustly hurts our sense of self; it devalues us and brings with it a loss of personal self-esteem and self-confidence. This triggers a moral crisis—we feel humiliation and shame, and in these emotions we realize that our sense of identity depends on the recognition of others. These hurt feelings motivate us to struggle for recognition to dispel this emotional tension and repair the

---

[257] Honneth, *The Struggle for Recognition*, 144.
[258] Honneth, *The Struggle for Recognition*, 135-136.

damage done to our positive relations-to-self, which Honneth believes can be repaired only by recognition.[259] Struggles for recognition then seek either to restore previous recognition relations or to find new recognition relations that will soothe the hurt feelings and establish positive ones.

It makes sense that one is motivated to struggle for recognition only if one feels one has been hurt by not receiving recognition. However, tying struggles for recognition to hurt feelings is not unproblematic. Fraser[260] criticizes Honneth's account as vague and problematic in its reliance on internal psychological effects and states. Fraser proposes instead a theory based on classifying recognition as institutionalized patterns of status equality and classifying misrecognition as institutionalized patterns of status subordination. Fraser makes it clear that she sees misrecognition as relayed only through social institutions, not through deprecatory or freestanding discourse between individuals. Fraser categorizes misrecognition as institutionalized status subordination, believing we need to locate the wrong of injustice in social relations rather than in individual or interpersonal psychology. She believes this is necessary to escape the problems of Honneth's psychological model for explaining struggles for recognition. Fraser's focus on institutions rather than individual emotions is valuable in adjudicating between genuine and false grievances, and it helps strengthen Honneth's weakness on this point. But our ability to judge that a social group has a legitimate claim of misrecognition does not help us answer what motivates a struggle for recognition. On this question, Honneth's model of an emotional response to experiences of misrecognition holds more promise. Fraser's position is that injustices "impede parity of participation in social life,"[261] claiming that injustices are not best interpreted as violations of personal identity.[262] But Honneth does have a point. How can an injustice not threaten an individual's personal identity? We can talk about degree of effect, but the threat and the effects of misrecognition on personal identity are real.

---

[259] Honneth, *The Struggle for Recognition*, 138.
[260] Fraser and Honneth, 198-236.
[261] Fraser and Honneth, 222.
[262] Fraser and Honneth, 204.

Fraser says that her view of recognition and misrecognition is a matter of justice and that Honneth views them as a matter of self-realization. Fraser is correct to warn against grounding a normative framework on one privileged set of experiences, but her implication that this is what Honneth is doing is unfair. Fraser's critique is that Honneth grounds his recognition theory in a moral psychology in which prepolitical suffering caused by denial of recognition is the single motivation underlying discontent.[263] True, as Fraser says, motives underlying personal discontent come from a wide range of resentments, aversions, and antipathies other than suffering from one's expectation that one's personal identity be recognized; but Honneth is not saying that all discontent comes from a denial of personal identity. His position is that the motivation for discontent stems from, ironically, what Fraser suggests—the expectation that one be treated fairly. Understanding that Honneth's idea of recognition is linked to our broad normative expectations of how we are treated rather than expectations of a specific personal identity dissolves Fraser's objection.

Fraser's theory may be helpful in cases of unjust distribution of objective resources, but Honneth is correct that struggles for recognition are not only about addressing redistribution but also about experiences of misrecognition within social relations. The latter cases are better analyzed with models of conflict that start from the moral feelings over unmet normative expectations.[264] As Zurn says, Honneth's recognition theory has important advantages in that it provides a clear account of the motivational wellsprings behind struggles in which individuals sacrifice their personal interests to promote the general welfare beyond the abstract demands of morality. Individuals engage in these risky struggles because there is an internal connection between social structures of moral regard and individuals' practical sense-of-self.[265] Connecting the moral feelings of violation with the need for personal integrity is, Zurn says, how

---

[263] Fraser and Honneth, 203.
[264] Honneth, *The Struggle for Recognition*, 163-165.
[265] Zurn, *Axel Honneth,* Kindle location 1910.

recognition theory overcomes the problems of theoretical idealism and the impotence of abstract oughts. Although Fraser has valid concerns about the incompleteness of Honneth's accounts of self-esteem and identity formation, Honneth's argument is still valid that the motives for social resistance against injustice are formed in the context of individuals' moral experiences.[266]

But if, as I do, we adopt Honneth's idea that hurt feelings help motivate an individual to struggle for recognition, there are still problems. Honneth's descriptions of hurt feelings from misrecognition reveal a dilemma for his theory. He lists three forms of misrecognition. One is when individuals are physically abused, such as rape or torture.[267] These individuals are deprived of autonomous control of their own bodies or personal space. Another form of misrecognition, typified by social ostracism and denial of legal rights, injures subjects' self-respect, and they lose their ability to relate to themselves as an equal interaction partner with other individuals.[268] A further form, degradation, robs subjects of opportunities to attribute social value to their abilities.[269] For Honneth, individuals suffering from any of these forms of misrecognition are diminished in their capacity to act in ways that would allow them to realize their own needs and are diminished in their ability to interact with others. Honneth identifies the loss in individuals who have been deprived of autonomous control of their own body or personal space as the loss of confidence in themselves and the world.[270] These individuals, he says, are severely diminished in their capacity to act in ways that would allow them to realize their own personality and in their ability to interact with their fellow humans as equals because the experience of misrecognition has injured their self-respect.[271] These individuals have, by Honneth's definition, impaired autonomy. Honneth then interestingly says that "the

---

[266] Fraser and Honneth, 29-33.
[267] Honneth, *The Struggle for Recognition*, 131-139.
[268] Honneth, *The Struggle for Recognition*, 133.
[269] Honneth, *The Struggle for Recognition*, 134.
[270] Honneth, *The Struggle for Recognition*, 132-133.
[271] Honneth, *The Struggle for Recognition*, 134.

negative emotional reactions accompanying the experience of misrecognition could represent precisely the affective motivational basis in which the struggled-for recognition is anchored."[272] These are the hurt feelings that Honneth sees as the motivations for struggles for recognition.

This leaves Honneth with the dilemma in which an individual, being damaged by misrecognition and lacking the recognition he says is necessary for one to be autonomous, nevertheless has some capacity to struggle for recognition. Honneth's position is clear that individual autonomy comes only from recognition; he states that "social recognition represents the necessary condition for subjects being able to identify with their valuable qualities and, accordingly, develop genuine autonomy."[273] Autonomy requires the extension of individual possibilities through social cooperation, and individuals need to experience recognition from their social world if they are to develop a feeling of social inclusion and autonomy. An individual, Honneth argues, cannot fully develop his or her autonomy merely through possession of economic goods[274] but also must receive three modes of recognition—love, legal rights, and esteem—from society to develop individual autonomy. If misrecognition damages one's relations-to-self, as Honneth holds, and the recognition necessary for autonomy is lacking, how can one respond to misrecognition with a struggle for recognition?

The other part of the dilemma is why it is that not all individuals who suffer hurt feelings from misrecognition are motivated to undertake struggles for recognition. As Honneth states, "The experience of being [misrecognized] can become the motivational impetus for a struggle for recognition," but, as he also admits, this only *can* happen but does not *have to* happen.[275] The question is, how does one move from the realization that one is misrecognized to a motivation to struggle for recognition? Honneth answers that it is necessary for the individual to have access to an existing social movement in his or her cultural-political

---

[272] Honneth, *The Struggle for Recognition*, 135.
[273] Honneth, "Grounding Recognition," 515.
[274] Fraser and Honneth, 176-177.
[275] Honneth, *The Struggle for Recognition*, 138, emphasis his.

environment through which that individual can articulate moral-political feeling:

> Empirically, whether the cognitive potential inherent in feeling hurt or ashamed becomes a moral-political conviction depends above all on how the affected subject's cultural-political environment is constructed: only if the means of articulation of a social movement are available can the experience of disrespect become a source of motivation for acts of political resistance.[276]

What exactly qualifies as a "social movement" Honneth does not entirely specify, but he consistently links it to collective acts of political resistance.[277]

Certainly, an existing social movement engaged in political resistance against misrecognition would assist misrecognized individuals in understanding their hurt feelings and would give them an outlet for their need for recognition. That the addition of a social movement does not solve the dilemma is evidenced by the fact that not all misrecognized individuals who have access to an existing social movement of political resistance actually engage in a struggle for recognition. The addition of a social movement only transfers the dilemma to the question of why and how an individual would accept the movement's relevance to his or her life and join it in acts of political resistance. A social movement can provide an interpretive structure by which individuals can interpret their experiences of misrecognition, and it can encourage an individual to struggle for recognition; however, it cannot make the individual accept the notion of a struggle or decide for the individual whether to engage actively in a struggle. The dilemma remains even if we remove Honneth's requirement of a social movement and adopt the plausible idea that individuals have access to a more generic normative surplus within recognition that depicts the way in which norms extend beyond the individuals to whom they are applied. That individuals have access to

---

[276] Honneth, *The Struggle for Recognition*, 138-139.

[277] Honneth, *The Struggle for Recognition*, 93, 128, 138-139, 143, 162-167, 170. Fraser and Honneth, 131-134.

something does not mean that they will partake of it. Also, a social movement cannot be a necessary condition for struggles for recognition because we need to account for the coming into existence of any social movement that struggles for recognition. What motivates individuals to start movements of political resistance? Plus, why does Honneth assume that individuals' hurt feelings from misrecognition can be articulated only within a social movement of political resistance? Those questions I will address in chapters 2.3 and 2.4 in which I discuss what forms struggles for recognition may take. First, there is still the issue of how an individual damaged by misrecognition could undertake a struggle for recognition.

What is at work when an individual moves from hurt feelings to a struggle for recognition? For individuals damaged by misrecognition to undertake a struggle for recognition, something must enable them to activate their potential to struggle. Does that something reside within the individual, the social environment, or both? Honneth and others would say that his account does not preclude individual actions, and this is true, but the issue is not a preclusion of individual agency; the issue is an underestimation of its importance for a theory of recognition. I agree with McBride that: "It would be a mistake to allow ourselves to be diverted from the deeper connection between individual agency and social recognition."[278] Discussion of misrecognition and struggles for recognition are incomplete without incorporating individual agency. The individual must be able to respond to misrecognition if he or she is to be able to undertake a struggle for recognition.

Even if struggles are not possible without an existing social movement, the individual must still be able to respond to the movement. Similarly, the positive effects of recognition are possible only if an individual is capable of responding to affirmation positively. Again, nothing in Honneth precludes individual agency, but he does not include it sufficiently. Honneth's philosophy of recognition circles the concept of individual agency, but he does not engage it. His reluctance seems to stem from his oft-stated opposition to standard liberal accounts of human

[278] McBride, 115.

autonomy that he finds overly individualistic. Honneth feels a need to set his philosophy of recognition against the modern liberal notion of the isolated individual. If, instead, we take it as given that the old paradigm of the isolated subject is invalid, then we are freed to pursue expansion of recognition theory. I am content to stop beating the dead horse of the Cartesian subject and take as a given that individuals are embedded in a social world that affects all of their thoughts and actions.

A theory of struggles for recognition needs to include that individuals have the potential to respond to their environment for their own sake, and such an account needs to be compatible with the need for individuals to receive recognition to be autonomous. What is needed is a view of struggles for recognition that includes an individual's capacity to respond to both the negative and positive aspects of the social environment with a struggle for recognition. Having such a view only points to the possibility for an individual to respond to an unfavorable environment and still does not indicate that an individual actually would respond with a struggle for recognition. I am seeking, here, something akin to what Bader refers to as a "general, minimalist capability of making experiences, of judgment, and agency without which human beings would be cultural dupes and not agents in any meaningful sense able to feel unjustly treated and complain/act against all different kinds of injustice."[279] It cannot be assumed in every case that a victim of misrecognition can draw on a previously achieved autonomy he or she received from recognition. Something is needed beyond hurt feelings to motivate an individual to struggle for recognition. The beginning of an answer can be found in Honneth's own words, and I will endeavor to encapsulate those ideas in a way that Honneth does not.

Honneth adopts the response model of recognition,[280] which states that recognition responds to and brings forward potentials already possessed by individuals and that receiving recognition helps individuals develop their autonomous self-determination. Recognition, Honneth says,

---

[279] Bader, 253.

[280] Honneth, "Grounding Recognition," 507, 509-510.

brings individuals into the social lifeworld, the normative recognition order that he calls a "second nature" into which individuals are socialized.[281] For the response model to work, though, there must be an inner personal component that is that to which recognition is responding and is that from which individuals respond to recognition. Honneth's argument assumes that individuals have a personal sense of self that can be suppressed by being abused and developed by receiving recognition and care. There must be something within an individual on which recognition can gain traction to assist that individual toward positive relations-to-self and autonomy, and it is from this inner something that an individual can respond to negative misrecognition with a positive struggle for recognition. Honneth never makes the connection between that prior personal sense of self and the presence of personal agency, but that connection must be established for any theory of struggles for recognition to work.

Recognizing someone requires an action from the recognizer. Honneth describes it as "the expression of a freestanding intention,"[282] and the individual's conscious intentions are what drive the dynamic relations of recognition attitudes and actions. This formulation fits with Honneth's agreement with Laitinen[283] about the need to locate recognition in the space of reasons, in which recognition is motivated by moral reasons and evaluates another individual's value.[284] However, if we, as Honneth does, place the necessary conditions for individuals to identify what is morally valuable exclusively within the norms of culture—the social lifeworld—we run into two problems; one Honneth addresses, but the other he does not. Fortunately, his answer to the first problem can also be used to address the second. The first problem is that, as Honneth is aware, placing the learning of moral norms within a social lifeworld means that the certitudes of the social norms are not immutable but can change over time. To counter the danger of relativism, he postulates a conception of

---

[281] Honneth, "Grounding Recognition," 508.
[282] Honneth, "Grounding Recognition," 506.
[283] Arto Laitinen, "Interpersonal Recognition: A Response to Value or a Precondition of Personhood?" *Inquiry*, 45, 2002, 463-478.
[284] Honneth, "Grounding Recognition," 507-508.

historical progress wherein human values expand—we recognize new valuable properties that we perceive people as having. This developmental path, Honneth believes, allows for justified judgments regarding the transhistorical validity of a specific culture of recognition, solving the problem of relativism.[285] Progress in social acts of recognition, Honneth believes, is indicated by increases in "individuality and social inclusion."[286] The social lifeworld can be understood as the emergence in the ongoing course of history of a "second nature" in which we are socialized and oriented into a changing space of reasons that allows us to evaluate changes in normative values over time. For example, Honneth sees capitalism as an improvement over estate-based social order in increasing the possibilities of individuation and recognition, without suggesting that capitalism is a perfect system.[287] This notion of progress in the social lifeworld's second nature, Honneth believes, answers the charge of value relativism. In our socialization into a normatively progressive second nature, we learn to recognize valuable qualities in others, the normative level of our recognition relations rises, and our opportunities for identifying our own abilities and autonomy grow.[288]

This notion of a second nature helps solve, in part, what I see as the second problem that arises from Honneth placing what is morally valuable exclusively within the norms of culture, which links with the agency dilemma I identified earlier. This problem is that it is true that individuals cannot judge anything about themselves as a valuable quality unless they learn from their society what is considered valuable, but if we say that social content completely determines what and how people make judgments, then we may render the individual incapable of possessing self-respect, self-realization, or autonomy. To maintain a concept of an individual's general, minimalist capability of making experiences and judgments, we should look more closely at this notion of a second

---

[285] Honneth, "Grounding Recognition," 508.
[286] Honneth, "Grounding Recognition," 511.
[287] Fraser and Honneth, 185.
[288] Honneth, "Recognition as Ideology," 333-334. See also Honneth, *Reification*, 23-33, and Honneth, "Grounding Recognition," 509.

nature—a social lifeworld that gradually socializes individuals into normative values. Honneth states that this socialization embeds individuals in a network of social relations in which they recognize other people as "both autonomous and individuated, equal and particular persons."[289] However, such mutual recognition is not a given within a society but must be manifested by individuals through their purposefully intended attitudes and actions. The notion of a socialization into a second nature implies the existence of something within individuals that enables them to learn from society and orient themselves in the second nature's space of reasons. Nothing is learned by an individual from the social lifeworld without the individual's involvement. Individuals perhaps almost cannot help but conform to what is being imposed on them by the normative recognition order of the second nature, but even enculturation requires reciprocation from an individual's own capabilities and choices. As McNay says, the individual's self-realization is one of "inherence and mutual determination rather than a unidirectional causality" of society on the individual.[290]

The idea of socialization into a second nature is more useful as an explanation for misrecognition and struggles for recognition than as an answer to relativism. Individuals are socialized to recognize valuable traits and contributions in themselves and others, but because of normative discrimination, an individual may not see him- or herself as having those properties. It becomes second nature for these individuals, and for others, not to see them as valuable. What critical theory needs to solve is the question of how the victim, despite being socialized into a negatively discriminatory second nature, is able somehow to make the connection that positive norms nevertheless should apply to him or her. Honneth is unclear about how we can get anyone to see that the victims of normative discrimination victims have valuable traits and contributions. There must be some capability for individuals to make the effort to overcome socialization and recognize the people whom society teaches them not to recognize. To make sense of struggles for recognition, we need to include

---

[289] Honneth, *The Struggle for Recognition*, 175.
[290] McNay, *Against Recognition*, 142.

a personal component that enables some people to respond to misrecognition with a positive struggle for recognition. We need not immediately explain why some individuals respond to misrecognition with a struggle for recognition while others do not. First we need to show how such struggle is even possible if recognition is needed to act autonomously. I think this missing link is something similar to autonomy—individual agency. The concept of individual agency I am discussing here is only in the context of the current discussion of recognition theory, bearing in mind that the concept can have various uses and mean various things. For my purposes here, I am attempting to establish a concept of individual agency as an individual locus of actions that will strengthen an overall theory of recognition and struggles for recognition.

Honneth considers autonomy but not individual agency. Yes, to achieve autonomy and self-realization, certain conditions external to the individual are prerequisite. Individuals need protections from injurious forces such as physical violence, but that protection is necessary because there is something internal to the individual that must be protected from these external forces. Honneth acknowledges that autonomy is intersubjective but neglects to include the individual's contribution adequately. Honneth is correct that "the freedom associated with self-realization is dependent on prerequisites that human subjects do not have at their disposal, since they can only acquire this freedom with the help of their interaction partners"[291]; but this is only half of the story. Freedom also has the prerequisite that individuals possess agency and choose to use it. The power that recognition has is to assist an individual to achieve autonomy by directly recognizing that individual as a being possessing individual agency—a recognition that fits within the response model. It is not autonomy that we are recognizing, but the internal agency of an individual. To recognize an individual, we must acknowledge him or her as a person possessing individual agency and thereby being capable of autonomy and self-realization. Recognition of a person's individual

[291] Honneth, *The Struggle for Recognition*, 174.

agency is part of the social recognition that enables a person to realize positive self-affirmation of his or her positive qualities. Therefore, recognition theory benefits from a greater emphasis on acknowledging individuals' inherent capabilities to strive for recognition and autonomy.

I agree with Honneth that "we attribute to every human being an interest in being able to freely determine and realize his own desires and intentions."[292] I believe he fails to explicate adequately what this entails—the reality that humans are beings who make choices and act on those choices. He also speaks of "basic self-confidence [that] represents the basic prerequisite for every type of self-realization in the sense that it allows individuals to attain, for the first time, the inner freedom that enables them to articulate their own needs."[293] Such a statement is made sensible when paired with a concept of individual agency. To say that there is something within the individual that responds to recognition, and to which recognition is responding, is not falling back into an individualistic bias, nor does it preclude a social approach to human autonomy. Any view of individual agency that makes sense must include that the individual is embedded in a social world and that to navigate successfully in the social world, the individual needs to engage in mutual recognition with others. Acknowledging the synergy between individual agency and recognition relations in which both individual agency and social autonomy are affected by recognition and misrecognition strengthens our view of recognition.

In a more recent work,[294] Honneth, writing with Joel Anderson, has amended his earlier discussions of the damages from misrecognition by directly acknowledging that it also affects agency. However, he does not connect these ideas on agency to the question of struggles for recognition; his concern instead is arguing that agents' dependency on recognitional

---

[292] Honneth, "Grounding Recognition," 516.

[293] Honneth, *The Struggle for Recognition*, 175.

[294] Joel Anderson and Axel Honneth, "Autonomy, Vulnerability, Recognition, and Justice," in *Autonomy and the Challenges to Liberalism: New Essays*, ed. John Christman and Joel Anderson (Cambridge, UK: Cambridge University Press, 2005).

infrastructure for their autonomy creates an obligation on society that must be included in standard liberal accounts of justice. Honneth could take his conceptions of damage to self-confidence and tie them to agency by arguing that the trauma of rape and torture causes a loss of individuals' own perceptual capacities of their own feelings, desires, and convictions.[295] Extreme misrecognition does damage individuals, and, as Honneth remarks, autonomy is vulnerable to anything that diminishes self-trust.[296] That Honneth admits that individual agency, in addition to relational autonomy, is affected by extreme misrecognition is a step toward a fuller view of how misrecognition affects individuals, but Honneth does not go further. Now we need a more robust picture of the role of individual agency in individuals' responses to misrecognition. The capability of undertaking struggles for recognition must lie within those individuals who resiliently respond to the suffering from misrecognition with a positive struggle for recognition. This resilience must stem from an individual's agency because what has changed from the experience of misrecognition is not the external environment but the feelings of the individual toward him- or herself and the social environment. This is why it is proper for Honneth to base social movements on the moral feelings resulting from experiencing misrecognition. Violations from misrecognition can damage one's relations-to-self, which, in turn, diminishes autonomy, but as long as an individual's agency remains, so does the possibility of motivation to engage in a struggle for recognition.

To craft a view of individual agency compatible with Honneth's insights on the need for recognition, I will turn first to McNay's interpretation of Bourdieu's concept of habitus as an answer to Honneth. Like Fraser, McNay has problems with Honneth's psychological story of struggles for recognition, claiming he has a "naïve, spontaneist account of action."[297] But McNay also rejects Fraser's objectivist theory of

[295] Anderson and Honneth, 133-134.
[296] Anderson and Honneth, 135.
[297] McNay, *Against Recognition*, 127.

recognition as lacking any orientation to the subjective dimensions of identity.[298] McNay proposes habitus—the process through which power relations are incorporated into embodied agency—as a new ground for mediating between objectivist and subjectivist accounts of recognition. Habitus grounds "an analysis of subjectivity and agency in the possibilities and constraint of embodied existence" within a social world.[299] Habitus shares Honneth's insight that a phenomenological emphasis on experience is needed to understand the effects of misrecognition and resistance to it. But McNay says that Honneth's model conflates experiences of suffering with the capability for the critical awareness of injustice, which he in turn conflates with agency. She rejects Honneth's position that suffering misrecognition leads to opposition to misrecognition. I think that this criticism is correct, that critical agency is not an inevitable effect of misrecognition, and that Honneth's account is unsatisfactory.

For McNay, the question in struggles for recognition is what would bring an individual to oppositional consciousness. McNay is correct that suffering misrecognition does not necessarily lead an individual to political insight about injustice or resistance to it. McNay says that the symbolic resources with which to formulate agency are also needed. For example, McNay credits the success of the women's movements in the '60s and '70s to feminists drawing on symbolic and linguistic resources to transform gender consciousness.[300] Because she holds that all experience is shaped by preconstituted discourses, she concludes that oppositional consciousness and agency are "determined by the specific configuration of symbolic and material relations—the space of possibles and structure of positions—in a given field of action."[301] But McNay's account does not explain two important questions. The first is where the symbolic and linguistic resources in opposition to the preconstituted discourses of patriarchy arose. The second is how, after symbolic and linguistic resources in opposition to patriarchy arose, some individuals in the same

---

[298] McNay, *Against Recognition*, 160.
[299] McNay, *Against Recognition*, 13.
[300] McNay, *Against Recognition*, 137.
[301] McNay, *Against Recognition*, 140.

field of action developed an oppositional consciousness while others did not. If resistance to injustice were a matter of the presence of symbolic and material relations, then McNay's theory exchanges Honneth's cause—suffering—for another—symbolic and material relations. Why would an individual take in those symbolic resources and respond with a struggle for recognition?

McNay's criticism is correct that Honneth does not consider the importance of power structures and power inequalities in keeping individuals from undertaking struggles for recognition, but she does not offer a workable mechanism to explain individual motivation for struggles for recognition. In fact, her conception of power structures' effects on individuals offers no sensible conception of how an individual could ever struggle against prevailing power structures. The problem is that if individuals' identities are repressed and colonized by the power structure, then where is there room for resistance? McNay points to individual agency as a way out of this problem, but her view of agency is lacking, a deficit that also appears in Bourdieu's conception of habitus. To say that opposition to misrecognition is "determined by the specific configuration of symbolic and material relations"[302] is no more reliable a predictor of individual motivation or action than is Honneth's reliance on the cultural-political environment to catalyze hurt feelings from suffering moral injuries. Both accounts suppose that agency, despite being called internal to the individual, is a spontaneous effect of external forces. Such reductionism lacks the hoped-for explanatory power of why social resistance does or does not happen. The presence of symbolic resources is insufficient to cause an individual to engage in a struggle for recognition similar to the way in which the experience of suffering is insufficient. Even if we were to say that it is a combination of hurt feelings and symbolic resources that motivate an individual to a struggle for recognition, we could still point to individuals who have suffered misrecognition and have access to symbolic resources but acquiesce rather than struggle. Suffering and symbolic resources are both necessary

---

[302] McNay, *Against Recognition*, 140.

components to motivate an individual to struggle for recognition, but there must still be something else operating in addition.

Regardless of the shortcomings of McNay's account, the notion of habitus can still be helpful. McNay is correct that habitus, because it views individual agency as embodied and embedded in a social world, mediates between objectivist and subjectivist accounts of recognition. I read habitus as how an individual is in the social world, is affected by the social world, and develops tendencies and dispositions in response to the social world through which the individual perceives and responds in deliberate reflective ways to the world. An individual's habitus internalizes the society's second nature and space of reasons from which the individual makes decisions, and, importantly, habitus responds to recognition and misrecognition. We still need to steer clear of a social determinism and not reduce habitus to rote mimesis but understand the individual's role and capability to act from his or her habitus in the social world. It was, after all, not some abstract entity called "feminists" who developed opposition consciousness by drawing on symbolic and linguistic resources to transform gender consciousness. Individual women drew on those resources, and each woman transformed her own personal consciousness and her own personal habitus to overcome constraints and embrace possibilities in order to struggle for increased recognition for women's rights. The locus of actions resides in each individual woman.

For suffering and symbolic resources to help motivate a struggle, an individual must have the ability to respond to them with actions, and an account of individual agency must be added to habitus. Kelly Oliver correctly observes that critical theorists who discuss subjectivity in terms of recognition lack a full realization of the ability to respond to and address others, an ability she calls "response-ability."[303] Her contention is that discussing recognition in terms of a subject-object dichotomy that is fundamentally antagonistic undermines the intersubjective dialogue on which recognition theory places great emphasis. Oliver's theory of response-ability separates subject positions from subjectivity. Our social

---

[303] Oliver, x.

interactions and cultural positions constitute our subject position, which varies as our relations and circumstances change. Subjectivity is our sense of agency and response-ability in our encounters with our social environment. Our experience of ourselves is maintained in the tension between our subject position and our subjectivity, which are always profoundly interconnected. Our subject position is historically determined and shaped by our experiences, but our subjectivity has (at least the appearance of) infinite response-ability. The issue here is the individual's ability to respond, and, in particular, the individual's sense of being able to respond. Oliver agrees with Honneth that being subordinated or oppressed affects an individual at the level of what Oliver calls his or her subjectivity, which is necessary for his or her sense of agency. Misrecognition compromises one's sense of one's agency. Victims can be rendered docile or speechless if their sense that they can respond to others is annihilated. We are by virtue of others, Oliver says agreeing with Emmanuel Levinas, that we are responsible for the other's responsibility, for the other's ability to respond, and for continually opening and reopening and not closing down possibilities for their responses.[304]

I believe that Oliver's concept of individuals having a response-ability that is enhanced and strengthened through positive dialogues of address and response is one way to add a concept of agency to habitus. The concepts of response-ability and habitus connect in that they both acknowledge the effects of power structures and the social environment on individuals. One's subject position shapes one's habitus, but one's subjectivity and dialogic relationships with others are where an oppositional consciousness can arise. Individuals always bring to their interactions their dispositions and capital (Bourdieu's economic, cultural, and social capital) from their position in the social field, but they also bring their ability to respond. Interpersonal interactions are mediated by the social field and also by individuals and their responses. Response-ability refers to a conscious agency that can oppose misrecognition by connecting with and using symbolic resources. It acknowledges that

---

[304] Oliver, 17-19.

individuals have the ability to respond to other individuals, to the suffering of misrecognition, and to symbolic resources with either dialogue or antagonism. That this ability to respond can be damaged by misrecognition but can still survive misrecognition highlights the individual's capability while appreciating his or her social vulnerability. Oliver's concept of response-ability, though an important addition to a theory of misrecognition, has limited use for two reasons. One is that Oliver places it in opposition to her problematic depiction of recognition as a pathological antagonism generated by oppression.[305] The other is that she places it within a broader concept she calls "witnessing" that depends heavily on her idiosyncratic interpretation of psychoanalysis. Those notions diminish the contribution that response-ability, as it stands in Oliver's theory, can make to a view of individuals being able to overcome misrecognition.

Another possible theoretical resource we could add to habitus is Korsgaard's concept of the self-constitution of individual agents. This concept gives us a way to think about individuals as being the authors of and responsible for their actions without making the mistake of thinking that there is a subject prior to or separate from socialization. Korsgaard's view is that

> it is as the possessor of personal or practical identity that you are the author of your actions, and responsible

---

[305] Oliver, 11-12, 24. Oliver claims that "it is only after oppressed people are dehumanized that they seek acknowledgment or recognition of their humanity" (26). This seems incorrect. As I will argue in chapter 2.4.1, we all seek recognition of our humanity and identity prior to being recognized or misrecognized. I suspect that what Oliver is trying to capture here is a notion of a transformational struggle that is undertaken only when one is misrecognized. Far from condemning recognition, as Oliver thinks, her statement reveals a struggle for recognition in response to normative discrimination. In this case, recognition is sought to rectify oppression. Yes, if there were no normative discrimination, there would be no need for a struggle for recognition, but if there were recognition as a human, there would be no oppression. Oliver's position seems to be that recognition is portrayed as something needed from the dominant culture, which may be, as she seems to assume, Charles Taylor's position, but she fails to see that we need recognition from someone to come to understand our own subjectivity.

> for them. And yet at the same time it is in choosing your actions that you create that identity. What this means is that you constitute yourself as the author of your actions in the very act of choosing them.[306]

She acknowledges that this sounds paradoxical but says that this apparent paradox of self-constitution is in fact no paradox because charges that self-constitution is voluntarism are false. "The picture here is not of a craftsman who is, mysteriously, his own product. The picture here is of the self-constitutive process that is the essence of life."[307] Life, Korsgaard says, does not create itself but in its biological processes is continually maintaining itself through its actions.[308] For humans, this means that, in addition to the animal activity of continually making ourselves through processes like taking in nutrition, we also must continually maintain our social practical identity. There is no *you* prior to your choices and actions because your practical identity is constituted by your choices and actions in response to your environment. We also are capable of reflecting on our responses and of considering whether to do one thing or another, yet to say we are capable is the wrong emphasis. We are *compelled* to respond to our world—it is our plight; and we use our human rationality to respond.[309] Our self-constitution is not a state that we achieve and then act from[310]; like breathing, it is continual motion, not a static condition. It is the plight of being human that we must continually choose and act and make ourselves the authors of our actions by the way that we act.

Key to the concept of self-constitution, and its application to our problem of struggles for recognition, is to understand practical identity as a socialized identity under which one, as an individual, values oneself and finds one's actions worth undertaking. One's practical identity is, as

---

[306] Korsgaard, Kindle locations 375-377.
[307] Korsgaard, Kindle locations 703-705.
[308] Korsgaard, Kindle locations 600-618.
[309] Korsgaard believes that correct actions are "not just any actions but actions that are most genuinely in accordance with the principles of practical reason." Korsgaard, Kindle locations 738-739.
[310] Korsgaard, Kindle locations 734-735.

Korsgaard understands, composed of one's roles and relationships, membership in social groups, associations with causes, professions and positions held, and so on. We value our roles and relationships; therefore, our conceptions of our practical identity, in Korsgaard's words, govern our choice of actions because to value ourselves in a certain role is at the same time to find it worthwhile to undertake certain actions for the sake of certain ends.[311] An individual, as possessor of a practical identity, is the author of his or her actions, and in choosing those actions, creates his or her identity by drawing on the normative resources in society.[312] This deliberate practical choosing and acting is what makes us human. That humans constitute their practical identity is why it makes sense to hold them accountable for their actions. Although it should not have to be said, I will belabor the point that Korsgaard is not suggesting that humans make up their practical identities out of whole cloth or on their own. Our practical identities are contingent on experiences and the environment from which we learn them and acquire our practical identities. Some practical identities we are born to environmentally, and others we adopt, but our practical identities are made by our active experiences of them. If you continue to endorse the reasons the identity presents to you, and observe the obligations it imposes on you, then it is you.[313]

Adopting the concept of self-constitution does not commit us to Korsgaard's lengthy recitation on Aristotle and Plato in the rest of her book, *Self-Constitution*. She, in fact, all but ignores the concept in the last three-quarters of her book despite its title. Because the key to understanding self-constitution is the concept of one's practical identities, we can instead place the concept of practical identity within Honneth's conception of recognition relations and keep both concepts grounded in the social world. An individual's practical identity is continually influenced by

---

[311] Korsgaard, Kindle location 384.

[312] "When you deliberately decide what sorts of effects you will bring about in the world, you are also deliberately deciding what sort of a cause you will be. And that means you are deciding who you are." Korsgaard, Kindle locations 371-372.

[313] Korsgaard, Kindle locations 424-425.

conflicting social forces, including incidents of recognition and misrecognition, and the individual must assimilate these experiences and deal with their effects through continual self-constitution. We can see how receiving recognition is important to one's practical identity by affirming one's roles and relationships. Receiving recognition gives individuals the social understanding and the self-confidence that facilitate their practical identities. Korsgaard says that we learn many roles, each of which one might think of as a set of principles or dos and don'ts, the interpretation of which can be thought about and debated.[314] Most of the roles within our practical identity are outcomes of circumstances—we are born to particular parents and as citizens of a particular country, for example. With these roles or subidentities of child and citizen come responsibilities that I did not choose but that I endorse whenever I willingly act in accordance with them, and in endorsing them, I affirm that I am them. Acts performed under duress, physical or psychological, are probably not endorsements, but they still contribute to what we are and affect our practical identity. We can combine this with Honneth's insight that when we act in accordance with our responsibilities, we are affirmed—recognized—by others for doing so. Recognition socializes us into our roles, which form our practical identity. We can also see how when we act in accordance with our responsibilities, we are affirming our own self as a good example of the role we have learned. With each such action, we affirm our practical identity, and this makes us who we are. It is a continuous feedback loop between an individual and the world in which he or she is embedded. This is what I take self-constitution to be.

Understanding the similarity of self-constitution to W.E.B. Du Bois's concept of double consciousness opens up a new understanding of what could motivate a struggle for recognition. Du Bois wrote that blacks developed the sense of always looking at themselves through the eyes of white Americans, of "measuring one's soul by the tape of a world that

[314] Korsgaard, Kindle location 390. Korsgaard actually uses "many particular practical identities," Kindle location 395, that we must unite into a coherent practical identity, but to avoid confusion, I am using the term "many roles" to describe components within our practical identity.

looks on in amused contempt and pity."[315] These experiences of normative discrimination misrecognition that denies their identities inflict moral injuries and hurt feelings in blacks, yet as Du Bois wrote, Blacks possessed a dogged strength to resist the strife of the normative discrimination and to attain self-consciousness. This was because they developed a double consciousness—the consciousness of one's self but also the consciousness of seeing one's self through the misrecognizing eyes of the whites. In later writings, Du Bois moved away from the terminology of double consciousness but retained the awareness of the internal struggle of blacks in a society that deems them inferior, ugly, congenitally stupid, and naturally criminal. This normative discrimination creates a low cultural status that is blacks' subject position in the social field of recognition relations, causing bitter inner criticism of themselves because it has become part of their habitus. Du Bois may have later despaired of the possibility of successful black resistance to racism, but he never lost the idea that despite the realities of white domination, the black retains a sense of the dichotomy between the normative discrimination expressed by the oppressors and a love for oneself that is not defined by white domination. This dichotomy is not a psychic split in the individual, but it enables a different way of thinking, feeling, and experiencing—a "gifted second-sight" and a subjectivity with which one can see both sides of the veil of normative discrimination and strive to affirm one's identity. The double consciousness of self and misrecognized self, with its accompanying double life and double duties, tempts the mind "to pretence or revolt, to hypocrisy or radicalism."[316] Du Bois rejects both of those paths as extreme and urges instead a merger of the double self into a better and truer self that does not deny historical and cultural realities but builds on them.

The black, Du Bois says, "simply wishes to make it possible for a man to be both a Negro and an American without being cursed and spit upon by his fellows, without having the doors of opportunity closed

---

[315] W.E.B. Du Bois, *The Souls of Black Folk* (New York: Dover Publications, 1999), 10.

[316] Du Bois, 156.

roughly in his face."[317] Fortunately, in this struggle for recognition, the black has the gift of second sight, which is a persistent conscious sensation of self and life on this side of the veil of misrecognition. Members of an excluded racial minority can look at each other without the veil of the color line that obscures the vision whites and blacks have of each other. Thus, people of color can see both themselves as they are and the white depiction of them and discern the difference. As Maria Lugones put it, the outsider necessarily acquires the flexibility of shifting from how he or she was constructed as an outsider by the white/Anglo world to how his or her life is constructed where he or she is more or less at home among fellow people of color.[318] This minority subjectivity has the potential to transform one's practical identity and the broader society by motivating striving and struggle within the political dimension in which minority subjectivity is formed.[319] Whichever path one takes—hypocrisy, radicalism, or affirming one's identity—one constitutes through one's actions a practical identity and affirms that identity.

How the concept of self-constitution helps us understand struggles for recognition lies within this issue of being affirmed in one's actions, which helps us understand why misrecognition matters and why some but not all would respond with a struggle for recognition. When my affirming myself through my choices is not reciprocated by others, this creates a dissonance that would create the hurt feelings Honneth describes. We can then expand the plight of having to choose and act identified by Korsgaard to include the plight of having to deal with the dissonance of being misrecognized. Placing these hurt feelings within the concept of self-constitution, we can see that a struggle for recognition is deliberately choosing an action that creates our sense of identity as one who struggles to affirm my self, my

---

[317] Du Bois, 11.

[318] Maria Lugones, "Playfulness, 'World'-Travelling, and Loving Perception," *Hypatia* 2 (2), 1987, 3-19.

[319] Nasar Meer, "Overcoming the Injuries of 'Double Consciousness,'" in *The Politics of Misrecognition*, ed. Simon Thompson, and Majid Yar (Farnham, UK: Ashgate Publishing, 2011), 45-66. "Political dimension" is Meer's phrase, but as I will argue in chapter 2.4.5, struggles for recognition can take place beyond the political dimension of social relations.

role, and my past choices. Our practical identity is the reason for the action of struggling for recognition, one reason among many reasons that make demands on individuals. In choosing the action of struggling for recognition, I constitute myself as one who affirms my self as worthy of recognition, and I demand that others reciprocate. Because being human means being constantly engaged in making who we are, a lack of recognition is a big deal. Misrecognition calls into question within ourselves our practical identity and our own choices to affirm that identity.

Connecting Korsgaard's concept of self-constitution with McNay's concept of habitus gives us a conceptual basis for how an individual could come to undertake a struggle for recognition. The human capacity for self-constitution is how the individual is capable of responding with critical agency to experiences of suffering. As a possessor of a practical identity constituted by action, an individual relates to society with inherence and mutual determination rather than as causally determined by society's norms. We all rely on recognition to come to a sense of our identity and to learn how to navigate the social world, but I agree with McBride that it is better for us to stress that we are recognition sensitive rather than recognition dependent because we always retain a degree of independence from the recognition claims made on us.[320] Similarly, we also retain some autonomy in the face of experiences of misrecognition, and we have the power to resist judgments on us by others. McBride says:

> The common idea that the actions of others must directly affect one's relation to oneself, and directly extinguish one's self-respect, seems to misconceive the way in which respect recognition works. I can retain my self-respect in the face of public assaults upon my dignity because my self-respect does not depend on others' reactions to me, but on my ability to recognize myself in light of the moral standards which I bring to bear upon my own conduct. When *I* violate these, I cannot recognize myself as a member in good standing of the moral community.[321]

---

[320] McBride, 136-137.

McBride's point is an important one that bears on the question of how we are to understand responses to misrecognition. Humiliation works when one can be convinced to misrecognize oneself. Humiliation is an attempt to convince people to think poorly of themselves by damaging their relation to themselves and their sense that they can respond to others, similar to Oliver's idea of our sense of response-ability being harmed. However, an individual can resist humiliation and all forms of misrecognition. My self-respect, McBride reminds us, is my judgment that I am entitled to be respected, and this is distinct from the judgment of others about me. As long as I retain my sense that I am entitled to respect, then the judgments of others do not supplant my judgments about myself. This is why, McBride says, one can preserve one's self-respect even in the face of the most appalling treatment by others. From this, McBride argues that

> no matter how recognition sensitive we are, it is still possible to maintain a degree of independence from any particular set of recognitive relations. As such, we are not passive recipients of recognition.[322]

McBride's insights lend credence to the argument that misrecognition is not determinative of either submission to or rebellion against that misrecognition. This is not to suggest that misrecognition has no effect on individuals, only that misrecognition is not determinative.

McBride introduces the idea of "virtual recognition," the human ability to retain a sense of being entitled to recognition and of this entitlement being recognized by a virtual community even if a concrete community misrecognizes and mistreats one.[323] McBride calls this a "virtual public" from which we are seeking recognition and to which we are appealing for recognition and from which we receive a "virtual recognition." This is not an appeal to a fantasy because, as McBride says, self-respect is my judgment that I deserve to be respected. Interestingly, Honneth has a similar concept that he calls the "generalized other." The

---

[321] McBride, 66.
[322] McBride, 66.
[323] McBride, 66, 156.

idea is that in forming one's identity, one takes on the perspective of a generalized other in which one identifies a relationship of mutual recognition in which one can know oneself to be confirmed as an individual in one's particular traits and abilities.[324] Honneth does not connect this idea with motivations for struggles for recognition, but McBride's formulation shows that it can be, and McBride links it to Kant's kingdom of ends and Adam Smith's impartial observer. We can, McBride says, appeal "over the heads" of those who refuse to recognize our claims to the authority of a virtual public. We deem those who reject us as not competent to judge our claims (which very well might be true), and we think that another, unbiased audience would be. Obviously, McBride says, this could be wishful thinking, and we must be careful not to mislead ourselves. But, McBride stresses, an appeal to a virtual public for virtual recognition is not a retreat into subjectivism but is critical thinking about what reasonable people would accept.[325] The virtual public is vital for our understanding of the reasons that others could present against recognizing our recognition claims. We cannot help but be guided by this sort of virtual recognition to help us make sense of the feedback we receive from actual experiences of social recognition and misrecognition.[326] This virtual public serves an important function within recognition relations as a necessary response to the very real possibility that the actual public we deal with is for one reason or another too incompetent to judge our recognition claims correctly. Others are not unbiased in their judgments of our claims to recognition because they too have a lot at stake in recognition claims. Through an inner dialogue with a virtual public, we can judge the responses of others to our recognition claims.

Dori Laub and Shoshana Felman[327] offer a similar idea that they call an "inner witness" that makes subjectivity and agency possible. Individuals develop an inner witness through internalizing their dialogues

[324] Honneth, *The Struggle for Recognition*, 88.
[325] McBride, 156.
[326] McBride, 156.
[327] Shoshana Felman and Dori Laub, *Testimony: Crises of Witnessing in Literature, Psychoanalysis, and History* (New York: Routledge, 1992).

with others in which they learn a sense of self as an agent, a process similar to that of mutual recognition described by Honneth. Laub and Felman say that if the inner witness is annihilated, such as by torture or extreme subordination, subjectivity and the possibility of addressing another is lost. Individuals can be colonized by misrecognition and come to believe that they are not entitled to be treated well. Individuals can come to internalize the misrecognition and side with it. There must be something within an individual that is the source of resistance to conforming to societal pressure to form one's identity in a particular way. Mutual recognition enables dialogue with others and makes dialogue with oneself possible, which further enables dialogue with others. Relations of reciprocity with others are possible when a positive interpersonal dialogue is internalized. Misrecognition damages both interpersonal and internal dialogues, but the inner witness gives one the perspective to be both outside and inside one's oppression and begin to overcome the moral injuries from misrecognition.[328]

An important part of our struggles for recognition is our assertions of our sense of identity. Even if we were to adopt the position that individual identity is wholly shaped by external forces, it would still be the case that individuals are interacting with their culture with the expectation that their sense of identity is accurate. When the views others have of them are in conflict with their sense of identity, their natural reaction will be to assert what they think is correct. Such disparate treatment motivates a struggle for recognition to reassert one's sense of identity. A struggle for honor is "based not on a violation of an individual assertion of rights, but rather on a violation of the integrity of the person as a whole"; it is an appeal for the recognition of one's integrity.[329] When an individual struggles for honor, an appeal is being made on two levels. One is to the idea that all individuals have an integrity that should be respected; but it is also an appeal to something personal and immediate to the individual—*my* integrity should be respected—*I* have value, and *I* have a right to say so.

---

[328] Felman and Laub, 57.

[329] Honneth, *The Struggle for Recognition*, 22.

Each of these declarations takes place within a social environment. They are expressions of power, or desire for power, made within an existing power structure. Struggles for recognition emerge not just from specific misrecognitions but also from the basic idea in our self-constitution of being deserving of respect—that even if no one does, someone should recognize me.

Habitus fleshes out the concept of self-constitution by placing individuals' practical identities fully within the preconstituted discourses that permeate all social experiences. With habitus and self-constitution, struggles for recognition can be seen as expressions of an individual deciding what sort of person he or she will be by incorporating symbolic and linguistic resources to transform his or her consciousness into oppositional consciousness to the preconstituted discourses and then taking action. We can then see that what motivates a struggle for recognition is not "I have hurt feelings from being misrecognized"; it is "I wish my actions to be an expression of someone who can be more than one who suffers hurt feelings." A struggle for recognition is a purposeful movement with cognitive content that claims available symbolic resources to struggle toward receiving the recognition that enables the individual to constitute his or her self as an autonomous individual. It would be morally wrong and factually incorrect to say that individuals cannot undertake this purposeful movement.

Zurn makes the astute observation that individuals can develop a degree of relevant practical relations-to-self even in the absence of full social recognition by tapping into the normative potential within society's unequal recognition order. Similar to McBride, Zurn says that individuals can anticipate full recognition from the community even in the face of misrecognition from the broader society.[330] The capability of individuals to tap into society's normative surplus and potential, anticipate full recognition, and then act toward that end can motivate struggles for recognition. This is the role I take individual agency to have in moving an individual to a struggle for recognition. To be human is to be a living

[330] Zurn, *Axel Honneth,* Kindle locations 1883-1885.

being who authors actions. It is the human ability to be a locus of actions and to act intersubjectively in a conscious and well-directed manner that constitutes one's practical identity. Agency is the means by which one engages with one's particular recognition relations, realizes that these current recognition relations are misrecognitions that cause one to suffer and that this suffering goes against moral norms, imagines the potential for recognition and the end of suffering, and acts in accordance with this alternative social reality by engaging in a struggle for recognition. Therefore, recognition theory benefits from acknowledging individuals' inherent capabilities to strive for recognition and autonomy.

The issue of the individual's perspective has an important role in struggles for recognition that is largely absent from Honneth's account. Honneth is correct that experiences of misrecognition are interpreted according to the prevailing recognition norms. Therefore, misrecognition is experienced in terms of objective social norms. However, it is also the case that experiences of misrecognition are interpreted by the individuals who experience them by personally comparing their experiences to the norms that they have learned. Instances of recognition and misrecognition are also matters of interpretation: Individuals must themselves interpret recognition norms and apply them to particular situations. According to the earlier mentioned response model (which I endorse), recognition is also an individual's interpretation of what qualities another individual is manifesting. It makes sense to extend this idea to misrecognition as an interpretation of other individuals' behaviors. That responsiveness and interpretation are part of recognition is why the earlier discussion about engagement with norms and individuals is important to understand recognition and misrecognition. The response model also reinforces that recognition is a relation among individuals to which all involved contribute and the conclusion that individual agency is necessary for struggles for recognition.

Joining individual agency with social recognition provides a fuller account of how individuals struggle for recognition and achieve autonomy. It is the ability to interact in a conscious and well-directed manner that enables an individual to struggle for recognition, and individual agency is a necessary but not sufficient condition for engaging in a struggle for recognition: necessary because no one can struggle for recognition without agency, but not sufficient because one can choose not to struggle for recognition. Individuals struggle for recognition because agency is not sufficient to attain autonomy—there are prerequisites of autonomy that must be acquired through interaction with partners. An individual can be called "free" in the full sense of the word only when that person has received recognition from others that enables him or her to achieve the goal of autonomy and when the individual has decided to exercise autonomy. We can view struggles for recognition as fueled by the feeling that others are unjustly failing to recognize our capability and right to act from our individual agency. When an individual's intention to struggle for recognition takes root in a social environment where that individual receives recognition from other individuals, the individual's chances of achieving self-realization and autonomy are enhanced. Both individual agency intending toward recognition and the receipt of recognition are necessary for autonomy.

This discussion leaves unresolved the problem of why some people engage in a struggle for recognition while others do not, but it provides a way forward to an analysis of this important question. The ideas of the individual as self-constituting within social norms and of habitus as embodied agency are theoretical tools that could move us toward a more robust and fine-grained picture of struggles for recognition. These ideas create for critical theory more complexity than Honneth's narrative, and they also provide critical theory with greater explanatory power.

2.3 - Honneth's Political Movements Problem

I turn now to the question of the ways individuals express their motivation to struggle for recognition. Struggles for recognition are social actions that require interaction with other individuals and, in some cases, social institutions. The most discussed social actions of struggling for recognition are collective political movements for legal justice, social equality, and access to social and economic resources. For Taylor, political movements for recognition are also the endeavors of marginalized groups demanding public recognition of their particular cultural identities above and beyond equal legal rights. Taylor sees the politics of recognition as the tension between a group's demands for particular recognition of their authentic cultural identity and the modern idea of universal respect and treatment.[331] Honneth disagrees with Taylor's distinction between particular recognition and universal respect and rejects the distinction between legal interest–based politics and identity politics,[332] claiming that the majority of identity-political demands for recognition can be grasped only as expansions of legal recognition.[333] However, his own approach is similar to Taylor's in seeing that struggles for recognition are political struggles of marginalized groups for recognition.

On why struggles for recognition manifest as political movements, Honneth begins with his premise that hurt feelings motivate one to a struggle for recognition because humiliation leaves one in a state of emotional tension that can be dispelled only by regaining the possibility of active conduct.[334] This makes sense—when we are suffering, we are motivated to act to alleviate that suffering. Interestingly, Honneth moves immediately to the assumption that active conduct takes the form of political resistance. The contingency for him lies not in whether one can be motivated to forms of praxis other than political resistance but in whether the injustice done to one will be disclosed enough cognitively to motivate political resistance:

> Empirically, whether the cognitive potential inherent in feeling hurt or ashamed becomes a moral-political conviction depends above all on how the affected subject's cultural-political environment is constructed: *only if the means of articulation of a social movement are available can the experience of [misrecognition]*

[331] Taylor, 27-28.
[332] Honneth, *The Struggle for Recognition*, 123-124.
[333] Honneth, *The Struggle for Recognition*, 161-170.
[334] Honneth, *The Struggle for Recognition*, 138.

> *become a source of motivation for acts of political resistance.*[335]

That Honneth does not by "means of articulation" mean the availability of conceptual resources but an existing social movement is shown by his similar expressions of the idea elsewhere:

> Whether the cognitive potential inherent in the feelings of social shame and offence evolves into a moral conviction depends largely on the form that the political and cultural environment of the subjects in question takes. If the experience of [misrecognition] is to *become a source of motivation for acts of political resistance, then there must exist a social movement* by means of which it can be articulated and thus manifest itself in positive form.[336]

These passages make clear Honneth's position that feelings of being unjustly treated can lead to political resistance only if there exists a social movement that is already articulating those feelings of injustice. It is worth noting here as confirmation that Renault, true to Honneth's theory, declares that a social movement "must be endowed with specific forms of organization and an internal public space ... in which the work is done of reflection about normative expectations and values that animate the movement."[337] The Honnethian-Renaultian conception is that an existing organized social movement is needed to supply means of articulation of hurt feelings caused by misrecognition.

Both passages occur in conclusions to chapters in which Honneth outlines his typology of misrecognition as the contrary of his three modes of recognition and describes the manner in which the different forms of misrecognition damage personal identity and integrity.[338] His stated goal in

---

[335] Honneth, *The Struggle for Recognition*, 138-139, emphasis mine.

[336] Honneth, *The Fragmented World of the Social*, 260, emphasis mine.

[337] Emmanuel Renault, *The Experience of Injustice: A Theory of Recognition*, Richard A. Lynch (tr.), (New York: Columbia University Press, 2019), 59.

[338] Honneth, *The Struggle for Recognition*, 131-139. Honneth, *The Fragmented World of the Social*, 247-260.

both chapters is to show that the negative emotions in response to experiences of personal misrecognition are the motivations for social resistance and are a moral driving force in the process of societal development.[339] The common thread for Honneth is his attempt to link internal hurt feelings due to violated expectations with the motivation to external acts in society. The problem I see is that Honneth argues from effect to cause—from the reality of political resistance movements to a theory of what motivates and interprets motivations in terms of political resistance movements. This connects private feelings with collective action but leaves out a large section of phenomena, including what other paths the motivation to struggle against injustice can take and the complex connections between those motivations and political resistance movements. Honneth never clearly defines political resistance or what makes a struggle for recognition political resistance aside from ascribing political actions to the institutional sphere of the political public sphere.[340] I define political resistance as attempts to change social institutions, practices, and recognition norms, usually in terms of laws, though also in terms of social attitudes. Not all struggles for recognition are political, as I will discuss more fully in chapter 2.4.5. In this chapter, I will critique some of Honneth's theoretical assumptions regarding political resistance and how they limit his account of struggles for recognition.

Honneth may want to reserve the term "struggles for recognition" for political movements, arguing that only struggles at that level are normatively relevant to social progress. There are two problems with such a view. It theoretically admits only the waves atop the turbulent ocean of moral crises without addressing the active conduct percolating under the political surface. Plus, we would then require a different term to describe all struggles that seek recognition outside the political arena. It is preferable to see political movements as a form of struggles for recognition that moves into the political sphere. Recognition and

---

[339] Honneth, *The Struggle for Recognition*, 132. Honneth, *The Fragmented World of the Social*, 248.

[340] Honneth, *Freedom's Right*, 127.

misrecognition behaviors cut across Honneth's spheres; therefore, struggles for recognition do also. Social conflict does not occur only at the macrosocial level of the cultural and political. Honneth identifies social experiences that generate struggles for recognition but fails to recognize that these experiences of moral injury motivate struggles in interpersonal and small-group levels of interaction as well. Honneth's account acknowledges only a limited number of individual acts as struggles for recognition.

One strength of focusing on collective political movements is that it avoids the theoretical pitfall of chasing episodic feelings of outrage by a few individuals.[341] To avoid this unproductive pitfall, we must limit our inquiries to those expressions of resistance to misrecognition that pass a threshold of significance. The question is what that threshold is. It would be incorrect to say the threshold is a certain level of political success. Honneth criticizes Fraser's view of social movements as being reductive for considering as social movements only those social conflicts that have attracted the attention of the political public sphere.[342] Putting aside the question of whether Fraser is guilty of Honneth's charge, Honneth faces a similar criticism in considering as struggles for recognition only collective political movements. Honneth seems to be reducing all social struggles to those violations of normative expectations that attract the attention of a significant number of subjects within a social group to become a collective movement. There is a difference between attention from the larger political public sphere and attention from a particular social group, but there is a qualitative similarity between Fraser and Honneth on this point. Honneth is guilty, as he accuses Fraser, of his theory relying on the contingent success of a certain level of social awareness—in Honneth's case, for moral injuries to be articulated collectively in a political movement.

For both Fraser and Honneth, restricting theoretical consideration to only those social movements that achieve a certain size is counterproductive for critical theory. A line is still being drawn whether it

---

[341] Zurn, *Axel Honneth,* Kindle location 1889.
[342] Honneth, 117-125.

is drawn at a society-wide level or a group level. So the question for Honneth is, at what level of collective sharing do moral experiences become a legitimate focus of inquiry for critical theory? Is there not a danger of saying to some that "your moral suffering is not being acted on by enough people for our theory to consider it significant?" It seems that moral experiences are of limited interest to Honneth until they have coalesced into a collective movement, yet to me it seems obvious that moral experiences must be experienced on an individual level before they can coalesce into a social movement. A rough analogy would be if we were to study those suffering physical disease but limit the scope of what we consider a disease to either those who have a foundation receiving government grants or those who have established mutual support groups. Honneth wants to expand the theoretical focus into feelings of misrecognition deeper than current social theory does. This is good, but the next necessary step is to drill down deeper than the group level and fully include the moral experiences of individuals and the way in which individuals are both influenced by and influence social movements.

I believe the crux of Honneth's political movements problem is an unnecessary collapsing of interpretive structures and collective political movements. It is correct to require an existing interpretive structure for individuals to develop normative expectations and understand when these expectations are disappointed, but an interpretive structure would not require an existing social movement of political resistance. What shows subjects that they have experienced an injustice rather than bad luck is a semantic structure that enables such an understanding. The language must exist that enables the interpretation that certain experiences are a result of injustice, and subjects must be exposed to that language for them to understand that they have been misrecognized and have experienced an injustice. This linking of the ability to articulate feelings with existing language is uncontroversial. Without a moral language with which to understand and articulate the feelings of being injured by another person, individuals will not be able to link their experience of hurt to the concept of an unjust action by another person. Individuals learn from their society a semantic structure of moral language by which they evaluate the moral content of their experience and by which they communicate to others their feelings and moral judgments. Honneth's position is that individual feelings of being hurt by misrecognition can exist but are fragmented and private until they are structured by communal experience, motivating collective resistance against injustice. Within Honneth's conception that recognition norms guide the socialization process, the reasoning here is sound. For Honneth, the principles of recognition provide a basis from which individuals can understand that they have experienced undeserved and unjustifiable misrecognition and that allows them to assert their grounds for greater recognition.[343] It is through the language of recognition norms that individuals learn what is appropriate behavior and what is inappropriate behavior. Therefore, misrecognition is knowable only through the experience of existing moral language from which they can interpret behavior directed at them as a moral wrong. Constructive responses to misrecognition also require a semantic structure of moral language that provides individuals with the capability to evaluate the institutions and customs of their culture with a view to whether they are morally justified and whether they can or should be changed.

Honneth needs to overcome the difficulty that an unjust recognition order probably will not provide a semantic structure that informs individuals that they are being treated unjustly. An unjust society would have negative recognition norms that socialize individuals into a semantic structure that justifies misrecognition and the harm it causes. The semantic culture in an unjust society will communicate to individuals that the various forms of misrecognition they receive are "normal" if not deserved. In an unjust society, the feelings of psychological injuries will not find an easy means of articulation, and individuals will remain unable to understand their hurt feelings as the result of injustice.

To deal with this problem, Honneth posits that a subculture that is attentive to those valuable traits and contributions of individuals that the mainstream culture overlooks can provide the needed semantic structure

[343] Fraser and Honneth, 144.

for individuals to articulate their negative feelings. Because he holds that individuals learn social norms through social experience, he also holds that individuals learn the semantics to express hurt feelings similarly. Learned from the dominant culture in a society are recognition norms that include pathological recognition and normative discrimination that lead to misrecognition. Within a subculture, though, one can learn from a community of those who have been similarly affected by misrecognition. Experiencing injustice can bond individuals in a subculture of shared feelings and interpretive ideas. These interpretive ideas of a shared social community

> generate a subcultural horizon of interpretation within which experiences of [misrecognition] that, previously, had been fragmented and had been coped with privately can then become the moral motives for a collective 'struggle for recognition.'[344]

Subjects can compare the shared experiences within their subculture with the experiences of those outside it and interpret their experiences as divergent from those of the broader culture, which can motivate a struggle for recognition to rectify the divergence. It is unclear whether Honneth is suggesting that shared experiences of recognitional disappointment necessarily lead to a shared social community. It is also unclear whether he is suggesting that a "subcultural horizon of interpretation" will necessarily lead to a collective struggle for recognition or is simply a prerequisite for one.

The problem with Honneth's position is his assumption that the only conduit for hurt feelings is a collective resistance movement that provides a framework for the individual to see him- or herself as a typical member of that group. Honneth's strong position stems from his contention that one needs recognition from one's community to engage successfully in any social action. As mentioned earlier, Honneth sees personal identity and relations-to-self as dependent on the individual's experiences of social recognition. Honneth sees individuals as developing their personal

---

[344] Honneth, *The Struggle for Recognition*, 164.

identities and their view of their place in society within the context of recognition norms that socialize individuals into an understanding of what recognition is. Therefore, he sees misrecognitions as understandable only in the context of social norms. From this, he holds that one can engage in resistance to misrecognition only if one can access a semantic structure in which to identify one's feelings of being treated unjustly. If subjects cannot receive the interpretive structure from the society at large, they must then receive it from an existing social group.

> Hurt feelings ... *become the motivational basis* for collective resistance only if subjects are able to articulate them within an intersubjective framework of interpretation *that they can show to be typical for an entire group*. In this sense, the emergence of social movements hinges on the existence of a shared semantics that enables personal experiences of disappointment to be interpreted as something affecting not just the individual himself or herself but also a circle of many other subjects.[345]

This line of argument, though seeming to place a semantic framework as a prerequisite to social movements, commits Honneth to seeing all struggles for recognition as being properly understood more as collective movements of group concerns than as expressions of individual concerns because a shared group semantic framework is required to enable personal interpretation.

Struggles for recognition, in Honneth's view, are struggles between social groups—a subculture struggling to expand the circle of recognition and/or change the recognition norms. Within Honneth's recognition order, because norms are established institutionally, they must be changed institutionally.

> It is by way of the morally motivated struggles of social groups—their collective attempt to establish, institutionally and culturally, expanded forms of

[345] Honneth, *The Struggle for Recognition*, 163-164, emphasis mine.

> reciprocal recognition—that the normatively directional change of societies proceeds.[346]

This is why Honneth sees collective social movements' struggles for recognition as a means of macrosocial historical progress in keeping with the tradition of critical theory and Honneth's own conception of a social recognition order. Honneth holds that struggles for recognition seeking to repair damaged relations-to-self must be collective struggles because individuals can convince themselves of their moral and social worth only within public acts of collective resistance. In Honneth's model, the solidarity of the collective resistance movement gives individuals the recognition that will restore the individual abilities that were misrecognized. Collective resistance can bring individuals out of the crippling effects of passively endured humiliation and help them toward new and positive relations-to-self.[347] Honneth's narrative of motivations for struggles for recognition is, therefore, a story of how an individual would be motivated to join an existing social movement of political resistance. An advantage of Honneth's model, from the perspective of social theory, is that if we place all motivations from misrecognition within collective movements, we avoid the risk of thinking that any feeling from any perceived slight could legitimately be a struggle for recognition. Honneth's move maintains a theoretical grounding of feelings of misrecognition in objective social normativity.

Much of the above criticism leveled at Honneth's conception of struggles for recognition can also be fairly leveled at Charles Taylor and Emmanuel Renault. Both Taylor and Renault consider injustice and struggles for recognition almost exclusively in terms of social movements manifesting predominantly in demands for political action. A detailed critique of their arguments is beyond my scope here, focused as it is on Honneth, but I do not find in either Taylor or Renault (who agrees with Honneth in many areas) any resources that correct the shortcomings in Honneth's account of struggles for recognition.

---

[346] Honneth, *The Struggle for Recognition*, 93.
[347] Honneth, *The Struggle for Recognition*, 164-165.

Honneth is vague about what political resistance is, and I will attempt to overcome this vagueness with an expanded view of struggles for recognition. In some areas, Honneth's claim that struggles for recognition must exist within collective political resistance is correct. For example, if I wish to get a law changed in my community, I will need the help of a social movement beyond my individual experience to manifest this change. Honneth's view can be defended by pointing out the connection between personal development and recognition and by pointing out that collective resistance movements provide solidarity that repair damaged relations-to-self and expand recognition. The problem with this view is that it assumes a consequence—collective resistance movements—before an antecedent—the motivation that instigates a collective resistance movement. A collective resistance movement must have one or more catalysts motivating enough to engender a social movement that goes against the prevailing social order. Honneth's model offers an explanation for why an individual could be motivated to join an existing collective resistance movement but not how such movements are formed. Honneth offers no substantial account for how a subculture moves from its experiences of misrecognition to a political movement. Within critical theory, we also need an understanding of how such movements begin.

Honneth consistently speaks of morally motivated struggles in terms of social groups. Honneth contends that social struggles are a structuring force in the moral development of society by way of the morally motivated struggles of social groups. This contention rests on Honneth's view that in modern society individuals' worth is recognized according to the status group to which they belong. The social standing of the status group is graded hierarchically in comparison with other status groups according to the predetermined worth of properties and the purported collective contribution of the status group.[348] From this view, Honneth sees struggles for recognition as the collective efforts of a status group to seek expanded recognition for their status group and contends that these social

[348] Honneth, *The Struggle for Recognition*, 123-125.

movements are the social actors of historical change. Collective attempts to establish expanded forms of reciprocal recognition generate the pressure by which normative change of societies proceeds.[349] Thus, Honneth's view is that a subject's self-esteem can be acquired only on the basis of collectively shared goals.[350] Therefore, struggles for recognition are group endeavors conducted with the solidarity and mutual esteem of collective social movements.

This leads to two questions—what would motivate a group to interpret the misrecognition they receive as morally wrong, and what would motivate an individual within a social group to follow its interpretations and actions? On the first question, a subcultural group whose members have been similarly affected by misrecognition could certainly develop the language to articulate the shared feelings and semantic ideas about the injustices they have experienced. But what indicates that every subculture will use that language to generate a social movement to expand the circle of recognition and/or change the recognition norms? Could they not instead use their interpretive language within the group to help each other cope with their feelings of being misrecognized without taking political action? On the second question, within a subculture, not every individual is engaged in an active struggle, even if it is correct to say the group as a whole is. We cannot oversimplify our view and assume that within a subculture that is, as a whole, engaging in a struggle for recognition that every member of that subculture is a contributing part of that collective resistance movement.

The issue I am raising is not whether struggles for recognition are exercised mostly in social groups (they are) but that Honneth has a chicken-and-egg problem similar to the one he has in the agency problem. Honneth believes that every collective act of social resistance can be traced to a set of moral experiences of being misrecognized, but he also claims that these feelings of being misrecognized can be expressed only in terms of political resistance movements. There is no question that the

---

349 Honneth, *The Struggle for Recognition*, 93.
350 Honneth, *The Struggle for Recognition*, 178.

grounds for claims for recognition are always socially shaped and that the content of individuals' expectations is always influenced by institutionally anchored principles of recognition.[351] A semantic structure must exist to enable individuals to articulate their experiences of hurt feelings from being misrecognized. Social movements can provide the symbolic resources by which individuals can see that their experiences of misrecognition are not idiosyncratic misfortune but experiences shared by others. It is from this realization, Honneth believes, that the potential emerges for collective action of resistance and revolt aimed at expanding social patterns of recognition.[352] The question is if struggles for recognition can come only from an existing collective social movement that is struggling for recognition, then how could any such social movement ever start? Honneth has included only one path, albeit the most common one, for an individual to undertake a struggle for recognition. We need to address the questions of how political resistance movements and struggles for recognition arise and why some injustices are not struggled against. Honneth's theoretical approach to struggles for recognition limits his ability to answer this question adequately.

Focusing on political movements simplifies our inquiries, but it risks discounting important phenomena. Honneth has a theoretical shortfall that can be seen in his response to Nancy Fraser in *Redistribution or Recognition?* Honneth states that he is focused on the question of which theoretical language is best suited to reconstruct and normatively justify present-day political demands within a framework of critical theory. Honneth wants to establish the theory of recognition as the "link between the social causes of widespread feelings of injustice and the normative objectives of emancipatory movements."[353] His theory of recognition, he argues, avoids the "abstractive fallacy" of theoretical attachment to publicly articulated goals (such as in Marxist theory) and instead focuses on the everyday dimension of moral feelings of moral injuries and

[351] Fraser and Honneth, 145.
[352] Honneth, *The Struggle for Recognition*, xix.
[353] Fraser and Honneth, 113

injustice, which, Honneth says, makes it clear that what is called "injustice" in theoretical language is that which is experienced by those affected as social injuries to their well-founded claims to recognition. He calls his approach a "phenomenology of social experiences of injustice."[354]

I read this argument by Honneth with interest but wonder where is the actual phenomenology for which he calls. If a theory of recognition is to take up the everyday dimension of moral feelings, then it needs to be a deeper phenomenology that takes seriously the implications of the important idea that the experience of moral injuries is what defines injustice and is the motivational source of social resistance. Honneth's move to locate the core of all experiences of injustice in the withdrawal of social recognition is a worthy theoretical approach, but to complete this move, we need to take in fully the experiences of individuals when they endure injustice, feel the effects, and respond to it. The shortfall in Honneth's approach is that his consideration of individuals' moral experiences of injustice focuses on the macrosocial side of struggles for recognition without sufficient attention to the individuals' experiences as the loci of struggles for recognition. Honneth is correct that his theoretical approach is one level beneath Fraser's argument,[355] but to fulfill the promise of his approach, we need to go further into the microsocial level.

Honneth is focused on how normative structures inform the feelings of subjects but with inadequate attention to how the feelings of those subjects inform the normative content of emancipatory movements. Honneth is not completely neglecting the moral experiences of individuals, but his consideration of them is limited by his theoretical reliance on a functionalist interpretation of social movements. Collective interpretation and action are required to transform experiences of injustice into a political resistance movement, but the feelings of an individual about the injustice he or she has suffered is what is being collectively interpreted and acted on. Zurn's example is the feminist struggle against the legal doctrine of coverture, whereby a woman lost her legal personality to her husband on

---

[354] Fraser and Honneth, 113-114.
[355] Fraser and Honneth, 134.

marriage, leaving her without recourse against economic and physical exploitation, including marital rape.[356] The determined feminist struggle and focused legal activism that overturned the marital exception to rape laws was a collective struggle based on the particular experiences of individual women, and these individual women and/or individuals close to them are who instigated the struggle for recognition of the rights of women in marriages.

We need a more robust picture of the roles of social movements and individuals in struggles for recognition. Returning to Honneth's account that both experiences of moral injuries and social movements are prerequisites for individuals to be motivated to struggle for recognition, Honneth's model is unclear about the division of labor between feelings of moral injuries and preexistent social movements. If both are prerequisites for manifesting struggles for recognition, then how do they intersect to bring them about? Is the preexistent social movement partly responsible for the feelings of misrecognition? Perhaps so, if the semantic structures of social movements are required to articulate the feelings into moral motives. Honneth touches on the difference between the private and the public without delving into the connections and mechanisms. It also seems that it is not the case, within Honneth's model, that there is a motivation to struggle separate from a motivation for acts of collective political resistance because Honneth sees all struggles as collective political actions. Could a lone individual not feel humiliated by misrecognition and feel motivated to correct the perceived injustice absent a preexistent social movement? It seems apparent that an individual can have feelings that are too diffuse to express effectively and also that an individual can have clear feelings but no constructive social outlet for them. Even if Honneth is arguing that his narrative addresses what motivates a particular individual to join a struggle for recognition, this still leaves unanswered the question of how social movements for recognition begin. Because Honneth considers social movements as the manifestation of struggles for

---

[356] Zurn, *Axel Honneth,* Kindle locations 1732-1740.

recognition, he needs an account of how these collective movements come to exist in the first place, which he does not provide.

If, as Honneth contends, a social movement hinges on a shared semantics of personal experiences, that does not mean that a set of shared semantics requires a social movement. This is because a subcultural semantics can exist without it being a part of a social movement of collective political resistance. Individuals, unable to receive recognition from their society's recognition order, can find a form of recognition and self-respect within the community of shared social status—but a subculture can exist as a source for reciprocal recognition without undertaking any struggle for increased recognition from the larger society. We therefore need to separate the notions of a semantic subculture and a social movement.

Honneth is correct about the need for a subcultural horizon of interpretation, but Honneth derives too much from the truth of the necessity of moral language. Honneth collapses interpretive structures, which he calls "subcultural horizons of interpretation,"[357] with social movements and presupposes both, leaving him without an account for their genesis. Certainly, a subculture and an interpretive structure are mutually supporting and influencing, but they are separate and do not spring up together fully formed. It makes more sense to separate social movements and motivations for struggles for recognition and say that a subcultural horizon of interpretation is involved in both. It is true that an individual can engage in resistance to injustice only if the moral language of norms, injustice, and resistance to injustice is available to the individual, but it is part of the larger picture—there is still the need for the individual to act. The interpretive language enables an individual to understand, but it itself does not create collective action. The intention of individuals to unite in common cause is facilitated by language, but it remains for the individuals, not the language, to decide whether to join in common cause. The environment alone cannot force a struggle for recognition in an individual much less in a social movement. We need a phenomenology of social

[357] Honneth, *The Struggle for Recognition*, 164.

experiences of injustice that can illuminate better how individuals respond to misrecognition. It is to that phenomenology that I now turn.

An interpretive structure within a subculture explains how individuals can communicate with each other about their moral experiences. But Honneth's claims are about more than whether one can communicate one's suffering to another. They are also about whether one will be motivated to struggle for recognition. Struggles for recognition are more than acts of communication; they are acts of resistance and defiance. For a struggle for recognition to exist, it must arise from, and be, a response to misrecognition that is a "yes, but." The "yes, but" acknowledges the misrecognition and the prevailing social situation and recognition norms behind it (the "yes") but calls for change (the "but"). It is at the same time an empirical acceptance and a normative rejection. The "yes, but" is different from two possible versions of "no" as a response to misrecognition. One "no" denies that what is happening is misrecognition, probably out of reluctance to admit one's situation or blame those responsible for the misrecognition. The other "no" acknowledges the misrecognition and resists without attempting to change the situation. This second type of "no" is still motivated by hurt feelings caused by moral injuries and is another reason why Honneth's account needs to be expanded. A "no" can be resistance to misrecognition, but it is not a struggle for recognition. I could call this a "yes, no"—a "yes" acknowledging the misrecognition and a "no" of not seeking to change the situation, though "yes, no" seems unnecessarily awkward. The "no" is defiance, perhaps manifesting as a stubborn refusal to cooperate, but is not actively seeking recognition or change. It can be valuable and meaningful for the individual who, in resistance, says "no" and may be a first step toward a struggle for recognition. However, defiance against misrecognition is not the same as demanding recognition and change; it is a type of action that has limited consequences. The "yes, but" is akin to Fanon's "yes" to life, love, and generosity accompanied by a "no" to scorn, degradation, exploitation, and the butchery of freedom.

Key to Fanon's "yes," and to my "yes, but," is that individuals are being actional rather than reactional.[358] The "yes, but" is an individual response that may or may not be assisted by an existing social movement. Either way, the "yes, but" is predicated on the capability of individuals to act in response to their situation. As McBride says, all individuals are social actors who are guided, but not determined, by social norms.[359] We interpret and apply social norms; they do not interpret or apply themselves. For example, an individual woman, McBride says, must work out for herself how to define and inhabit the roles in her life "and to cope with the inevitable mixture of recognition and misrecognition that must accompany her judgment."[360] We find ourselves in a world of other individuals and, what is more, in a plural world of differing and conflicting claims. McBride says that we rely on recognition norms to guide our actions but that we are free to assess each particular situation in which we find ourselves. Our plight is that we must decide for ourselves what actions to take. When others claim to have the authority to recognize us, McBride says, "We are always agents who must endorse the authority claims of others before their recognition is of any value to us."[361] Similarly, when we are misrecognized, our plight is to decide whether that misrecognition is valuable to us, or whether to reject it, and decide what action to take. If an interpretive structure is available, an individual can interpret that language as applying to her life. She can then say "yes, but" in response to the misrecognition she is receiving. If a social movement is available to her, she could decide to take action to join it. If no social movement is available to her, she could decide to take action on her own. An individual cannot create a struggle for recognition out of nothing, but the individual agent is an important and necessary ingredient in struggles for recognition.

---

[358] Fanon, 222.

[359] McBride, 157.

[360] McBride, 161. Also: "The social world does not address us with a transparent and coherent set of normative expectations. Consequently, we cannot hope to hand over the authority to resolve struggles for recognition to the 'community.'"

[361] McBride, 7.

To postulate that social movements are required for all struggles for recognition would be making the mistake of arguing from effect to cause. There is no unequivocal rationale to argue that a struggle for recognition requires a social movement, even if we say that it requires a set of shared semantics.

In the discussion of the dimensions of misrecognition, I talked about the importance of a dimension of action. A dimension of action also applies to struggles for recognition because the capability to act can actualize in varying degrees of action. Feelings that one has been misrecognized do not necessarily manifest as acts of misrecognition behavior. Similarly, feelings from moral injuries do not necessarily manifest as struggles for recognition. An interpretive language provides the tools that individuals can use to articulate their feelings of moral injury but does not mean that an individual *will* articulate his or her feelings. Even if individuals do find the language, they may not articulate their feelings to another individual. A teen bullied at school could know how to express that he is being misrecognized but decide to keep his thoughts to himself or express it in words that he does not share with anyone. When two or more individuals begin to communicate about their feelings of being misrecognized, they may find solidarity and common cause. They could, though, go no further than conversation without taking any action beyond commiseration. The move from conversation to action is a big one. It may be too psychologically or materially demanding to press one's legitimate recognition claims. We do not need to resort to Marxist ideology theory to explain reluctance to engage in political resistance. The risks are high, the odds of success are low, and individuals have other needs that require tending.

We also need to include nonrational reactions to misrecognition. The emphasis throughout critical theory has been on describing social pathology and the remedy to it in terms of rationality. As helpful as that is for a theoretical approach, in everyday life, rationality is not the source of all individual actions, and that includes responses to misrecognition. Emotional reactions of rebelliousness can also motivate individuals to engage in a struggle for recognition and could also spur the development of the semantics needed to interpret behavior. In such a case, emotional actions could facilitate rational interpretation as members of the subculture seek to interpret the emotional reactions of others. Social movements can be sparked by individuals who act having reached their breaking point of tolerance for misrecognition, and that emotion-fueled action encourages others to, either emotionally or rationally, join in actions of resistance. The 1969 Stonewall rebellion in Greenwich Village, New York City, began as a spontaneous emotional reaction against police oppression. The initial riot sparked street protests the next night and led to an organized social movement in Greenwich Village that struggled for recognition of gays and lesbians. The nonrational riot led to a rational rebellion and struggle for recognition. The movement for gay rights spread nationwide, then worldwide. The initial emotional reaction to misrecognition is widely acknowledged as the beginning of the gay liberation movement and is commemorated by a national monument.[362]

These types of emotional responses are different from the hurt feelings that Honneth sees as motivations for struggles for recognition. Despite the emotional content, Honneth considers an individual's hurt feelings as motivational grounds only if they are *rationally* articulated in terms of "universal ideas and appeals in which individual actors see their particular experiences of misrecognition eliminated in a positive manner."[363] By contrast, the type of emotional reaction to which I am referring is not rationally articulated and has no basis in rational reflection. A lack of rational content or rational justification does not mean that an act cannot become motivation for others to struggle for recognition. Another point worth making is that, in Honneth's account, negative emotional reactions arise only when rational normative expectations are disappointed. In 1969,

---

[362] David Nakamura and Juliet Eilperon, "With Stonewall, Obama designates first national monument to gay rights movement" *The Washington Post*, June 24, 2016. Accessed September 17, 2016, https://www.washingtonpost.com/news/post-politics/wp/2016/06/24/with-stonewall-obama-designates-first-national-momument-to-gay-rights-movement/?utm_term=.c253021955bb.

[363] Honneth, *The Struggle for Recognition*, 163.

society gave homosexuals no rational normative expectations that they would receive recognition. So what rational normative expectations of theirs were disappointed? Certainly, one could respond that any denigrated and excluded person can rationally link the general idea that all human beings deserve recognition with the reality that they are excluded from that recognition. Again, though, that does not mean an individual would make that rational connection, especially given the prevailing normative discrimination that socializes individuals into a seemingly rational recognition order.

From the foregoing, it makes sense to consider a narrative of struggles for recognition that places social movements within a much broader social process. Widespread and persistent misrecognition generates marginalized subcultures. The relative insularity of these subcultures generates an interpretive structure within society's larger set of established norms that supplies the language with which members of the subculture can speak of their experiences as a marginalized subculture. The interpretive language *could* speak of the marginalization of the subculture as a moral wrong. If so, then individuals within the subculture *could* draw on the resources of the interpretive structure as a motivation to struggle against the moral wrongs of their marginalization. If enough individuals come to be similarly motivated, they *could* coalesce as a social movement resisting injustice. Then that existing social movement *could* inspire other marginalized individuals to join the movement to struggle for recognition. The multiple "coulds" of this formulation are not hand waving but reflect the real-life variations in marginalized subcultures that must be accounted for within critical theory. How much and in what ways a subculture is in dialogue with the mainstream culture is different for each subculture. Within what dialogue there is, it would be incorrect to assume that any particular subculture is struggling for increased recognition from the general society.

Honneth misreads the role of individuals in struggles for recognition because he believes that hurt feelings are not necessarily morally valuable unless they are rationally articulated according to social norms. Honneth distinguishes individuals articulating their experiences in the democratic public sphere from individuals "living them out in a counterculture of violence."[364]

> The sense of no longer being included within the network of social recognition is in itself an extremely ambivalent source of motivation for social protest and resistance. It lacks any normative indication or direction that would stipulate in what ways one would struggle against the experience of [misrecognition] and humiliation.[365]

There is a problem with structuring the normative value of emotional response in this way. A subculture that is not included within the network of social recognition is almost certainly also excluded from the socially acceptable modes of rational and emotional expression. Structures of dominance dictate the normative direction allowable to marginalized groups. This includes how they should respond to their social treatment and status. The ways a marginalized group would be permitted to struggle against their experiences of misrecognition and humiliation would be restricted, including in political avenues. In the U.S. South during segregation, there was little to no legal or political path allowed for blacks to struggle within the legal or political system against misrecognition and humiliation. Even when avenues of redress were not closed by the letter of the law, such as they were for black South Africans under apartheid, prevailing norms of discrimination prevent many marginalized groups from having fair access to the legal and political systems. For Honneth to say that the victimized, misrecognized, and ostracized should have the "individual strength to articulate their experiences in the democratic public sphere, rather than living them out in a counterculture of violence"[366] misses the reality that being victimized, misrecognized, and ostracized usually also means being blocked from articulating one's experiences in the democratic public sphere.

---

364 Honneth, *Disrespect*, 77-78.
365 Honneth, *Disrespect*, 77.
366 Honneth, *Disrespect*, 77.

McNay justifiably accuses Honneth of neglecting power structures and power inequalities that keep individuals from undertaking struggles for recognition.[367] To improve Honneth's theory, we must include the reality that power structures use recognition norms to suppress individuals and that individuals must work outside those recognition norms in order to struggle against misrecognition. This could mean gauging a spectrum of behavior from acting outside proper etiquette to the extreme of actual violence. It is true that well-behaved women seldom make history, and women have had to resort to a variety of "unacceptable" behaviors in their struggles for recognition. The American civil rights movement was an expression of individuals who were not being included within the network of social recognition and, thus, who were forced to conduct actions that were outside the behaviors stipulated as acceptable for them. Commendably, they largely did not resort to violence, but must we condemn the Palestinian intifada and other struggles for justice because they did? Perhaps we must, but that is a question that needs to be considered separately for each particular conflict.

The possibilities for response to misrecognition are wider than social movements. Honneth is correct that it is "only by regaining the possibility of active conduct that individuals can dispel the state of emotional tension into which they are forced as a result of humiliation."[368] However, active conduct toward this end does not have to be political or even social. A woman who has been humiliated by sexual or physical abuse has a number of avenues to take action to dispel her moral crisis aside from partaking in a political movement to change the legal system. At the most personal level, women survivors of abuse can seek personal recognition for their moral injuries from friends and family or a counselor. Only if the woman sought changes in the broader culture would she require a social movement. At a small-group level, Zurn mentions "Take Back the Night" or "Reclaim the Night" marches that are not waged through the legal system but are directed at cultural attitudes that enable the minimization of

---

[367] McNay, *Against Recognition*, 132cf.
[368] Honneth, *The Struggle for Recognition,* 138.

abuse of women[369] and are also designed to raise awareness about sexual assault and rape prevention. Some U.S. university campuses have created a safe zone or rape-free zone.[370] Such zones do not, in themselves, attempt to change the laws, but they do provide solidarity for women who have been, or fear being, assaulted and abused. Despite their group coordination, such social efforts would fall short of the definition of a political resistance movement, yet these active efforts have the potential to empower women and give them a sense of solidarity and self-confidence.

These types of active conduct on the personal and small-group levels are struggles for recognition, and such personal acts of struggling for recognition are what lead to social and political struggles for recognition. Social movements do not spring up out of nothing. They arise from small groups of individuals discussing their experiences and what they hope and intend to do in response. These small groups arise when individuals, maybe even just one, start communicating their moral feelings and normative expectations. The semantic structure of moral language that is required to motivate a struggle for recognition is enacted only when individuals communicate; therefore, the genealogy of all social movements is individuals communicating. Social movements and political resistance movements bubble up from these communicative interactions among individuals.

We need to consider the possibility that moral injuries can be motivating without being politically motivating—meaning attempting to change legislation or governments. It is not a given that individuals who are motivated to struggle for recognition will choose to act to affect the political institutions in their society. What goes into their decisions is difficult for theory to discern without delving into an individual's personal life. McNay observes that "it is not possible to understand what makes an action political or not, or indeed what disinclines individuals to behave in a political manner in the first place, without engaging with their own

[369] Zurn, *Axel Honneth,* Kindle locations 1745-1746.

[370] See for example, Brooke Eidenmiller, "'24-Hour Rape-Free Zone' set for October 7, 8 at UNC-CH," accessed September 21, 2016, http://www.unc.edu/news/archives/sep99/rapefree092899.htm.

understandings and interpretations of self and world."[371] We can begin to engage with how individuals understand and interpret themselves and their world through a phenomenology informed by the multidimensional view of misrecognition and our emerging rethinking of struggles for recognition. Only by letting the individual inform us about him- or herself can we hope to begin to understand his or her choices. How an individual views the political and his or her relation to it factors into that individual's willingness to take on the political. Individuals may feel that attempting to change their recognition relations in the political sphere is too difficult or dangerous. They may instead opt to change their recognition relations with other groups on a more interpersonal level outside of political means. In such a case, the laws of the society do not change, and the subculture does not see expanded legal recognition, but individuals may win increased personal recognition from others within their social circles. Political recognition is not the only type of recognition that people seek.

Looking at some other examples, we can see that the importance of social movements is slightly different from what Honneth portrays. Social groups are not required to struggle for recognition, but depending on the social level of the misrecognition, they can facilitate individuals' responses to misrecognition, especially in the ability to communicate. If a friend misrecognizes me, I do not need a social movement to articulate to my friend my experience of being misrecognized. My struggle for recognition is part of an interpersonal relationship between my friend and me, and I can hope to communicate directly with my friend about my normative expectations. Beyond personal relationships, obstacles to communicating my normative expectations usually amount to a matter of access to those who can hear and act on my complaint. My workplace may not have a procedure for dealing with employee grievances, and my supervisors may be inaccessible. I may need the help of a labor union to be heard and recognized at work. Fundamentally, in a struggle for recognition, what is sought are visibility and the understanding from others that is needed to have our recognition claims answered. Existing social movements

---

[371] McNay, *The Misguided Search for the Political*, 98.

facilitate struggles for recognition in situations in which direct personal communication is not possible, such as changing a nation's laws. If I want to change a law, my elected officials may not be able or willing to hear me. I may need the help of an organized advocacy group whose numbers can attract attention. The dynamic involved is the difference between horizontal recognition—individuals relating to another individual or a small group—and vertical recognition—the individual relating to cultural and legal institutions. An individual cannot easily take on "the system" on her own, though she could, on her own, make recognition claims on another individual or a small group.

Social movements are needed to overcome obstacles to being heard in one's struggles for recognition but are not needed for the struggle itself. The lone protestor standing outside the council office or the White House is struggling for recognition of his or her cause, even if no one notices or cares. It is when those who struggle are noticed and get other people to care that social movements emerge. Honneth ties struggles for recognition to political movements, but it is better to see struggles for recognition as manifesting along a continuum. Individuals enter the political arena out of necessity, and perhaps only out of necessity. Even when they do enter the political arena, struggles for political recognition of ethnic, religious, and cultural diversity are ultimately struggles for personal security and well-being within a more inclusive culture. All struggles over personal identity and cultural recognition operate along a continuum of social scale. It is in this sense that Honneth's social spheres make some sense, but their usefulness is limited because the boundaries are diffuse and fluid and relative to individual circumstances. I propose that it is better to think of struggles in terms of social avenues through which individuals act—the personal, small groups, or social movements, which do not map directly to the tripartite structure of family, civil society, and state.

Honneth's contention that struggles for recognition manifest as political resistance movements does not address the question of whether an individual is motivated actually to join such a movement. Honneth has no significant account of how political resistance movements begin, and he does not provide a clear account of why an individual would join a social movement. I contend that we must not lose sight of the reality that individuals are the social forces that initiate, build, and continue struggles for recognition. I agree with Zurn who warns that the view that social change is simply a case of ideals being worked out in practice hides the actual social struggles and serious conflicts involved in realizing such ideals of expanded recognition.[372] I stress that these struggles and conflicts are undertaken by individuals and point to the examples previously given.

All told, the resistance to misrecognition is more complex than Honneth's mapping them exclusively to collective social movements involved in political resistance. Joining a collective movement is only one way to resist injustice, and, even if an individual has joined a group, it is the individual who has engaged in that course of action to articulate his or her personal struggle for recognition. That preexistent social movements motivate individuals who have experienced misrecognition and facilitate individuals in struggling for recognition is certainly true, but the question of what generates social movements for recognition remains. One answer would be that social movements are generated by historical processes and are a product of progress. Another is that they are generated by individuals who decide to act on their feelings of being misrecognized and engage in struggles for recognition. Both are possible, and probably both contribute to the generation of each particular social movement for recognition.

2.4 - Expanding the Story of Struggles for Recognition

Building on the discussion of misrecognition and struggles for recognition, I now seek to craft a narrative of struggles for recognition that solves problems within Honneth's account. In this chapter, I will blend the strengths of Honneth's account of recognition with the multidimensional account of misrecognition and the discussion on the problems in Honneth's account of struggles for recognition to craft a more robust view of what is involved in recognition, misrecognition, and the struggles to correct injustices. Struggles for recognition are both how individuals

[372] Zurn, *Axel Honneth,* Kindle locations 1794-1796.

become themselves and how societies change, both of which Honneth's theory acknowledges. What I see as a central problem in Honneth's theory is that although his guiding intuition is that intersubjective recognition is the normative structure of human personal development and ethical life, Honneth's theory fails to include the full importance of individual contributions to intersubjective recognition. It is true, from one perspective, that social institutions are present and individuals are thrown (in a Heideggerian sense) into that social structure, but we would be negligent not to admit that as individuals interact they affect that social structure. That individuals have an effect on society and, thus, have the potential to change social structures and norms is crucial to the concept of struggles for recognition. It is true that individuals become who they are only through interacting with others, and it is also true that society becomes what it is only through individuals interacting with each other. Perhaps no one would dispute that second point, but I argue that more emphasis needs to be placed on it. An expanded view of struggles for recognition is a step in that direction.

The agency and political movements problems show the need to expand the concept of struggles for recognition. Honneth's formula of a *struggle* for recognition—the response to feelings of being misrecognized manifesting through a social movement seeking political change—is only part of the story. Individuals seek transformation of relations dominated by misrecognition in a variety of ways. Not all of these ways can be classified as political and/or collective struggles for recognition. Honneth could argue that struggles for recognition, because they are responses to social misrecognition, require a social movement. If this were true, it would be true only for macrosocial institutional misrecognitions—for example, apartheid or women being denied equal legal rights—situations in which systematic, mostly legal, change would be required. To be true to the phenomena of social life, we must acknowledge that some social struggles occur outside of social movements and for reasons other than effecting political change. It is a better expression of Honneth's basic concept of struggles for recognition to expand the model of these struggles to include the wider variety of individuals' efforts to restore healthy recognition relations. By tying struggles for recognition to collective political movements, Honneth creates a lacuna that hides other forms and aspects of struggles for recognition—most specifically, the very personal aspects that we can find in struggles for recognition. By decentralizing struggles for recognition from collective political movements and adding the concept of individual agency, we can craft a more robust picture of struggles for recognition.

To expand a view of struggles for recognition that takes into account the above issues, I begin by identifying two types of struggles for recognition—affirmational and transformational. I argue that the presence of affirmational struggles in individuals' lives is a resource that helps bridge the gap in Honneth's theory between hurt feelings from being misrecognized to undertaking a transformational struggle for recognition. I then turn to how struggles for recognition are shaped by social power relations and the vying for the authority to claim recognition. These insights help us explain the ways that struggles for recognition extend beyond political resistance into personal relations that either connect or divide individuals. Finally, I address a further dilemma in Honneth's account of struggles for recognition: how it is that individuals who have not suffered misrecognition would join other individuals' struggles for recognition.

2.4.1 - Affirmational and Transformational Struggles

The discussion so far about struggles for recognition indicates that there is more to the story of struggles for recognition than is present in Honneth's account. Honneth predominantly uses the term "struggles for recognition" to refer to collective political resistance, but he also mentions Hegel's notion of an ongoing struggle for recognition. In Honneth's version of Hegel, an individual's ethical progress toward self-realization unfolds within the Hegelian tripartite structure. The three Hegelian stages impose on individuals increasingly demanding patterns of mutual recognition as they gain positive confirmation of their identity. Hegel's public spheres structure the intersubjective struggle for recognition, and an individual must progress through each of the three stages in turn. When Honneth uses "struggle" to describe the individual's ethical progress through the Hegelian-defined three stages of individual development, he is referring to an intersubjective struggle to gain positive relations-to-self in that dimension of one's identity. Honneth sees Hegel as establishing

> that ethical progress unfolds in a series of three levels of increasingly demanding patterns of recognition, and that an intersubjective struggle mediates between each of these levels, a struggle that individuals conduct for the purpose of having their identity claim confirmed.[373]

This kind of struggle for recognition drives communalization among individuals by making them aware of their subjective normative claims. The struggle for recognition within the three spheres is a mechanism of social integration that rationally informs individuals not only about their differences but also about their similarities; it both individuates and communalizes individuals, allowing them to form rational conceptions of themselves as individuated subjects.[374] Not surprisingly, this ongoing process of confirming oneself Honneth describes as "an agonistic relationship that requires a permanent 'struggle' for recognition."[375]

We need to ask what distinguishes a *struggle* for recognition from the constant *seeking* of recognition. We seek recognition always, even from infancy, Honneth says, and yet what Honneth means by a "struggle for recognition" is clearly something different from the everyday need for recognition. The everyday seeking of recognition needs to be parsed out and its relation to what Honneth means by struggles for recognition explored. The permanent ongoing struggle to confirm identity claims I will term "affirmational struggles." They are the ongoing efforts of individuals to seek recognition that constructs and affirms their personal identities and their place in society. Whether or not we adopt the concept of self-constitution mentioned earlier, affirmational struggle is the intersubjective

---

[373] Honneth, *Disrespect*, 132-133.
[374] Honneth, *The Struggle for Recognition*, 28-29.
[375] Honneth, "Grounding Recognition," 502.

social process through which individual practical identity is constructed. The second type of struggle I will term "transformational struggles." They are responses to circumstances or instances of misrecognition that seek to rectify perceived injustices and transform recognition relations.

Both types of struggle involve the intersubjective quest for recognition, but they differ in an important way. The affirmational struggle is a need prior to any particular social interaction and is the constant general condition of being a social individual. A transformational struggle is a specific response to a specific situation—a moral struggle to correct a perceived injustice or heal a moral injury—and it answers needs that arise subsequent to a particular social interaction. We can also view the distinction in these terms: Transformational struggles are secondary attempts to repair interruptions and interferences with the ongoing process of primary affirmation of social relations and belonging. In other words, there is cause for a transformational struggle only when something goes wrong, whereas the affirmational struggle remains necessary even if all is well. We could summarize that an affirmational struggle is necessary to and inseparable from social life, and a transformational struggle is a contingent response subsequent to social life going wrong. This distinction remains even if we were to argue that things always go wrong in recognition relations.

This distinction between affirmational and transformational struggles for recognition clarifies without contradicting Honneth's theory and helps us understand the motivations for different struggles for recognition. The differentiation is between a struggle for affirmation and a struggle for justice, with the former being in service of the latter. Much of Honneth's discussion of struggles for recognition can be placed under the label of transformational struggles that seek to change social conditions. Other accounts of struggles for recognition, such as those outlined by Taylor and Renault, also describe transformational struggles. The distinction also helps us understand the agency and political movements problems mentioned earlier by seeing them in terms of the relationship between transformational struggles and affirmational struggles.

Affirmational struggles can be seen as the process through which individuals affirm their practical identities, which coincides with Korsgaard's concept of self-constitution. We do not come into the world with a constituted identity, but through seeking and receiving affirmation we continually constitute our social practical identity, and this makes us who we are. Absent from Korsgaard's account is a full appreciation of the difficulties involved in maintaining a practical identity. Korsgaard does admit that it is our plight that we are *compelled* to respond to our world.[376] But beyond our existential plight is our continual practical plight that we must continually act in accordance with our normative responsibilities associated with our social roles. Especially in today's world, protecting and enhancing our social relations are imperatives; therefore, seeking recognition from others is imperative. Affirmational struggles are a struggle because of the nature of recognition relations. We are compelled not just to respond to the world but to interact with others and maintain healthy and beneficial relations with them. The normative structure of society continually places demands on us, which places our practical identity at risk. These demands increase the more we interact with others, also increasing the risk to our social standing and autonomy.

Understanding the importance of affirmational struggles provides an answer to the objection that recognition assumes human relations are essentially warlike, thereby making it problematic to imagine that struggles for recognition can lead to peaceful recognition relations.[377] Affirmational struggles are not necessarily struggles against others, and they do not reflect a war of all against all. Mostly, affirmational struggles are an attempt to fit in, to belong, and to be accepted, so they are the opposite of oppositional struggles. Certainly, there is competition among individuals for honors and prizes, but competitions for esteem are different from the need to affirm one's sense of identity and sense of belonging. Many of us do want to be exceptional, to be a winner and acknowledged as

---

[376] Korsgaard, Kindle locations 371-372.
[377] Kelly Oliver makes this objection in *Witnessing: Beyond Recognition*, 4.

such, but our sense of identity probably does not depend on being seen as exceptional.

The idea of affirmational struggles can be further unpacked by using McBride's "interactionist" approach to recognition in contrast to what he calls Honneth's "developmental" approach. McBride's approach "focuses on the way recognition-sensitivity is a basic aspect of social interaction, and of the daily *exercise* of individual agency, rather than of the way we come to achieve this competence."[378] McBride uses the term "recognition-sensitivity" to describe a basic aspect of all individuals in the social world. McBride observes that the role Honneth ascribes to recognition in the acquisition of autonomy and social capacities implies that the work of recognition is over when relevant capabilities have been acquired. McBride says that "the developmental approach appears to treat recognition as a sort of scaffolding necessary to the construction of personhood, but which then becomes redundant once personhood has been achieved."[379] McBride likens Honneth's developmental approach to the view of an individual as an empty vessel that must be filled by the various modes of recognition in order for the individual to function in the social world. Honneth does mention that continued recognition is needed not just to develop relations-to-self but also to rebuild healthy relations-to-self damaged by misrecognition and to regain the confidence to function in the world. McBride acknowledges this, but asks what purpose recognition continues to serve if we currently have basic functioning capabilities. The developmental approach seems to leave no reason for individuals to continue to want to seek recognition but they clearly do continue to seek it. I think McBride's comments show that Honneth's account is too inclined toward the view of the individual as a passive empty vessel that recognition makes autonomous and misrecognition renders nonautonomous. Such a view does not sufficiently describe how recognition works in everyday lives as an active ongoing interactive process.

---

[378] McBride, 138, emphasis his.
[379] McBride, 138.

McBride's interactionist approach sees recognition as a guide for learning how to act in ethical space and as social feedback that allows us to correct our actions.[380] Our recognition-sensitivity, McBride says, helps us get our bearings in the normatively constituted world that we inhabit. As we interact with others in our everyday lives, we adapt and revise our understandings and expectations of appropriate behaviors, others, and ourselves. McBride says that individuals seek recognition because recognition is a resource in our everyday interactions with others. Thus, we desire recognition not just to feel good about ourselves but to function fruitfully in society. Our interactions with others form a continuous feedback loop in which the more we receive recognition the better we are able to function in the social world, which earns us more recognition, which hones our social functioning, and so on. We can convert respect and esteem into power and wealth, which explains why individuals continue to pursue recognition interactively after they have achieved autonomy. We can see the truth of McBride's description in that within recognition of one's capabilities are different kinds of recognition. For example, recognizing one's capability to do tasks does not necessarily include the recognition that one is capable of doing them unassisted. Thus, an individual may develop the self-confidence to do a certain activity but only with guidance or only in certain safe social situations. An individual's social life is a web of recognition relations, with shifting connections and dispositions. We learn different roles and identities for different circumstances—child, sibling, spouse, employee, friend, and so on—and we learn how to express ourselves through our roles. As much as we assert ourselves and our sense of our identities, however, we remain dependent on the recognition of others to assess our performance and affirm us in our roles; and, ultimately, our community is the arbiter of whether we are playing our roles properly. Thus, every life is a constellation of affirmational struggles in continual interaction with others.

Affirmational struggles are constant and formative. To be a social individual means that recognition claims are inescapable because one

---

[380] McBride, 140.

cannot function in a culture without receiving recognition from others as a member of that culture. This means that being involved with affirmational struggles for recognition is an "ineliminable feature for social life and the exercise of our autonomy."[381] There are a bewildering and almost frightening number of norms by which one will or will not be recognized as behaving properly, from not committing violence to how one should blow one's nose in public. If we run afoul of cultural conventions, we pay a price in negative judgments from others, which could affect our interactions with them. It is our plight that we are compelled, not only to respond to the world, but to seek its response to us. Complicating our plight, our culture does not always give us a clear and coherent set of normative expectations and feedback. Part of our affirmational struggles is to understand and interpret what is expected of us. We are forced to learn to become adjudicators of the norms and the various interpretations of how to apply them and affirm ourselves through them.

In the process of socialization, individuals become accustomed to the seeking of recognition as a constant in their lives. Learning recognition norms, learning how to interpret normative claims, and developing a practical identity are continual processes that take place in social life. In the socialization process, we all learn our culture's recognition norms and what behaviors on our part bring us recognition. Experiences of affirmational struggles for recognition structure individuals' normative expectations and how they see and interpret their world. As an individual experiences instances of recognition and misrecognition, that individual constitutes his or her worldview and sense of identity. When we do not receive the affirmation we need and believe we are entitled to, we may seek other individuals from whom and communities from which we can receive it. Achieving recognition is a social skill that is necessary to navigate social life and must be learned through the socialization process. As social beings, individuals cannot help but develop at least some skill in affirmational struggles; to fail to gain that skill is to fail at life.

---

[381] McBride, 159.

2.4.2 - Affirmational Struggles as Foundation for Transformational struggles

We saw earlier that experiencing moral injuries from misrecognition is insufficient motivation for an individual to undertake a struggle for recognition. The presence of a subcultural interpretive structure and language is also insufficient to move an individual to a transformational struggle. The individual's movement to a struggle for recognition remains insufficiently explained, and I think that reframing the issue by including the presence of affirmational struggles in an individual's everyday life will help answer it. Honneth's framing is too optimistic, which ironically creates difficulties for his theory. He never explicitly says subjects are in a condition of positive relations-to-self from receiving recognition prior to experiencing moral injuries, but that is implied from his idea of a subject moving through the spheres of recognition, beginning with the love recognition one receives from one's mother. We can recall Honneth's idea that after recognition is learned within the family sphere, other relations of recognition are "merely filled out at later stages through the acquisition of conceptions about the reciprocal ascription of abilities and rights."[382] The suggestion throughout Honneth's work is that misrecognition happens to a previously recognized subject whose society has, through recognition, given it an understanding of normative expectations and can for these reasons understand it is being misrecognized. The social reality is that individuals do not go from experiencing a positive state of relations-to-self, then experience a negative state of misrecognition, only to be ready to respond with a positive struggle for recognition. Instead, individuals constantly need recognition; constantly are engaged in seeking it; and, in real ways, constantly lack recognition.

I view the individual's movement to a struggle of political resistance as a movement from one mode, a continual affirmational struggle, to another mode, a contingent transformational struggle. There is still a gap between affirmational and transformational struggles, but that gap is not as wide as is the one in Honneth's account. Honneth relies on individuals

[382] Honneth, "Rejoinder," 392.

being convinced by an existing political resistance movement, but he cannot explain how this movement came into existence, nor does he adequately explain how the presence of a movement provides an internal resource for the individual to move toward engaging in a transformational struggle for recognition. We can rely instead on individuals having the internal resources that they have developed through their past affirmational struggles for recognition. The human need for affirmation of being socially adept and accepted is ever present. Affirmational struggles are constant, but transformational struggles are not, even if they seem to be always around the corner. The former are necessary, even when recognition relations are healthy, but the latter are contingent and require a "yes, but" decision and action.

Recognition and misrecognition are personal rather than abstract instances for us. As Honneth is correct to point out, the experience of misrecognition is an emotional injury more than an intellectual issue. What we can add to that picture is that misrecognition also interrupts the everyday affirmational struggle. The state of emotional tension that Honneth identifies results not only from a rational comparison of experience to normative expectations but also from a disruption of relations-to-self and practical projects. Honneth's insight that emotional experiences are at the core of struggles for recognition is enhanced by including the frustration of interruption in our daily lives. Whether or not we have rational reasons, we have a natural expectation that events in our lives will unfold as we desire. When that desired for flow of events is interrupted, we take action to rectify the situation, often emotionally. Individuals perceive moral injury more in terms of a hindrance of their involvements than as a violation of society's norms. I concede there is a legitimate concern that we not lump the normative concerns of recognition and justice with the mundane concerns of everyday activities—being misrecognized is not equivalent to one's appliance malfunctioning; however, the human responses to these very different events are not entirely dissimilar. The point is that human responses to misrecognition are usually not high-minded and normatively guided rational political struggles but instead are a more personal struggle limited to restoring a personal sense of well-being or basic functioning, such as food riots.

Because affirmational struggles are constant in our lives, we are familiar with recognition being an issue for us even if we do not think of it in rational, theoretic terms. Affirmational struggles for recognition are an important part of intersubjective relations and the fabric of human society, and we cannot conceive of social life without them. As social beings, we are recognition-sensitive beings and because affirmational struggles are constants in our lives, we are also sensitive to transformational struggles for recognition. Individuals are already exercising their agency to varying degrees of action in their everyday affirmational struggles, and they can draw on these experiences to overcome moral injuries, a possibility not accounted for in Honneth's theory.

That we are all familiar with affirmational struggles still does not answer why one individual engages in a transformational struggle while another does not. This is where we return to the "yes, but" described earlier, and we can see that it is the prelude to a transformational struggle for recognition. Affirmational struggles are a struggle for recognition from others, ideally based on successful engagement with recognition norms. In this way, affirmational struggles are acts in accordance with those with whom we interact. As responses to misrecognition, transformational struggles are acts in conflict with those with whom we interact. The move from affirmational struggles to transformational struggles takes place in response to a misrecognition that violates our normative expectations, harms our identity claims, and interrupts the expected flow of our lives. The "yes, but" is a rejection of acquiescence to one's situation along with an active attempt to change it. That individuals desire recognition and are sensitive to misrecognition is not enough for them to struggle for recognition when it is denied them. An individual must draw on his or her agency and make a decision to undertake a struggle for recognition.

What is the "yes, but" act founded on? I described earlier how the concepts of self-constitution and habitus give us a conceptual basis for how an individual could come to undertake a struggle for recognition. An individual acts out of individual agency and draws on an interpretive structure, but, also, the individual draws on the practice that comes from participating in affirmational struggles. By learning how to participate in affirmational struggles, an individual develops skills that are a reservoir from which to draw on for transformational struggles. We continuously try to be seen by others in the right way in terms of recognition. From this familiarity, we can move to transformational struggles that are also about being seen in the right way but in response to misrecognition. Affirmative struggles are ways to avoid misrecognition; transformational struggles are ways to correct misrecognition. Affirmational struggles are preemptive, and because we are already in this mind-set of continually avoiding misrecognition, we can switch our efforts into how we can correct misrecognition when it occurs. We can directly connect our transformational struggles with our ongoing affirmational attempts to stave off misrecognition, and we are capable of using our agency to move from one struggle to the other. Honneth has no such account.

The constant of recognition in our lives gives us internal resources to draw on when faced with misrecognition. These resources enable us to relate better to transformational struggles, understand the recognitional issues involved, and move toward action. Our familiarity with affirmational recognition struggles gives us intersubjective resources to draw on so that we can respond to injustice with something other than brute force. Acknowledging this partially fills the gap in Honneth's account. An acknowledgment of individual agency is still needed to explain the move from suffering misrecognition to struggling for recognition, but now that move is not as far as it is in Honneth's account. We saw earlier from McBride the idea of virtual recognition—the idea that one can imagine virtual recognition. Because we can imagine the cessation of experiencing misrecognition, it may motivate us to take action toward that end and consider what steps we can take to minimize misrecognition of ourselves and rectify the damage done to us by it.

The role of affirmational struggles in transformational struggles also helps us to think about where to place the emancipatory interest in struggles for recognition. Honneth argued that critical theory must acknowledge that the emancipatory process must manifest itself in the moral experiences[383] of the individuals involved and that the impairment of an individual's freedom must be pretheoretical[384]; individuals must "experience an impairment of what we can call their moral experiences, i.e., their 'moral point of view,' not as a restriction of intuitively mastered rules of language, but as a violation of identity claims acquired in socialization."[385] This is true because we do not live according to theory, nor do we live primarily reflectively. Individuals also do not act in response to theory; they act in response to their moral experiences, which theory only helps to interpret. We can better understand this through affirmational and transformational struggles. A weakness in much of critical theory is that it places the emancipatory interest in social class, not in individuals. We can remedy this by turning the focus to the microsocial level, redefining emancipatory interest in terms of individuals' practical projects within their everyday affirmational struggles. Individuals desire to understand and be understood, to recognize and be recognized, mostly in terms of fulfilling their everyday needs. Methods of understanding and being understood by others are learned through experience, and this learning is necessary to manage one's involvements in the world successfully. The "yes, but" of transformational struggles comes from individuals who desire an end to their suffering from misrecognition. They draw on their familiarity with everyday affirmational struggles for identity and social belonging to seek changes in their circumstances. Again, misrecognition can not only injure an individual's self-esteem but also interrupt the everyday affirmational struggle. A very simple motivation for transformational struggles can be to return one's situation to what is perceived as normal. Not everyone is motivated by high-minded conceptions of justice for one's social class.

---

[383] "Appear as a moral state of affairs in the experiences of…" Honneth, *Disrespect*, 70.

[384] "If the Left Hegelian model of critique is to be retained at all, we must first reestablish theoretical access to the social sphere in which an interest in emancipation can be anchored pre-theoretically." Honneth, *Disrespect*, 66.

[385] Honneth, *Disrespect*, 70.

We can also see how the power structure can exploit individuals' needs for recognition and their familiarity with affirmational struggles. Critical theory has long shown an interest in the question of why the class struggle has not resulted in a revolution by the proletariat. Honneth's theory about why it has not happened is that in response to workers' demands for justice, the dominant class uses a combination of social mechanisms to narrow the possibilities for the suppressed proletariat to articulate their experiences of injustice rationally. In this sense, capitalism has evolved into a "new capitalism" that has romantically charged the idea of individualism and, changing the recognition norms, shifted the onus for bettering their circumstances onto individuals. Workers are no longer recognized for fulfilling hierarchically defined roles within a large enterprise, Honneth argues. Now, workers must become "entreployees"—entrepreneurs of their own labor—showing self-motivated initiative and bringing their abilities and resources to individualized projects to seek recognition for their achievement and move their career ahead.[386] What Honneth has astutely noticed is how capitalism and corporations have learned a way to channel employees' personal affirmational struggles into serving the interests of the capitalists. The normative structure of new capitalism is that workers are responsible for whether they are noticed and appreciated by employers, so workers are responsible for whether they are hired or fired, promoted or not, their employment status now tied to their need for affirmational recognition. The structural contradictions of capitalism are "no longer even perceived as those of capitalism as such, since subjects have 'learned' in their role as entreployees to assume responsibility for their own fate."[387] Meanwhile, the actual freedom and compensation given to workers by the system is not commensurate with the promises made to workers if they adopt the new labor paradigm. Capitalism has managed to divert consciousness of economic exploitation and workers' emancipatory interest from transformational struggles into affirmational struggles.

---

[386] Honneth, "Recognition as Ideology," 343. Honneth, *The I in We*, 175.
[387] Honneth, *The I in We*, 176.

It makes sense, theoretically, to view transformational struggles for recognition as closely related to affirmational struggles and even as a further expression of affirmational struggles. What this does for us is place the transformational struggles undertaken by social movements in the context of personal affirmational struggles, bridging the gap between the political and the personal. The extent to which an individual is already engaging in affirmational struggles contributes to his or her capability of undertaking a transformational struggle. When we explore particular incidents of transformational struggles for recognition, we see how they can be sparked by an individual act and how political movements depend on those individual acts. The Montgomery bus boycott is an example. It began at a particular moment in time: December 5, 1955, inspired by the solitary act of resistance a few days earlier by Rosa Parks. Within Honneth's framework, we can ask whether a political resistance movement already existed and whether that movement was what motivated Parks to act. The particular political resistance of the boycott did not exist at the time Parks acted, though her solitary act did spark a social movement to begin such resistance. Parks did have an interpretive structure—her church community and her involvement in the National Association for the Advancement of Colored People (NAACP). Honneth could argue that the NAACP constituted a broader social movement that motivated Parks to act despite there not being a particular political movement to boycott the Montgomery City Lines bus company.[388] However, the language of rights and justice had been there for centuries—even language that addressed the

[388] Arguments can be made as to whether the Montgomery bus boycott was a political movement. In the strictest sense, it did not directly deal with the affairs of government or law and, therefore, could be argued as being not political but a movement of economic resistance directed at a business. I argue, however, that given that the African-American participants in the boycott were well aware that they did not have fair access to the political system and that the system was inherently unfair to them, they had to resort to nonlegislative action to counter the misrecognition directed at them. In a fairer society, they could have petitioned the government for redress, but because that was not possible, they had to try to force political change through economic action. Therefore, the Montgomery bus boycott qualifies as political resistance.

injustice and misrecognition directed at the black community. Similarly, the interpretive structure of Marxism has existed for decades, and the predicted rising up of the proletariat has not occurred. This is why some point to power structures as the force that squelches resistance.

Why did Rosa Parks act that day? Honneth's resources to answer that question are external factors such as existing political resistance movements. I expand the resources by including Rosa Parks's capacity to use her own embodied agency within a particular social situation to respond to misrecognition. For Honneth, the question is how a collective political resistance movement influenced Rosa Park's actions on the bus. For me, the question expands to include what Rosa Parks herself felt, thought, and did on that bus. Both external forces and individual agency must be taken into account to explain what makes struggles for recognition possible. Did Parks need a social movement to feel motivated to resist? She needed an interpretive structure, but what else she needed was, as she said, determination:

> When that white driver stepped back toward us, when he waved his hand and ordered us up and out of our seats, I felt a determination to cover my body like a quilt on a winter night.[389]

How are we to understand what Rosa Parks experienced and the action she performed that evening? To say she could act only if there was an existing political movement around her would be to render her without power or autonomy. To say she could act entirely spontaneously would be to neglect the realities of her being embedded within and socialized by the power structure. The answer lies between the extremes: Despite the power structure and the long history of misrecognition of blacks, women, and her personally, Rosa Parks, a self-constituting black woman, exercised her agency that day. There was no existing political movement, but she was involved in affirmational struggles, both to affirm her own practical

---

[389] Donnie Williams and Wayne Greenhaw, *The Thunder of Angels: The Montgomery Bus Boycott and the People Who Broke the Back of Jim Crow* (Chicago: Chicago Review Press, 2005), 48.

identity in her own life and with the NAACP to affirm a social identity for blacks. Thus, she could, at that fateful moment on the bus, draw on her agency and familiarity with struggle to become determined to resist.

Parks called on what McBride terms a "virtual public," appealing "over the head" of the bus driver who refused to recognize her claims. She could, as Zurn says, anticipate full recognition from her community, even in the face of misrecognition from the broader society.[390] That Parks had reasonable expectations that her subcultural community would support her undoubtedly contributed to her determination. But, ultimately, it was her on that bus at that time who made the decision to act, not in opposition to how the white power structure had defined her as an actor, but to act instead from her love for herself that was not defined by white domination. She was "tired of giving in"[391] and said "yes, but." A social movement can help individuals by affirming them in developing more positive relations-to-self, giving them a better position to say "yes, but," and this is part of what the NAACP was doing for individuals like Parks. Ultimately, though, individuals need to act.

Honneth would hardly disagree that Rosa Parks made an individual decision to act, but lacking an adequate account of individual engagement and agency, he is unable to explain how struggles for recognition can begin. Political resistance movements cannot bear all of the weight of moving an individual from hurt feelings to actions that struggle for recognition. By including individual agency, we can construct a narrative for struggles for recognition in that an individual, suffering hurt feelings for misrecognition and having individual agency and familiarity with affirmational struggles, responds to his or her misrecognition with "yes, but" and overcomes socialization to act and attempt to change the situation. If the individual receives from others recognition that he or she is seeking change (a recognition that can come only from other individuals who use their own agency to overcome socialization), it actualizes and

---

[390] Zurn, *Axel Honneth,* Kindle locations 1883-1885.

[391] Rosa Parks and James Haskins, *Rosa Parks: My Story* (New York: Dial Books, 1992), 116.

strengthens the individual's struggle for recognition, enabling the individual to take further action, which could lead to further recognition of the struggle from others, and so on. Perhaps others recognize in the individual's struggles that they have suffered similar misrecognition and can use their agency to engage with the emerging transformational struggle against a shared injustice. Individual engagement is crucial for struggles for recognition to begin, and because Honneth does not talk about individual engagement and agency, he misses one of the necessary elements of struggles for recognition. Amending Honneth's account with individual agency enhances his theory and provides us with more resources to explore how individuals' capacities and dispositions may motivate them to resist or not to resist.

There is a further move from transformational struggles to social movements. What motivates struggles for recognition is being an individual embedded in a culture. What motivates social movements is individuals joining in common cause in response to perceived injustices within their culture. Rosa Parks's action precipitated a political movement only because others joined with her in a transformational struggle to change social conditions and their culture's recognition norms. The paths from individual acts to social movements are complex, the discussion of which requires considerable further study. However, the emerging picture of struggles for recognition that I outline here can inform that deeper study of those paths.

2.4.3 - Power Relations in Misrecognition and Struggles for Recognition

Obviously, a struggle for recognition is not as simple as an individual's decision to act because individuals are embedded in a social environment that is influenced by a power structure. Recognition relations are shaped by social norms that are intertwined with a power structure. The dynamic interactions between norms and individuals, including misrecognition and responses to misrecognition, play out within a social environment of institutionalized patterns of cultural value. We therefore must have at least some conception of how power structures affect recognition relations.

Honneth has been criticized for not having a sufficient conception of power in his theory of recognition. McNay says that Honneth's limited view of power binds agency with identity, which dilutes the effects of power on subjectivity, particularly how power mediates the relation between agency and identity.[392] Petherbridge also criticizes Honneth for an inadequate conception of power, though she observes that Honneth prefers Foucault's relational theory of power over the one-dimensional notion of structural power in Althusser and Adorno. Honneth, writing with Hans Joas,[393] saw Althusser's theory of power as limited to the manipulative strategies and procedures of the state. Honneth and Joas prefer Foucault's concept of the "microphysics of power," which places the genesis of power relations in local-level confrontations such as in factories, families, and schools. Foucault's theoretical model is a great advance, Honneth and Joas believe, because it reveals that power relations are reproduced and maintained in a society's everyday conflicts between opposed interests; indeed, this is the sole way through which a social system of power maintains itself. Honneth, on his own in *The Critique of Power*, agrees with Foucault that power is not something that can be possessed but is a relation, "a fragile and open-ended product of strategic conflicts between subjects."[394] Honneth also agrees with Foucault's idea that power lies at the everyday level of social life, formed in the strategic changes of everyday conflicts.[395] These important conceptions of power, included by Honneth in his early work are, Petherbridge claims, largely dropped in his later work. I agree with Petherbridge that the radical contingency and indeterminacy of the human condition revealed by Foucault's "micro-analysis" of power opens up questions concerning Honneth's critical project.[396] I believe Petherbridge is also correct that Honneth has tended to

---

[392] McNay, *Against Recognition*, 163-167.

[393] Axel Honneth and Hans Joas, *Social Action and Human Nature*, trans. Raymond Meyer (Cambridge, UK: Cambridge University Press, 1988), 148.

[394] Honneth, *The Critique of Power*, 155.

[395] Honneth, *The Critique of Power*, 160.

overlook the complexity of the constitutive dimensions of power.[397] This leaves Honneth's theory without a robust account of forms of productive power at the level of intersubjective relations.[398]

Recognition is bound up with power. As Allen says, "a state of human intersubjectivity that is completely free of power relations and is structured entirely by mutual recognition is an illusion, and a pernicious one at that."[399] Petherbridge is correct that recognition may only be enacted within the context of power relations and that it might be the case that the normativity of recognition must always exist within the context of power relations.[400] Importantly, Petherbridge and Allen both state that not all forms of power are forms of domination but that some are constitutive and enabling. It makes sense to think that individuals seek to avoid dominating power and acquire enabling power by acting strategically within the context of power relations. Because individuals are embedded in a social environment, and expressions of recognition and the seeking of it are shaped and restrained by power relations, it is in individuals' self-interest to act in accordance with the prevailing recognition norms. Allen correctly observes that:

> if individual identity is always constituted and sustained through intersubjective recognition, then we will have an interest in sticking with those modes of communication and recognition that serve to stabilize and confirm our identities, whether they are systematically distorted by asymmetrical relations of power or not.[401]

When seeking recognition, individuals have little choice but to work within their culture's recognition norms.

---

[396] Petherbridge, 62.
[397] Petherbridge, 191.
[398] Petherbridge, 197.
[399] Allen, 91.
[400] Petherbridge, 77.
[401] Allen, 105.

Petherbridge argues that "Foucault's 'micro-analysis' of power enables a consideration of power as a modality of everyday relations and forms of interaction,"[402] a consideration she thinks that Honneth would have done well to consider in his theory of recognition. I agree with Petherbridge that Honneth's theory of intersubjectivity is conceptualized only within the normative terms of recognition and that, consequently, he does not pursue a more multidimensional theory of sociality and interpersonal interaction that includes power relations and strategic action within those relations.[403] It seems almost self-evident to view recognition relations within power relations, though perhaps they are one and the same. If, as McBride argues, recognition includes a struggle for authority, then recognition is about power. Struggles for recognition, both vertical and horizontal, are then struggles about and for power—the power for the authority over recognition relations and norms.

If power produces the social, then recognition and misrecognition contribute to the social. Petherbridge's notion of productive power in subject-formation and intersubjective relations is useful here.[404] Power not only can oppress and dominate individuals but also can enable their productive capacities and relations-to-self. Petherbridge refers to constitutive or productive power and says, on the basis of Foucault, that it is distinguishable from forms of domination by always being changeable, reversible, and unstable. How I interpret this idea as fitting into recognition and misrecognition is that behaviors of recognition and misrecognition are expressions of intersubjective power, both dominating power and productive power. Individuals are vying for power in their everyday interactions, and this power struggle is part of affirmational struggles. When power within intersubjective relations is changeable and reversible, healthy recognition and productive affirmation are possible. When power relations are not changeable and reversible, such as in pathological recognition and normative discrimination, misrecognition is

---

[402] Petherbridge, 46.
[403] Petherbridge, 6, 8.
[404] Petherbridge, 194-198.

inevitable. Dominating power impedes intersubjective relations, which renders us irrelevant in our interactions with others; it impedes our capability to contribute to and appropriate our own practical identity, and it disturbs our relations to ourselves and the world.[405] Affirmational and transformational struggles both use productive, enabling power within intersubjective relations both in terms of using the power structure in service of one's own interests and in developing countercultural identities, communities, and even institutions.

There is a tension between power relations and recognition relations, but there is also a strong connection between them. Like recognition, power is a relationship. When we see that they are interactive elements within interpersonal relations, we get a fuller picture of intersubjective relations. Foucault's view of intersubjectivity is as mutually constructing subjectivity, in which each individual's subjectivity is constructed through his or her relations with others.[406] At times, Foucault's notion of the social construction of the subject reduces the individual to an entity subjected to control by others and tied to the identity created by others for him or her, which is a problematic view if taken to extremes. If intersubjectivity means anything, it cannot mean that an individual is affected only by others but produces no effects. At other times, Foucault steers clear of this problematic view, saying that "to live in society is to live in such a way that action upon other actions is possible—and in fact ongoing."[407] The possibility of action that affects other actions is what makes social struggle possible. As Foucault also says, "power relations are rooted deep in the social nexus, not reconstituted 'above' society"[408]

---

[405] Rahel Jaeggi calls this impedance of our capability to appropriate "alienation." Rahel Jaeggi, *Alienation (New Directions in Critical Theory)*, trans. Frederick Neuhouser and Alan E. Smith, ed. Frederick Neuhouser (New York: Columbia University Press, 2014), Kindle locations 1107-1112.

[406] Michel Foucault, "The Subject and Power," in *Michel Foucault: Beyond Structuralism and Hermeneutics*, ed. Hubert Dreyfus and Paul Rabinow, 208-226, 2nd ed. (Chicago: University of Chicago Press, 1983), 212-213.

[407] Foucault, 222.

[408] Foucault, 222.

Combining these thoughts with the idea of recognition as an intersubjective relation shows that recognition, and especially struggles for recognition, is an issue of power aiming to influence the constitution of subjectivity in oneself and others. Recognition operates within power relations because both recognition and power relations work within normative structures. By construing recognition as the valuing of others, we can see how recognition carves out a space of significance within relations, including power relations. Struggles for recognition are not only struggles against domination or subjectification but also struggles for meaning and significance. Our intersubjective actions construct us as individuals and construct our social world; we construct each other and the culture we inhabit. We act to modify the attitudes and actions of others just as they act to modify our attitudes and actions. These actions, both supportive and conflictual actions, construct and structure the field of our interactions and possible responses to each other. Struggles for recognition have ambitions other than changes in social institutions; they also seek to change the field of personal interactions. Struggles for recognition are complex and varied. Exchanges of recognition "may not merely enact forms of positive affirmation but exchanges may involve compromises, negative constructions, or even maintain power relations."[409]

Transformational struggles seek to change the recognition order and the power structure behind it. A central paradox of struggles for recognition is that for those struggles to exist at all, the individuals involved must act in a way that is contrary to the prevailing power structure. Transformational struggles are possible because the power structure does not completely determine individuals' actions. As Allen says, the regulatory regimes of power structures cannot maintain and reproduce themselves without the involvement of the individuals whom they regulate.[410] Individuals are not merely passive objects; they are social actors with their own involvements. When individuals come together in common cause to engage in transformational struggles, they cease to

---

[409] Petherbridge, 77.
[410] Allen, 77.

maintain and reproduce the power structure; and with persistence and good fortune, they can change their culture. Such change is possible because individual subjectivity is not entirely the product of the social process of recognition. As Honneth observes, if it was, there would be no space to consider the presocial constitution of the individual and no possibility to consider the force of negativity in the individual that is responsible for nonconformism, resistance, and revolt.[411] Resistance and revolt are correctly understood as a negative force in that they are an individual's negative response to his or her current situation. This negativity, though, is a means by which positive results can be won. A struggle for recognition is a negative response to a negative situation that attempts to create a more positive situation. If oppression is intrinsic to the social structure, then we cannot expect society to solve it. Oppression is a problem that can be solved only by individuals stepping outside the dominant power structure and acting separately from it. To fight injustice, we need continually to assess and reinterpret our perceptions and actions. This is a personal activity. Only we can do it.

Despite the prevailing power structure, power relations emerge from individual interactions and involvements. Social institutions are not the only sites of action and interaction—intersubjective relations are also. Recognition is usually discussed in terms of a state recognizing individuals, such as the recognition of same-sex marriage. Honneth's work opens up the importance of discussing individuals recognizing each other. What Honneth brings to critical theory is the possibility of normative-based resistance to power, though he places this possibility within collective political resistance. I believe that Honneth is correct that the consideration of a normative dimension is important in developing a theory of the social that can account for how a stabilization of power can arise out of social conditions of continual struggle. A consideration of power in interpersonal relationships is important in a theory of recognition and misrecognition because any recognition or misrecognition behavior takes place within a power dynamic that includes a struggle. But I suspect

---

[411] Honneth, *The I in We*, 218.

a difficulty for social theory arises if it adopts a particular characterization of struggle as being true among all individuals. I believe more work remains to develop an account of how the disparate instances of individual social action form a social order. I argue that it is more productive to characterize power within the dynamic tension of individuals' involvements that are played out in terms of physical actions, communications, and cultural expressions. Placing the focus on individual interactions and involvements will better illuminate the reasons for misrecognition and the effects on those who suffer from it.

2.4.4 - The Authority to Claim Recognition

Because recognition is a specific response to how a specific individual is, the question arises as to who has the authority to recognize another, and what is the authority that sets the standards for recognition norms? The temptation is to say that social institutions, perhaps the state, can and should establish and guard social norms. Aside from the question of the moral legitimacy of the state or other institutions imposing norms on individuals, there is the practical question of how much any institutional authority in practice dictates how individuals recognize the recognition norms. An institution can guide behavior only if individuals recognize the authority of that institution and follow its guidance. Whether an individual follows authority out of respect for the institution or fears negative consequences for not following, each is a kind of recognition.

Both affirmational and transformational struggles are not only over who receives recognition but also over who has the authority to grant recognition. As McBride says:

> At the heart of the struggle for recognition is a struggle for authority; authority, firstly, over our self-interpretations, and secondly, over the authority of the normative expectations which we have of others and of ourselves, and which others, in turn, have of us.[412]

---

[412] McBride, 136, 152cf.

There are two important insights in McBride's statement. The first is that recognition norms and our relations to them are subject to interpretation. The second is that the struggle for recognition is not just to receive recognition but to be able to influence recognition relations. Instances of recognition and misrecognition are inherently interpersonal, and interpersonal relations are inherently and inescapably bound up with recognition concerns. Likewise, struggles for recognition are inherently interpersonal. In seeking recognition from another, we recognize the other as having an amount of authority and power over us. We are seeking something that the other can give to us or withhold from us. The double-edged nature of recognition reveals that part of recognition is that we recognize another as having the authority and power to recognize us. Conversely, if we do not recognize another as having that authority and power, then whether he or she recognizes us would not matter much to us. I will get recognition from you only if I recognize you first. Recognition can happen only intersubjectively. This reason we need others (in addition to the many other reasons we need others) adds to the tensions surrounding recognition.

Many expressions of power, including domination and oppression, reflect conflicts about recognition norms and the authority over them. Targeted violence by whites intending to terrorize and subjugate blacks had, as Zurn says, a specific moral meaning that nonwhites were not worthy of the most basic consideration given to humans as humans.[413] This means that these acts of violence were about recognition: who should and who should not receive it. Collective movements in support of segregation of the races in the United States were struggles to support a recognition order that recognized the white race as superior to the black race, or, to be more accurate, recognized their conceptions of what white race and black race meant. To call collective segregation movements struggles for recognition would certainly be perverse, but that would reflect the perversity of the normative discrimination behind these collective movements. The American civil rights movement was a political resistance

[413] Zurn, *Axel Honneth,* Kindle locations 1756-1757.

movement against the segregation recognition order and was clearly by definition a struggle for recognition.

What are we to make of the white resistance to the civil rights movement? As repulsive as their racism and oppression was (and still is in some quarters), their struggle is based on recognition norms. Obviously, those norms are morally lacking, but we must not discount the fact that in the minds of those fighting to maintain norms of racial supremacy, their struggle is about recognition. We do not in any way condone their immoral bigotry by acknowledging this. The white supremacist movement is a struggle for recognition of normative discrimination and a fight against those who will not recognize those norms. White supremacists speak of defending the existence of white people and fighting against a "white genocide" they believe is coming because their meaning of American identity is under threat from civil rights being granted to nonwhites and the immigration of nonwhites to America. As Barbara Perry has argued, this movement is bound up with particular notions of race, gender, and sexuality that extol the virtue of reproducing the white race in the face of perceived threats to racial purity and white social supremacy. This putative virtue also is behind the white supremacists' opposition to abortion rights and homosexuality and requires the control of women.[414] Perry does not use the language of recognition, but I think what she accurately describes as the "age-old canons of the white-supremacist movement" are recognition norms. The white supremacists see themselves as defending a moral recognition order with a "white man's struggle" for the moral superiority of white male heterosexuals.[415] Perry concludes that the white supremacist movement is not the lunatic fringe we would like to think it is but reflects mainstream racist and gendered views that she calls asking "all

---

[414] Barbara Perry, "'White Genocide': White Supremacists and the Politics of Reproduction," in *Home-Grown Hate: Gender and Organized Racism*, ed. Abby L. Ferber (London: Routledge, 2004), 75-96.

[415] Within the white supremacist movement, white women are still subject to misogyny, and homophobia is strong. Both of these normative discriminations connect with the desire to increase the white race because independent women and homosexuals are perceived to cause reduced birth rates.

Others to conform to an artificial set of norms and expectations."[416] Perry's suggestion is that we counter this recognition order (my term, not hers) by ceasing to define different as inferior. I think this is correct, and the point I wish to take from this discussion of white supremacist movements is that racism is perpetrated by means of recognition and fought by means of recognition and that it is incumbent on us to discern which recognition is healthy. With forms of bigotry against difference, the discernment is easier, but I think it good to identify the general idea of struggles for and against pathological recognition for use in understanding social struggles in which the discernment may be less evident.

Struggles for recognition are not binary struggles over yes-or-no normative judgments. Often the struggles are over the interpretations of what the relevant norms are, how they are to be applied, and who the arbiter is of these questions; there is perhaps even a dispute over whether norms apply in a particular case. This interpretive process is also a question of authority. Certainly, social institutions offer an authoritative stance on questions about norms and their applications, but that authority is not as clear or strong as portrayed. Again, McBride cuts to the heart of the issue:

> The social world does not address us with a transparent and coherent set of normative expectations. Consequently, we cannot hope to hand over the authority to resolve struggles for recognition to the 'community.'"[417]

It is left to each individual to interpret the norms as they apply to particular circumstances. The question of whether recognition or misrecognition has occurred is a judgment that an individual needs to make. Even if an interpretive structure is available to help an individual, he or she still must make a judgment based on that structure. Our claims about recognition and misrecognition are also claims that we have the authority to make our claim. One's recognition of one's own authority extends to all aspects of

[416] Perry, 94-95.
[417] McBride, 161.

recognition in interpersonal relationships. If an individual cannot recognize his or her own moral authority, then he or she cannot bring him- or herself to demand, and perhaps not even to seek, recognition from others.

To be affirmed, we need guidance; support; and, of course, recognition. We learn to follow the authority of others, and we learn to trust others to guide us in how to behave and think, starting with our parents or guardians. We also sometimes learn not to trust others as reliable authorities, even those on whom we previously relied. In the constellation of our affirmational struggles, we are constantly switching between roles of claimant and judge[418] and constantly struggling over who has the authority in our recognition relations. This is the case even when all we are asking for is to be listened to when speaking: We are heard only after we are recognized as one worth hearing. The struggle for recognition is also a struggle for *sincere* recognition. We are less satisfied with the recognition of others if we learn that it is not sincere, and though it is difficult if not impossible to demand sincerity, we will press for sincere affirmation of ourselves and our contributions. Here too, we are forced to judge whether or not the recognition we receive is sincere. In seeking affirmational recognition, we seek out individuals from whom we can receive it. At the same time that we need support and approval from others, we also need to maintain some distance and autonomy from them. Struggles for recognition are often, if not usually, struggles to maintain autonomy and not be overly defined by others, and this requires enough authority to accomplish that. What makes true friendship special and prized is that, ideally, it is a relationship without struggles for power and authority or doubt about the sincerity of mutual recognition. Friendship is an intersubjective relationship in which two individuals are affirming each other in their affirmational struggles. A true friend values our autonomy, our viewpoints, and our desires, and we reciprocate.

We can make more sense of the complexities involved with the multidimensional approach by inquiring as to which norms are being

---

[418] McBride, 152.

engaged with, and to what extent, and which individuals are being engaged with and to what extent. All struggles for recognition are struggles over normative interpretation; even the question of whether a norm applies in a particular case is a normative question. This means that recognition relations have an ineliminable element of conflict. Perhaps, as Georg Bertram and Robin Celikates claim, recognition relations are constituted precisely in and through interpersonal conflicts.[419] This is easily seen in the political arena where political discourse and actions are defined by conflict. It is also fairly easily seen in the social competition for jobs or status within a group. Even among friends and family, only a completely ideal personal relationship would be without some level of conflict over recognition norms and their application.

2.4.5 - Struggles Beyond Political Resistance

Political resistance is but one variety of struggles for recognition, specifically a variety of transformational struggles. Renault stated that struggles against misrecognition are political and involve political normativity "only when individuals and groups are fighting against the denial of recognition produced by the institutions of social life."[420] This fits with my definition of political resistance as attempts to change social institutions, practices, and recognition norms, usually in terms of laws and political norms, that I see as a kind of transformational struggle. However, Renault, with Jean-Philippe Deranty, later claimed that "the normativity immanent in demands of recognition is not just ethical but political in nature, in that it questions the institutional contexts and contains the implicit potential for a universalistic project of community."[421] To say that the ethical or the personal is political is an admission of an important social reality, but another important admission is that individuals

---

[419] Bertram and Celikates, 15.

[420] Emmanuel Renault, "What Is the Use of the Notion of the Struggle of Recognition?" *Revista de Ciencia Política*, Volume 27, No. 2 (2007): 201.

[421] Jean-Philippe Deranty and Emmanuel Renault, "Politicizing Honneth's Ethics of Recognition," *Thesis Eleven*, Number 88 (February 2007): 92-111, 104.

experience in their social reality a division between their personal lives and the political sphere. In this chapter, I will discuss the reality of this division, especially for individuals in groups targeted by normative discrimination, revealing why many opt to struggle for recognition outside a political struggle for transformation of misrecognition.

Not all efforts to alleviate the effects of misrecognition are transformational struggles, and not all transformational struggles seek to change a culture's laws or recognition norms but may seek only to restore social balance within a local community. All transformational struggles attempt to revalue meanings, interpretations, and values,[422] but an extent and a scale are involved. The American civil rights movement or women's suffrage movements are archetypal political resistance movements in which there was extended involvement by large numbers of individuals and organizations to change society's laws and institutions. Struggles for recognition are conflicts, but not all such conflicts are large-scale political ones. They can also be more internal to a small group or between individuals. Joining an existing political resistance movement is just one possible path that individuals take in response to experiencing misrecognition. There may be little in Honneth or other critical theorists that directly denies other possible responses to misrecognition, but these other responses are certainly underexplored. This lacuna within critical theory leaves out important social phenomena, hindering critical theory's ability to understand individuals' actual social aspirations and conflicts as they seek relief from their experiences of misrecognition. This lacuna in turn hinders critical theory's ability to describe and explain social reality and diagnose moral problems in a way that contributes to positive social change. A robust theory of struggles for recognition needs to take into account the varying ways in which individuals struggle for recognition short of attempts to change social institutions.

Political theory understandably focuses on macrosocial political struggles, which are not entirely disconnected from individuals, but are often portrayed by theorists in terms of conflicts between groups. Taylor

---

[422] Zurn, *Axel Honneth,* Kindle locations 525-526.

speaks of a politics of recognition as conflicts between social groups in defense of their cultural identities. He describes misrecognition as a condescension by dominant groups toward other groups' cultural identities, harming those cultural groups. Similar to Honneth, Taylor says that

> our identity is partly shaped by recognition or its absence, often by the misrecognition of others, and so a person or group of people can suffer real damage, real distortion, if the people or society around them mirror back to them a confining or demeaning or contemptible picture of themselves. Non-recognition can inflict harm, can be a form of oppression, imprisoning someone in a false, distorted, and reduced mode of being.[423]

The potential harm we can do to others by withholding or denying recognition makes it a moral demand that we approach other cultures with a presumption of equal worth. Taylor, however, sees recognition and authenticity to be ideals in opposition to each other. Equality demands that we recognize individuals as possessing the same qualities, but authenticity demands we recognize individuals as distinct in their unique qualities. Taylor further argues that the view that everyone is equal means, ideally, that one's ethnicity or gender is politically and morally irrelevant. The problem is that Taylor's thinking about individual differences remains based on group identities—his example being the unique identity of the francophone Quebecois. Taylor's concern is for the identity rights of groups more than for that of individual persons. This is problematic because if the criticism is that distinct identity should not be subsumed to an idea of equality, this concern should extend not only to a group but also to individuals. If it is good to say that the distinct cultural identity of francophones should be respected within a liberal society and not subsumed under universalist norms, then it is also good to say that a particular individual's distinct identity similarly should be respected.

---

[423] Taylor, 25.

What would the case be to draw a line such that groups larger than a certain number deserve consideration of their distinct identity but groups smaller than that number and individuals themselves are beneath consideration? If we take autonomy seriously, then we must take individual differences seriously. However, it would be difficult to argue that every individual difference should take precedence over considerations of moral equality and that every individual claim of uniqueness must be accommodated. At what point would the idea of equality under universal norms be so eroded as to be meaningless? McBride argues that the focus on the "unfortunate association" between recognition and cultural identity politics has obscured the important interactions among recognition, social norms, and individual agency. I agree with McBride that the "relations of mutual recognition between us are not external to who we are and how we act, but are inextricably bound up with our relations to ourselves and our lives."[424] To me, that means that our critical theory must include microsocial interpersonal recognition relations and not be limited to macrosocial recognition relations among groups' cultural identities.

Taylor's picture of struggles for recognition as political conflicts between subcultures and the dominant culture identifies one set of phenomena. The question is whether a subculture would respond to misrecognition with a struggle against other groups or against the dominant social institutions. A marginalized subculture will not always respond to misrecognition with political resistance. Another path for the subculture, which may be a rational path in some circumstances, is to turn inward rather than try to win legal recognition through the social conflict of political resistance. As Du Bois describes, if individuals cannot see themselves positively through the conceptions of the dominant culture, it does not mean they cannot find worth in themselves. Individuals can cognitively understand the distinction between the attitudes and treatment they receive from members of their subculture and what they receive from those outside it.

---

[424] McBride, 137.

Melvin Rogers is correct that it is a theoretical mistake to assume that reciprocal social respect among members of marginalized groups is not sufficient to help individuals form positive relations-to-self. Social recognition from a community is possible even if the community is a subculture that is misrecognized and oppressed by social institutions, a possibility that Rogers says is not found in Honneth's account. I agree with Rogers that we need to take seriously the creative abilities of subaltern groups to forge meaning and to generate and define countercommunities, which constitutes a form of resistance that Rogers terms "counter-publics" that he distinguishes from subcultures actively engaged in political resistance.[425] Zurn observes that members of denigrated groups still may not have full and equal opportunities to develop healthy self-esteem and that positive mutual affirmation within a group denigrated by society may be the best one can hope for.[426] However, being esteemed by those closest to one should not be treated as a mere consolation. True, subcultures do not supply institutional legal rights, but contrary to Zurn, it is not impossible for members of a denigrated subculture to understand themselves and their characteristics and accomplishments as worthy.[427] A subculture provides an interpretive structure that members can draw on to develop positive relations-to-self. For this reason, members of a denigrated subculture may elect not to seek solidarity with the wider culture but take satisfaction in the mutual recognition of their social group. And if their recognitional needs are satisfied from others within their group, they might not feel motivation to struggle for recognition from the larger society despite the misrecognitions they receive from others outside their group. The humiliations will still hurt, but the emotional tension into which they are forced as a result of humiliation can be dispelled through active conduct within the group rather than through political resistance. As Rogers concludes, members of a subculture have the ability to build a community of mutual recognition that can sustain their psychological

[425] Melvin Rogers, "Rereading Honneth: Exodus Politics and the Paradox of Recognition," *European Journal of Political Theory* 8 (2), 2009, 196.
[426] Zurn, *Axel Honneth,* Kindle locations 1274-1275.
[427] Zurn, *Axel Honneth,* Kindle location 1278.

integrity and moral autonomy outside of the formal structure of recognition of which Honneth speaks.[428] This realization is important because we need to avoid the condescending view that for members of subaltern groups to develop positive relations-to-self, they must seek recognition from dominant groups.

Struggles for recognition are not limited to collective struggles for legal rights or social esteem; they include struggles over personal identity, which, though they have personal, social, and political dimensions, remain anchored in the individual. What is at stake in struggles for recognition is not only overcoming oppression and injustice but also using one's power to create meaning and value for oneself. If we couch the issue of recognition only within group dynamics, we miss what I argue is a principle motivation for struggles for recognition—the construction and maintenance of our sense of self and sense of the world in which we find ourselves. Recognition enables an individual to gain a sense of self, or a sense of practical identity, a sense that is molded by social norms and experiences. Our sense of self is a sense that is in relation to our social environment, especially in relation to the people who are most important in our lives. We are not born with a pure and transparent identity waiting to be discovered; it is constituted through our experiences and our responses to those experiences. It is an affirmational struggle because it is an ongoing effort to constitute our practical identity and our sense of self in terms of our community and its norms. Because we are unavoidably continually interacting with our social community and its norms, we also often run into our sense of self being misrecognized. It is to this personal transformational struggle that I now turn.

My sense of my identity is in tension with the identity that others attribute to me, both of which are potentially in tension with the norms of our culture. For each of us, recognition and misrecognition are judged by us not only in terms of the culture's recognition norms but also, if not more so, in terms of how we view ourselves. McBride writes of one important aspect of affirmational struggles:

---

[428] Rogers, 201.

> The struggle for recognition which we all experience, to some extent, in our lives centres on the ever-present possibility of a serious clash between how we recognize ourselves and how others recognize us.[429]

How we see ourselves is not always how others see us, and others may not understand our identity claims, much less grant them. What matters to us is not what the terms of the recognition are from a critical theoretical standpoint but whether they are the terms under which we want to be recognized. Quoting Hume, McBride notes that we accept praise from others only when their opinion agrees with our own self-assessments.[430] The clash between how we recognize ourselves and how others recognize us is an inextricable part of social life and a continuous source of tension. Each time it occurs, we ask ourselves how serious that clash is and what its repercussions are. When the clash occurs, we do well to ask ourselves whether the fault lies in us or in the other, even though the human tendency is to blame others for the clash.

The struggle for my sense of identity has a character different from that of other struggles. In a struggle for legal rights, for example, I know that the final arbiter is the applicable legal norm. But in the struggle to maintain my sense of identity, I feel that I am the final arbiter. There is good reason for this (or so I think): My identity is unique to me, it is a product of the collection of my personal experiences, it affects me far more than it affects anyone else, and who knows me better than myself? Or so I think. The problem with that view is that all of those truths do not mean that my view of myself is complete and infallible. This is why we have to say a "sense" of identity because our identity is not concretely known, even by us. In our interactions with others, we encounter others having a sense of who we are that may differ from our own. Generally, we would prefer that others see us the way we see ourselves, and as annoying as is someone else disagreeing with our sense of identity, a more troubling prospect is that the other individual's sense of us may be more accurate

---

[429] McBride, 41.
[430] McBride, 81.

than ours. Part of our socialization and development process is learning that others recognize aspects of ourselves of which we were previously unaware. We need to learn about ourselves from others, yet this disagreement is a risk to our sense of identity. Are we wrong about ourselves? Are what other individuals see in us really our own traits, or are what they see traits they are projecting onto us that are not part of us?

Our struggles for a sense of identity take place within a social environment. A significant threat to our personal identity is the culture of prevailing social norms, which could suppress our self-expression, especially if we are members of a group targeted by normative discrimination. As McBride points out, "To have the opportunity to be esteemed by others for one's traits and abilities one must have the freedom to present these features for social evaluation."[431] McBride gives the example of gay people who could not be openly gay and thus were unable to connect with some of their own traits through recognition from others. In the same vein, Allen gives an excellent example of one aspect of the social difficulties of a sense of identity:

> Having a coherent gender identity is, in a society such as ours, necessary for social recognition and thus for having a social existence at all. In this sense, given that the attainment of a coherent gender identity is predicated upon the disavowal of homosexual attachment, the subject's very identity is constituted by the disavowal of homosexual attachment.[432]

There is truth in this—our options for a self-identity are limited by dominant social norms—but Allen misses the dynamic that it raises. This scenario shows how identity is a dynamic tension between cultural norms and something personal in an individual. One struggles against the cultural identity because one's own sense of identity is at odds with it. If identity were not partly a personal sense, then there would be no struggle about whether to accept or avow the cultural identities. Conversely, this also

---

[431] McBride, 129.
[432] Allen, 79-80.

helps illustrate the impetus for the bigotry of homophobia—the idea of homosexuality as anything other than a perversion is threatening to a heterosexist identity that being heterosexual is "natural" while being homosexual is "unnatural."

Many of our struggles for recognition are personal struggles to affirm our own sense of identity or our place within our immediate social environment. For the most part, we are not involved in larger political resistance to change our culture's recognition norms, though the struggle for one's sense of identity certainly can become an attempt to change the recognition relations in which we are involved. When we acknowledge the power relations in which we find ourselves and our investments in them, we may decide to attempt to change the structure of those relations.[433] In this attempt, we are looking for more than affirmation from others; we are looking to change the ongoing recognition relations with others, and the struggle has moved from an affirmational one to a transformational one. These transformational struggles can take the form of political resistance or various other forms of social action.

Individuals must cross a line to engage in political resistance, a line that is difficult to define. There are several reasons why crossing the line into political resistance is difficult for individuals. One is that the political sphere is restricted if not closed to subaltern groups, such as homosexuals or racial minorities excluded by normative discrimination. Another reason is that struggles for recognition are usually interpersonal within one's community, whereas the political realm is outside our community and interpersonal relationships. We are used to affirmational struggles that occur within our everyday involvements, and we largely engage other individuals with whom we have direct contact. Despite the tensions inherent in affirmational struggles, we have familiarity with them. The issues around them, possible courses of action, and the effects of our actions are more readily discernable. Transformational struggles that seek to change the norms of small groups with which we have direct contact is more daunting but can be seen as a logical extension of affirmational

---

[433] Oliver, 69.

struggles. If one wants to change the culture of one's workplace, for example, there is a finite social scope with which one is engaging. To seek to change social institutions, such as laws, practices, or social attitudes, is a much larger task not just in terms of scope but also because direct engagement is more difficult. In the workplace, one can more easily speak directly with authority figures who have direct influence on the norms we seek to change. Such direct access is much harder to come by in political struggles, even at a local level. Political struggles at the national level are different situations in which social institutions are distant in social connections if not also in geography. We do not have direct access to most of the decision makers in legal and political institutions, nor do we have many relations with those with the power to influence those social institutions. The asymmetrical relations of power within society are strongest in the political sphere in which access and dialogue are granted to a favored few and others are largely excluded.

Engaging in political resistance requires stepping outside of one's subcultural sphere and into an uncertain world, which requires self-confidence and some understanding of how to proceed. The agency problem discussed earlier applies strongly to political resistance—how can individuals who are damaged by misrecognition undertake political resistance? An existing political resistance movement is certainly helpful, but even when a relevant movement is extant, the difficulties of political resistance are still a disincentive for individuals. The difficulties may not be alleviated by the potential solidarity they may find with others in a political resistance movement. It would seem that what is needed is the existence of a strong subculture already engaged in political resistance. This is what Honneth seems to hold, putting aside the dilemma of how such a subculture came into being, much less how it came to be moved into political resistance.

Subcultures do come into being, but not all are involved in political resistance. Other than political resistance, subcultures play a role in affirmational struggles.[434] Honneth emphasizes the importance of

---

[434] The topic of subcultures is broad, and though I think it is underexplored in the

community solidarity and shared values for an individual to develop self-esteem. Individuals develop self-esteem through being part of some kind of community and receiving recognition from others within that community. That individuals depend on a community to receive social recognition explains why they seek to belong to various forms of social associations.[435] But as Joel Anderson points out: "It remains somewhat unclear exactly what determines the boundaries of the community in Honneth's account—what if one is esteemed only by other Jews or other lesbians?"[436] This is an important question that shines more light on Honneth's problematic implication that struggles are significant only when they are collective political movements. Honneth's discussion of subcultural communities considers them in terms of the class struggle–oriented political debates and activities of 18th and 19th century bourgeois and proletarian social clubs.[437] It is doubtful that Honneth would hold that subcultures are produced only by class struggle, but a robust theory of struggles for recognition needs to be clear that class-based social groups are only one type of subculture. Communities of Jews, lesbians, and many other marginalized groups are subcultures in which individuals engage with each other in mutual recognition, providing success in affirmational struggles and perhaps providing support for transformational struggles directed outside their subculture. The composition of subcultures is deeply affected by economic class structure, but subcultures form in a variety of circumstances, especially in contemporary societies.

Mutual recognition can be shared in any subculture, but we can distinguish between subcultures of circumstance and subcultures of volition. Subcultures based on cultural divisions—race, religion, economic class, and so on—are not chosen, and their members are victims of circumstance. Individuals in oppressed groups are born into these

---

literature, I will be dealing only with the narrower scope of the role of subcultures in struggles for recognition.

435 Honneth, *The I in We*, 203.

436 Joel Anderson, "Translator's Introduction," in Honneth, *Struggle for Recognition*, xviii.

437 Honneth, *Freedom's Right*, 255-258.

subcultures and find themselves misrecognized by the dominant society without much opportunity to escape being so characterized. There are also voluntary subcultures, such as groups with common interests in music, art, or hobbies, which are certainly more accessible to individuals not in oppressed groups than to those who are, but nevertheless individuals can voluntarily associate with others and form groups of common interests. Individuals will seek recognition from groups on the basis of common interests either out of a perceived lack of recognition in their social lives or to supplement the recognition they already receive. A voluntary subculture can be an expression of struggles for recognition, certainly affirmational, but also possibly transformational. Subcultures can be sources of both affirmation and conflict, of both recognition and misrecognition. Many of the instances of recognition found within a subculture are affirmational struggles that do not challenge the marginalization of the subculture. These instances of recognition are still empowering to recipients, and whether or not they use the space provided by intrasubcultural recognition to undertake a transformational struggle beyond their subculture is up to them, and we have little right to judge them on it.

Voluntary subcultures form when individuals' experiences of recognition and misrecognition reveal their common interests. Individuals need to receive recognition to develop positive relations-to-self, particularly a sense of connection with others. Ideally, individuals receive recognition through healthy recognition relations within a morally healthy culture. The reality is, however, that the normative discriminations and pathological recognitions of a culture deprive many of recognition. I previously outlined some of the ways in which individuals experience misrecognition. Individuals certainly have the option to accept the limiting recognition offered by the stereotypes of pathological recognition or to accept living under the oppression of normative discrimination. Such concessions are insufficient, though, and individuals need to find recognition through other means. Alternatives to the prevailing recognition order are available to most individuals. When individuals do not receive recognition, one possibility for them is to "shop around" for others to recognize their identity claims, viewpoints, or behaviors. In response to misrecognition, some individuals will seek recognition where they can find it. It is a search for interpretive authority as much as for recognition. We form and join subcultures to increase our potential recognition relations. When we fail to receive the recognition we feel we deserve, we think that there must be the "right" group of people who, unbiased against us, will see clearly and agree with us. This shopping around for recognition is informed by the "virtual public" McBride talks about, and we seek a real recognition that corresponds to the virtual recognition we can imagine. One option is to find recognition within a subculture that provides recognition relations outside the prevailing cultural misrecognitions. Another option is to adopt behaviors and appearances to create at least a sense of recognition (which I will address in chapter 2.4.6).

Amidst the wide variety of subcultures, I will use subcultures coalescing around music as an example. Musical culture is a set of subcultures oriented around musical genres. Those who enjoy jazz and those who enjoy heavy metal are in different subcultures. Certainly, one can enjoy both genres of music, but the number of others with whom one can share the enjoyment of both is limited. One is probably attending jazz concerts with one set of friends and heavy metal concerts with a different set of friends. Fans of a particular artist constitute a subculture different from that of fans of another artist, even in the same genre. Directioners are fans of boy band One Direction, and this is a separate subculture from that of fans of boy band BTS, a social reality that the separate fan subcultures will eagerly verify. Musical subcultures can form countercultures that encompass more than music—clothing, slang, and other lifestyle choices mark each member as belonging to the subculture, with the accompanying concepts of group distinction and status. Teddy boys, mods, rockers, rude boys, punks, and Deadheads provide examples of such countercultures.

A significant drawback of many subcultures is that, although there is absolutely nothing wrong in having an extensive collection of Grateful Dead bootleg tapes, being an expert on Star Wars trivia, or having great cosplay outfits, it is difficult to get anyone outside the subculture to care about and recognize these activities. Certainly, we all should respect the right of individuals to express themselves and find satisfaction and self-esteem as they wish—no harm, no foul. But although one can demand an equal opportunity to gain esteem, one cannot demand being esteemed for a particular act or set of acts. The further a subculture's common traits diverge from the social norms of the prevailing culture, the less likely individuals in the subculture will be esteemed by members of society not part of their subculture, and the more likely they will receive normative discrimination misrecognition. Stamp collectors, no matter how obsessive in their hobby, are unlikely to suffer the same level of social disapproval as, for example, participants in the "living doll" subculture. Members in a subculture may experience increased isolation from those outside the subculture. If one's sense of identity is tied to a status that has very little symbolic capital in the wider culture, one may become increasingly dependent on the subculture for one's sense of identity and well-being, which could lead to negative consequences, including isolation, resentment, and conflict with the rest of society.

2.4.6 - Separating from Others: Subcultural Antagonism and Manufactured Recognition

In the discussion of subcultures, I touched on their positive role in affirmational and transformational struggles for recognition. Subcultures can provide the interpretive structure that enables struggles for recognition, but subcultures also can enable misrecognition. The impetus behind struggles for recognition can also manifest in antisocial and harmful ways. It is possible within struggles for recognition to descend into exclusion of and even cruelty to others. Struggles for recognition are not engaged in entirely for noble moral motives; the motives may be self-serving. Honneth portrays recognition in a positive light of a constraint of our actions in a nonegotistical manner such that we no longer oppose each other but join in solidarity with others and share experiences and agree on ethical goals. He assumes that "acts of recognition are oriented not towards one's own aims but rather towards the evaluative qualities of others."[438]

[438] Honneth, "Grounding Recognition," 513.

This assumption may help establish normative justification for social criticism, but individuals do not think and act in terms of theory, and the aims behind their recognition and misrecognition behaviors are also relevant.

Acts of recognition can be committed for personal aims, the most prevalent of which is that conducting acts of recognition are acts that earn one the recognition of being a respected person in one's community. The nature of mutual recognition is that, by according recognition to another, one is reciprocally recognized for it. Because recognition of recognition directly benefits the individual, and the individual would have been socialized into understanding that benefit, it is certainly more than possible that an individual would perform an act of recognition not out of respect for and observance of moral values but in service of his or her own aims and without engaging with others. Because recognition can come from other individuals or from a subculture, an individual can choose to behave in ways that would be disapproved of by society at large but that would find approval from a group of friends. A group of teenagers may vandalize property to receive recognition from each other, perhaps because they know their behavior would be condemned by society. The pull to descend into antisocial behaviors comes from the individual's need for affirmation from others and the social value of esteem. To possess both is to have social capital, which is desired for its own sake. Social capital comes from recognition from others, and if not received from the dominant culture, it can be received from a subculture.

For the most part, subcultures are not in open conflict with the rest of society, though as we saw earlier, members of a subculture may experience conflict directed at them in the form of normative discrimination and social ostracizing. The question is whether the subculture sees itself as simply separate from the mainstream or as antagonistic toward it. The punk movement was, as Renault astutely labels it, engaged in an agonistic struggle *of* recognition as opposed to a struggle *for* recognition from society. Punks wanted to deepen the conflict they had with the rest of society, Renault says, embedding the conflict in their music, words, and appearance.[439] As Honneth observes, "Social esteem can just as well be sought in small militaristic groups, whose code of honor is dominated by the practice of violence, as it can in the public arenas of a democratic society."[440] In social conflicts, enemies can be identified and targeted with reactive normative discrimination. Subcultures can also develop attitudes of overprotectiveness, resentment, and vengefulness. This is especially true in political resistance movements when those who are seen, rightly or wrongly, as those responsible for the oppression struggled against are targeted. Anger at the oppressors is understandable and, to an extent, necessary and commendable, but the moral aims of the struggle could be lost amidst the anger.

Anger and defiance against misrecognition from the dominant culture can manifest as a small group in opposition to the rest of society. The unequal distribution of justice and opportunities for recognition in the dominant culture can lead to "a counterculture of compensatory respect"[441] that recognizes the status of those within the group but not the status of those outside the group. It is this opposition to the outside world that makes a subculture a counterculture. Honneth believes such a counterculture is a limited, uncoordinated prepolitical reaction to misrecognition that will emerge only "so long as the identity-supporting milieu of a collective social movement is lacking." Honneth dismisses countercultures as inadequate expressions of social solidarity because they lack the coherent linguistic expression of a collective political movement. Honneth fails to appreciate the power of small groups of individuals to grow a counterculture in which individuals mutually support their identity claims organically from the constituting actions of individuals. No doubt, a small counterculture does not have as much capability as a large, coordinated social group to affirm its members' identities or engage in transformational struggles for recognition. Nevertheless, anger is an energy, and an attitude of "us against the world" is a source of solidarity that motivates actions that have real effects on individuals both within and

---

[439] Renault, "What Is the Use of the Notion of the Struggle of Recognition?" 200.
[440] Honneth, *The Struggle for Recognition*, 77.
[441] Honneth, *Disrespect*, 93-94.

outside the counterculture. A counterculture may engage in antisocial actions of hostility or destruction that manufacture a sense of solidarity and power to compensate for its marginalization from society. A street gang is not engaging in a collective social movement of political resistance, but its members are, in their minds, resisting society. A counterculture's limited capability to react to the dominant culture is in fact part of its identity, an embracing of one's status as a social outcast. Involvement in the counterculture becomes an affirmational struggle to be seen as belonging to it in the eyes of other members of the counterculture—the counter recognition norms of the counterculture replace the recognition norms of the dominant culture.

Compensatory respect is not limited to countercultures but is an attitude and action that any individual can undertake. When one feels a lack of recognition from others, one can compensate by engaging with recognition norms and esteem oneself. This type of behavior I call "manufactured recognition" because it is a self-recognition created by an individual for him- or herself, not recognition received from others. Manufactured recognition plays off of prevailing norms of honor or esteem that elevate individuals who display certain traits. Traditionally, the idea of honor was associated with certain individuals who were by their birthright worthy of honor and greater social esteem. As the values of liberal democracy have increased, the concept of honor associated with birthright has decreased, and social esteem has increasingly become associated with conceptions of earned worth, which in capitalist society, largely means accumulation of wealth. Awards, honors, privilege, and earning power now reflect accomplishments that are worthy of respect and reward. Manufactured recognition distorts and often inverts the relation between behavior and the rewards of recognition. Therefore, it is a distortion of affirmational struggles. Traditional ideas of social status have lingered, and wealth and fame, plus the trappings associated with them, still engender a sense that those with wealth and fame deserve recognition. In today's consumerist society, one may not have social wealth and power, but one can have at least some of the trappings of it. Plus, ideas of being "fashionable" and "on trend" have developed as new forms of social status. One can literally buy forms of esteem recognition by purchasing the right clothes, the right car, and not just a luxury watch but an X brand watch and by appearing at the right restaurants, clubs, or social gatherings, and so on. Corporations that produce consumer goods and services know this and are quite eager to sell this form of social status recognition. This "recognition for sale" is a social structure that can be exploited by individuals to give themselves a sense of recognition.

Manufactured recognition is different from positive self-esteem, healthy pride in one's accomplishments, or enjoyment of the finer material things in life. That is because there is a short path from manufactured recognition to misrecognition for the simple reason that it is a recognition drawn in terms of superiority to others. Self-esteem does not require the lessening of others, but the structure of manufactured recognition is "I have X and you don't, therefore I deserve more recognition than you." X can be a material item, a physical or mental skill, a belief or creed, or a social affiliation. The emphasis is less on solidarity with others and more on separation from others. If individuals cannot easily manufacture a sense of their own recognition, they can try to make themselves respectable by judging others as unrespectable. One can feel better about oneself despite being poor because at least one does not drink, one's daughter does not have a tattoo, or one is not a gossip like *those* people are. Marginalized whites can still feel superior to any black person, an insecurity-driven bigotry easily exploited by the corporate media and politicians. This denigration of others to tolerate one's own deficiencies is different from adaptive preference formation, in which poor people strive to be happy despite their poverty without needing to diminish others.[442]

It is not only those who are misrecognized who seek to manufacture recognition. Individuals are capable of desiring to receive more esteem than they deserve regardless of their social status. The middle class couple may desire to appear more wealthy and better connected. Men will act out attempting to draw attention to what they believe to be esteem-worthy

---

[442] Amartya Sen, *The Idea of Justice* (Cambridge, MA: Harvard University Press, 2009), 164-165.

expressions of masculinity such as misogynist acts toward women or bullying of others. Cliques, both teenage and adult ones, are ways to manufacture a sense of camaraderie that excludes and denigrates others. Parents push their children to excel in sports or the arts or to get into a good school more to increase their own social distinction than for the child's benefit. The social and personal benefits of recognition that encourage individuals to seek it also can encourage them to manufacture it. Like-minded individuals who seek to manufacture recognition in similar ways can form voluntary subcultures, such as elitist social clubs, to share their manufactured mutual recognition for their alleged superiority to those outside the group. Such a subculture lacks the social capital and power truly to perpetrate normative discrimination, but they still perpetrate misrecognition on nonmembers and cut off recognition relations with others. The influence of all forms of manufactured recognition on individuals should not be underestimated.

2.4.7 - Joining Others' Struggles

One more question involving struggles for recognition needs to be addressed. If the experience of moral injuries is a prerequisite for struggles for recognition, then how is it that anyone not so injured can join in solidarity with those who have been injured by misrecognition? Honneth's model is that struggles for recognition are social movements of groups suffering the same moral injuries who in their shared suffering find common cause. If experiences of a moral injury are a prerequisite to feel motivated to struggle for recognition, then would it not be the case that we would engage in a transformational struggle only in response to our direct experience of a moral injury? How and why would individuals join transformational social movements when they do not share the moral injuries that the common cause of the movement seeks to rectify? Why did white people join the American civil rights movement? Why do men join pro-choice movements? Why do heterosexuals join same-sex marriage legalization movements? Why do city dwellers march to save the rainforests? Broadening the question: Why would we ever join anyone else's struggle for recognition? This is an important question because the potential for collective political resistance exists when there is sufficient shared concern for a particular political cause. This includes, but is not limited to, shared experiences of injustice. Often, because groups victimized by injustice are in the social minority, political change cannot be achieved until those not directly affected by the injustice join in common cause, and this does happen. Sympathy from others is an important factor in struggles for recognition.

That there is a problem to be solved can be seen in the example of the recent dramatic changes in the struggle for recognition of gay rights, in particular same-sex marriage. The attitude of hostility toward homosexuals in prevailing social mores or normative discrimination against homosexuality encourages or at least enables hostility against that sexual identity. Given the prevailing social mores against homosexuality, we would expect, and indeed have historically seen, widespread hostility. We have even seen self-loathing among homosexuals caused by their society's prejudice. Opposition to same-sex marriage is partly due to cognitive dissonance from a perceived violation of the norm of patriarchal traditional marriage—if there is no man ruling over wife and kids who honor and obey that superior male, how can it be marriage? Given that there is entrenched normative discrimination against homosexuals and that homosexuals are a small minority (approximately 10 percent), we would think that the power structure is strongly against a transformational struggle for gay rights. Could we, however, say that in a society that condemns homosexuality that every individual is hostile toward homosexuals? No. We have seen in the past few decades a dramatic shift in public attitudes toward homosexuality, most concretely evident in the legalization of same-sex marriage in multiple countries. In Ireland, for example, same-sex marriage was legalized by popular vote.[443] How can we

[443] Henry McDonald, "Ireland becomes first country to legalise gay marriage by popular vote," *The Guardian*, May 23, 2015, accessed December 17, 2016, https://www.theguardian.com/world/2015/may/23/gay-marriage-ireland-yes-vote.

explain this change? The prevailing attitude was not removed by some force of nature; it changed from within.

One answer possible from critical theory is to say that rational awareness has reached the point at which the hostility has been replaced by rational acceptance. But this seeming explanation does not actually explain how this rational change was achieved, if indeed we could say it is rationally or was intentionally achieved, as the answer implies. Even if it is correct to say that a rational attitude has replaced an irrational attitude, we still must explain how that change occurred in defiance of the prevailing social mores. What forces could contribute to overcoming prevailing normative discrimination? Changes in the environment external to the society, or in technological development, could alter attitudes toward social norms. Social movements definitely change social norms, but the problem remains of why social movements would go against those social norms. To my mind, the best way to explain this is to understand that individuals have the agency to undertake transformational struggles for recognition beyond their own life experiences and the agency to care enough about others to join them in their transformational struggles for recognition. Enough people who were not homosexuals and were not personally harmed by misrecognition of homosexuals joined with homosexuals' struggles for recognition to struggle for recognition for gay rights.

Why do individuals join other individuals' transformational struggles for recognition? One possible answer for Honneth is that in his account, the semantic structure that motivates struggles for recognition does so because the moral language is shared—the individual understands misrecognition as affecting both him- or herself and others.[444] This is also Zurn's answer, which he expresses as recognition providing the connection between social structures of moral regard and an individual's practical sense-of-self, a connection the individual can use as a resource to make sacrifices to promote the welfare of others.[445] Honneth could also argue

---

[444] Honneth, *The Struggle for Recognition*, 163-164.
[445] Zurn, *Axel Honneth,* Kindle location 1921.

that the subspecies of recognition he associates with solidarity enables individuals to join the morally injured in their struggles for recognition. Or, if they are loved ones with whom we have intimate relationships, then perhaps the love relationship is the motivation for joining in common cause. Honneth rejects this latter idea, saying that because the enclosed goals of love relationships cannot be generalized into matters of public concern, love does not entail moral experiences that can lead to social struggles for recognition—what I am calling transformational struggles.[446] It seems odd to suggest that we would not stand up for our spouse, children, or friends out of love for them when they are wronged. Honneth, on the basis of his tripartite view of the recognition order and normative expectations, could say that if we stand up for a loved one, it is not out of love but out of the universal recognition of their legal rights or social value. In Honneth's account, the shared semantics of love do not transfer to the public sphere. This does not seem correct and cannot explain why we are more likely to support the social and legal struggles of those we are intimately involved with than of those we are not. It would seem that love relations do extend into matters of public concern. When we love someone, the goals of love are added to the recognition of rights and value. Perhaps it is the case that love makes the misrecognition more real to us. Ikäheimo's discussion of unconditional recognition for a loved one, not conditioned by prudential considerations, empowers us to struggle for their recognition. Or perhaps, if Honneth is correct about feelings of being treated unjustly being a motivation for struggles for recognition, when injustice happens to our loved ones, it is felt by us, and this feeling motivates us. None of this, though, explains why we would join a social movement in which neither we, nor someone we are in intimate relations with, belongs.

There seems to be a different kind of recognition at work in joining with others in their struggles for recognition. Our acknowledgment of legal rights, social worth, and even love, is not joining another in his or her struggle. When we see someone who has suffered from misrecognition, we

[446] Honneth, *The Struggle for Recognition*, 162.

may or may not join with that person in his or her struggle. If such individuals are engaged in a transformational struggle for recognition, we may wish to join them in their struggle. If they are not engaged in a transformational struggle for recognition, we may wish to struggle on their behalf—or we may do nothing to assist them. Joining another's struggle for recognition is a movement in addition to an understanding of circumstances, and this movement is informed by an interpretive structure that others are being misrecognized in addition to our recognizing them. Even if we both understood others as subject to misrecognition and recognized them, that is not sufficient to struggle actively for their recognition. It could be argued that, ideally, every individual who has had a legitimate recognition claim denied is worthy of our solidarity with their struggle for recognition. It would be impossible, though, for us to join every legitimate struggle for recognition—our time and energy are limited. Why, then, do we choose to support the particular causes that we do?

Even if we are not a member of the aggrieved group, in response to such movements, we could believe that marginalized people deserve recognition, and we could resolve to help them achieve the goals of their struggles for recognition out of human compassion. Many non-black people have joined the Black Lives matter movement in its struggle for recognition. One does not need to be black, much less harassed by police, to feel that black people deserve to not by mistreated. In joining someone else's transformational struggle, we recognize them, we observe that they are not being granted the esteem or legal rights they are due, and we act on our recognition. A social movement to defend the National Health Service could be termed a recognition of everyone's right to healthcare. But how far can this extension of recognition of others go? In joining an environmental social movement, do we recognize that others have a right to a clean environment and health and safety? Is the phenomenon of participating in walks to raise money for medical research to cure a particular disease a struggle for recognition? Breast cancer charities could be said to recognize the value of women and their health in resistance to cultural disregard for women's health issues. We could be connecting our sense of virtual recognition with the plight of others and come to sympathize with them, understanding to a degree how we would feel if we were in their situation. We may want to defend the National Health Service or promote cancer research not out of fear that we may need to benefit from these services, but out of compassion for those who do.

The decision of whether to join in another's transformational struggle for recognition is different from recognizing the legal rights of others or recognizing their accomplishments. Recognition behavior is a valuable affirmation of an individual's qualities and circumstances, whereas joining with an individual's transformational struggle is actively seeking to change his or her circumstances. The complicated decision-making process to join others' transformational struggles cannot be reduced to a single factor, but we can identify some. Aside from instrumental reasons—curiosity, political calculations, and so on—joining another's struggle could be a recognition of him or her as someone worth our time and energy. Or we could agree with a social movement that its members' goals would be good for some individuals or for society. Either way, it is a move out of the world of our personal concerns into the world of others' concerns. Such a movement is opening up to perceive others and allowing them to perceive us. Joining in others' struggles is connecting with them in solidarity and some degree of intimacy. Joining another's transformational struggle is a movement beyond affirmation into another's world of experiences and concerns.

To connect with and understand others, even others physically close to and similar to us, requires a journey that goes beyond a general feeling of moral responsibility to fellow human beings. Maria Lugones calls these journeys "world travelling," by which she means traveling from our "world" to another individual's "world" with a loving perception of identifying with and making connections with him or her.

> Loving my mother also required that I see with her eyes, that I go into my mother's world, that I see both of us as we are constructed in her world, that I witness her own sense of herself from within her world. Only through this traveling to her 'world' could I identify

> with her because only then could I cease to ignore her and to be excluded and separate from her.[447]

We need not require deep intimacy to come to understand each other. It is more an openness to see others for who they are both in their differences from and similarities to us. World traveling works at a group level in that individuals of one culture or subculture can connect with individuals of another culture or subculture by traveling to their worlds. Lugones's example is women of color traveling to the worlds (subcultures) of other women and seeing with their eyes. Such travels require dropping the arrogance of thinking oneself a privileged subject and instead being open to surprise and creativity—an attitude Lugones labels "playfulness."[448] Our possibilities for playfulness are limited by the power structures of our culture. As Lugones says, within a dominant culture where she, a woman of color, is marginalized, it is difficult for her to play in settings dominated by Anglo whites. In the language of recognition, a woman of color is not recognized by whites and is not included fully in recognition relations. To survive in a dominant culture, marginalized people learn that their opportunities to express themselves and travel are limited by the normative discrimination of the dominant culture, which includes a lessened ability to travel in the political sphere. Women of color, Lugones claims, despite being in different subcultures, have more room to express themselves and play in each other's worlds because they are not (to use Du Bois's language) on the other side of the veil of whiteness. In world traveling, we are energized by our relations with others. We learn to love and understand by means of such traveling, and experiencing hindrances in our travels and play awakens us to the need to change hierarchies. It is from such individual choices to reach out to others, understand, and join with them that transformational struggles can begin.

Cornel West insists that racism is a disease of the soul that cannot be overcome by arguments or analyses but can only be tamed by love and care. Love, he says, "has nothing to do with sentimental feelings or tribal

---

[447] Lugones, 8.
[448] Lugones, 16.

connections. Rather it is a last attempt at generating a sense of agency among a downtrodden people."[449] The movement into others' worlds is different from supporting a cause to make ourselves feel good—for example, a kind of manufactured recognition emblemized by the "slacktivism" of "liking" the page of a cause on Facebook. Such disconnected and self-limiting behavior is not productive either in working toward justice or in personal growth; it is simply behavior to give ourselves a sense that we have done something. It is a thin substitute for the world-expanding behavior of seeking to understand and join with others as we see in Lugones's idea of world traveling.

---

[449] Cornel West, *Race Matters* (New York: Random House, 1994), 29.

Conclusion and Future Foreword

The subtitle of this book, "Critical Theory Beyond Honneth," was suggested to me half in jest by a colleague, but it immediately resonated with me. Although I have in this book been critical of Axel Honneth, I recognize my debt to him for providing the groundwork for my investigations both here and in the future. My focus here has been to harvest Honneth's insights, fill in some of the gaps in his accounts, and build on his work to revise and extend critical theory. I believe that Honneth's account of recognition ultimately falls short not because he is wrong about what recognition means for an individual or for society, or is mistaken about its intersubjective nature, but because the account is insufficiently complex. Honneth expands social critique to include the intersubjective, personal experiences of individuals, but he does not fully embrace the implications of these experiences. Expanding the inclusion of individuals' experiences is primarily what I mean by critical theory beyond Honneth. I have not solved all of the issues that I have raised in this paper, but I have attempted to establish concepts on which we can base the further exploration of social justice and responses to injustice.

This study sets forward two main conceptualizations to assist future research in various fields of critical social theories. In Part One, I focused on the issue of misrecognition in order to clarify and expand a conception of how recognition relations can cause misrecognitions that lead to injustice. In Part Two, I focused on the issue of struggles for recognition to clarify and expand how individuals respond to injustice. The more we can clarify these issues, the more explanatory power our critical analysis will have.

The first conceptualization is that recognition and misrecognition behaviors are better understood along the dimensions of engagement with norms, engagement with individuals, and the engagement with action. The three dimensions of misrecognition are not formal categories but features that help us to understand the nature of misrecognition behaviors and enlighten us as to misrecognition's causes and possible remedies for it. In comparing misrecognition behaviors in this way, we can craft a better picture of social injustices by analyzing how they manifest within individual lives. In general, we can identify misrecognitions in which the problem is in vertical recognition, either disengagement from norms or engagement with problematic norms, and misrecognitions in which the problem is in horizontal recognition, during which there is insufficient or improper engagement with other individuals. That some injustices are perpetrated through engagement with recognition norms helps explain their persistence. Individuals have an incentive to adopt their culture's recognition norms in interpersonal relations, even when those recognition norms structure some of their relations as asymmetric and oppressive.

The second conceptualization set forward in this book is an expanded view of struggles for recognition that takes such struggles beyond identity politics and group political conflicts into everyday social experiences. The emerging picture of struggles for recognition that I have outlined here can inform a deeper study of the complex paths individuals take in response to injustice. The picture of struggles for recognition is a complicated one, with multiple reasons for why an individual would engage in a struggle for recognition and multiple ways an individual can undertake the effort to rectify injustices in his or her life. This is not surprising given that misrecognition is, as we have seen, a complex phenomenon. In his formulation of struggles for recognition, Honneth focuses on the individual's experience of moral injuries to his or her identity claims, but in that formulation are signs of a needed further shift. Honneth is seeking to explain political resistance and protest action, but these are not the only forms of struggles for recognition. Claims of moral injuries to normative expectations are not just collective claims—individual claims are also in play. Expanding the model of these struggles to include the wider variety of individuals' efforts to restore healthy recognition relations better helps us understand social conflict, including understanding transformational struggles for recognition as beginning with an individual's "yes, but," and the roles of subcultures.

The common thread in these two conceptualizations is the importance of individuals' normative experiences in ethical life and social change.

Zurn remarks that Honneth acknowledges that cultural factors alone cannot explain all social processes but does not really tell us what would provide such an explanation, and he calls for more work to be done in this area.[450] I agree and suggest that the two conceptualizations this study raises contribute to that explanation. The focus on individuals' experiences and involvements in misrecognition and struggles for recognition will help us understand how power operates in social relations. By going beyond abstract theory and into individual experiences, we can shed light on the ways power can structure intersubjective relations and contribute to recognition and misrecognition.

My hope is that this book's two main conceptualizations will assist in crafting an account of the causes of injustice. The multidimensional view of misrecognition overcomes Honneth's overly optimistic picture of recognition and shows how negative recognition fits into the normative structure of social life while acknowledging the positive value of recognition. The next step, I believe, is to understand that the causes of social injustice exist not only within macrosocial structures but also in individuals' intersubjective relations. Power structures shape social relations, but individuals are active in many forms of injustice because individuals act out of their own interests and perceptions, which are not shaped entirely by social processes. Increased attention to how individuals respond to power, norms, and each other in terms of their involvements will illuminate domination, exploitation, exclusion, and oppression, even when we can identify that the origins of those injustices lie within social institutions and structures.

Corollary to the question of the causes of injustice is the issue of responses to injustice. Honneth is correct that struggles against injustice are often attempts to expand recognition. The expanded account of struggles for recognition in this book shows that political resistance is only one possible path for those who experience misrecognition. Exploring the varied ways that individuals do respond to misrecognition will help us understand how social change happens and also how, at times, injustices

---

[450] Zurn, *Axel Honneth*, Kindle locations 5421-4522.

are not resisted. The study of struggles for recognition must also acknowledge the social reality that it is individuals who instigate social change, usually for personal emotional reasons. What historical progress has been made has come about not only from rational arguments and moral appeals but also from the pure stubborn love, sacrifice, and perseverance of many, many individuals.

The importance of recognition in individuals' lives and in social justice movements makes it a vital element in social and critical theory. Recognition theory can provide insights into a broad range of practical social issues. With the inclusion of a more robust account of misrecognition and an expanded account of struggles for recognition, recognition theory can be more effective within social justice theory in analyzing social problems and conflicts past, present, and future.

Bibliography

Allen, Amy. *The Politics of Our Selves: Power, Autonomy, and Gender in Contemporary Critical Theory*. New York: Columbia University Press, 2008.

Althusser, Louis. "Ideology and Ideological State Apparatuses." reprinted in *Lenin and Philosophy and Other Essays*, trans. B. Brewster. New York: Monthly Press Review, 1971.

Anderson, Joel and Axel Honneth. "Autonomy, Vulnerability, Recognition, and Justice." In *Autonomy and the Challenges to Liberalism: New Essays*. edited by John Christman and Joel Anderson, 127-149, Cambridge, UK: Cambridge University Press, 2005.

Appiah, Kwame Anthony. "Identity, Authenticity, Survival: Multicultural Societies and Social Reproduction." In *Multiculturalism*, edited by Gutmann, Amy,149-163. Princeton, NJ: Princeton University Press, 1994.

A.R., "Affirmative Action: Indian Reservations." *The Economist*, June 29, 2013, accessed November 25, 2016, http://www.economist.com/blogs/banyan/2013/06/affirmative-action.

Bader, Veit. "Misrecognition, Power, and Democracy." In *Recognition and Power: Axel Honneth and the Tradition of Critical Social Theory*, ed. Bert van den Brink and David Owen, 100-132. New York: Cambridge University Press, 2007.

Bertram, Georg W. and Robin Celikates. "Towards a Conflict Theory of Recognition," *European Journal of Philosophy* 23 (4), (2013): 838-861.

Bourdieu, Pierre. *The Field of Cultural Production*. Cambridge, UK: Polity Press, 1993.

Bourdieu, Pierre and Loïc J.D. Wacquant. *An Invitation to Reflexive Sociology*. Chicago: University of Chicago Press, 1992.

Butler, Judith. "Eine Welt, in der Antigone am Leben geblieben wäre," *Deutsche Zeitschrift für Philosophie*, 49: 587599, 2001.

Cavell, Stanley. "Knowing and Acknowledging." In *Must We Mean What We Say?* Cambridge, UK: Cambridge University Press, 1976. 238-266.

Cohen, Stanley. *Folk Devils and Moral Panics: The Creation of the Mods and Rockers*. London: Grenada Publishing, 1972.

Defense of Marriage Act. United States Government Printing Office. September 21, 1996. Accessed September 1, 2016.

Deranty, Jean-Philippe and Renault Emmanuel. "Politicizing Honneth's Ethics of Recognition," *Thesis Eleven*, Number 88, February 2007: 92-111.

Du Bois, W.E.B. *The Souls of Black Folk*. New York: Dover Publications, 1999.

Eidenmiller. Brooke. "'24-Hour Rape-Free Zone' set for Oct. 7, 8 at UNC-CH," http://www.unc.edu/news/archives/sep99/rapefree092899.htm, accessed September 21, 2016.

Fanon, Frantz. *Black Skin, White Masks*. trans. Charles Lam Markmann. New York: Grove Press, 1967.

Felman, Shoshana, and Dori Laub. *Testimony: Crises of Witnessing in Literature, Psychoanalysis, and History*. New York: Routledge, 1992.

Foucault, Michel. "The Subject and Power," In *Michel Foucault: Beyond Structuralism and Hermeneutics*, 2nd ed. edited by Hubert Dreyfus and Paul Rabinow, 208-226. Chicago: University of Chicago Press, 1983.

Fraser, Nancy and Axel Honneth. *Redistribution or Recognition? A Political-Philosophical Exchange*. London: Verso, 2003.

Friedan, Betty. *The Feminine Mystique: Contexts, The Scholarship on The Feminine Mystique*, edited by Kirsten Fermaglich and Lisa Fine. New York: W.W. Norton & Co, 2013.

Honneth, Axel. *The Critique of Power: Reflective Stages in a Critical Social Theory*, trans. Kenneth Baynes. Cambridge, MA: MIT Press, 1991.

Honneth, Axel. *Disrespect*. Cambridge, UK: Polity, 2007.

Honneth, Axel. *The Fragmented World of the Social*, edited by Charles W. Wright. Albany, NY: State University of New York Press, 1995.

Honneth, Axel. *Freedom's Right*, trans. Joseph Ganahl. Cambridge, UK: Polity, 2013.

Honneth, Axel. "Grounding Recognition: A Rejoinder to Critical Questions." *Inquiry: An Interdisciplinary Journal of Philosophy* 45 (2002): 499-519.

Honneth, Axel. *The I in We*. trans. Joseph Ganahl. Cambridge, UK: Polity, 2012.

Honneth, Axel. *The Pathologies of Individual Freedom*, trans. Lasislaus Löb. Princeton, NJ: Princeton University Press, 2001.

Honneth, Axel. *Pathologies of Reason: On the Legacy of Critical Theory*. New York: Columbia University Press, 2009.

Honneth, Axel. "Recognition and Moral Obligation." *Social Research*, Vol. 64, No. 1, The Decent Society (Spring 1997), 16-35.

Honneth, Axel. "Recognition as Ideology." In *Recognition and Power: Axel Honneth and the Tradition of Critical Social Theory*, edited by Bert van den Brink and David Owen, 323-347. Cambridge, UK: Cambridge University Press, 2007.

Honneth, Axel. *Reification: A New Look at an Old Idea*. Oxford, UK: Oxford University Press, 2008.

Honneth, Axel. "Rejoinder." In *Axel Honneth: Critical Essays,* edited by Danielle Petherbridge, 391-421. Leiden: Brill, 2011.

Honneth, Axel. *The Struggle for Recognition: The Moral Grammar of Social Conflicts*. London: Polity, 2003.

Honneth, Axel and Hans Joas. *Social Action and Human Nature*, trans. Raymond Meyer. Cambridge, UK: Cambridge University Press, 1988.

Horkheimer, Max. *Critical Theory*. New York: Seabury Press, 1982.

Ikäheimo, Heikki. "Conceptualizing Causes for Lack of Recognition: Capacities, Costs and Understanding," *Studies in Social & Political Thought*. SSPT 25 – Special Issue: Pathologies of Recognition (2015), http://journals.sussex.ac.uk/index.php/sspt/article/view/45, accessed November 17, 2016.

Irigaray, Luce. *I Love to You*. trans. A. Martin. New York: Routledge, 1996.

Jaeggi, Rahel. *Alienation (New Directions in Critical Theory),* trans. Frederick Neuhouser and Alan E. Smith, edited by Frederick Neuhouser. New York: Columbia University Press, 2014. Kindle.

Jütten, Timo. "Sexual Objectification." *Ethics* 127 (2016): 27-49.

Korsgaard, Christine M. *Self-Constitution: Agency, Identity, and Integrity*. Oxford, UK: Oxford University Press, 2009. Kindle.

Laitinen, Arto. "Interpersonal Recognition: A Response to Value or a Precondition of Personhood?" *Inquiry* 45 (2002): 463-478.

Laitinen, Arto. "On the Scope of 'Recognition': The Role of Adequate Regard and Mutuality." In *The Philosophy of Recognition: Historical and Contemporary Perspectives*, edited by Hans-Christoph Schmidt am Busch and Christopher F. Zurn, 319-342. Lanham, MD: Lexington Books, 2010.

Leeb, C. "Marx and the Gendered Structure of Capitalism." *Philosophy and Social Criticism* 33 (2007): 833-859.

Lugones, Maria. "Playfulness, 'World'-Travelling, and Loving Perception." *Hypatia* 2 (1987): 3-19.

Malpas, Jeff. *Heidegger's Topology*. Cambridge, MA: Massachusetts Institute of Technology, 2007.

Markell, Patchen. *Bound by Recognition*. Princeton, NJ: Princeton University Press, 2003.

Markell, Patchen. "The Potential and the Actual: Mead, Honneth, and the 'I.'" In *Recognition and Power: Axel Honneth and the Tradition of Critical Social Theory*, ed. Bert van den Brink and David Owen, 100-132. New York: Cambridge University Press, 2007.

McBride, Cillian. *Recognition*. Cambridge, UK: Polity Press, 2013.

McDonald, Henry. "Ireland becomes first country to legalise gay marriage by popular vote," *The Guardian,* May 23, 2015, https://www.theguardian.com/world/2015/may/23/gay-marriage-ireland-yes-vote, accessed December 17, 2016.

McNay, Lois. *Against Recognition*. Cambridge, UK: Polity Press, 2008.

McNay, Lois. "Having It Both Ways: The Incompatibility of Narrative Identity and Communicative Ethics in Feminist Thought." *Theory, Culture and Society* 20 (6) (2003), 1-20.

McNay, Lois. *The Misguided Search for the Political*. Cambridge, UK: Polity Press, 2014.

Meer, Nasar. "Overcoming the Injuries of 'Double Consciousness.'" In *The Politics of Misrecognition*, edited by Simon Thompson and Majid Yar, 45-65. Farnham, UK: Ashgate Publishing, 2011.

Mendonça, Ricardo Fabrino. "Recognition and Esteem: A Case Study of the Struggles of People Affected by Leprosy." In *The Politics of Misrecognition*, edited by Simon Thompson and Majid Yar, 145-167. Farnham, UK: Ashgate Publishing, 2011.

Mill, John Stuart. *The Subjection of Women*. Indianapolis, IN: Hackett Publishing, 1988.

Mills, Charles. "White Supremacy." In *Companion to African-American Philosophy*, edited by Tommy L. Lott and John P. Pittman, 269-283. Oxford, UK: Blackwell Publishing, 2003.

Nakamura, David and Juliet Eilperon. "With Stonewall, Obama designates first national monument to gay rights movement," *The Washington Post*, June 24, 2016. Accessed September 17, 2016, https://www.washingtonpost.com/news/post-politics/wp/2016/06/24/with-stonewall-obama-designates-first-

national-momument-to-gay-rights-movement/?utm_term=.c253021955bb.
OED Online. "pathology, n." Last modified December 2016. Oxford University Press. http://0-www.oed.com/view/Entry/138805? (accessed January 6, 2017).
OED Online. "pathological, adj. and n." Last modified December 2016. Oxford University Press. http://0-www.oed.com/view/Entry/138800 (accessed January 6, 2017).
Oliver, Kelly. *Witnessing: Beyond Recognition*. Minneapolis: University of Minnesota Press, 2001.
Parks, Rosa and James Haskins. *Rosa Parks: My Story*. New York: Dial Books, 1992.
Patterson, Orlando. *Slavery and Social Death: A Comparative Study*. Cambridge, MA: Harvard University Press, 1982.
Perry, Barbara. "'White Genocide': White Supremacists and the Politics of Reproduction." In *Home-Grown Hate: Gender and Organized Racism*, edited by Abby L. Ferber, 75-96. London: Routledge, 2004.
Petherbridge, Danielle. *The Critical Theory of Axel Honneth*. Plymouth, UK: Lexington Books, 2013.
Pinkard, Terry. "Recognition, the Right and the Good." In *The Philosophy of Recognition: Historical and Contemporary Perspectives*, edited by Hans-Christoph Schmidt am Busch and Christopher F. Zurn, 129-151. Lanham, MD: Lexington Books, 2010.
Renault, Emmanuel. *The Experience of Injustice: A Theory of Recognition*, translated by Richard A. Lynch, New York: Columbia University Press, 2019.
Renault, Emmanuel. "The Theory of Recognition and Critique of Institutions," in *Axel Honneth: Critical Essays,* edited by Danielle Petherbridge, 207-232. Leiden: Brill, 2011.
Renault, Emmanuel. "What Is the Use of the Notion of the Struggle of Recognition?" *Revista de Ciencia Política*, Volume 27, No. 2 (2007): 195-205.
Rogers, Melvin. "Rereading Honneth: Exodus Politics and the Paradox of Recognition." *European Journal of Political Philosophy* 8 (2009): 183-206.
Russon, John and Kirsten Jacobson. "Heidegger and Space: The Open in Which We Sojourn." In *Bloomsbury Companion to Heidegger*, edited by Francois Raffoul and Eric Nelson, 345-352. London: Bloomsbury, 2013.

Sayer, Andrew. "Contributive Justice and Meaningful Work." *Res Publica* 15 (1) (2009): 1-16.

Sayer, Andrew. "Misrecognition: The Unequal Division of Labour and Contributive Justice." In *The Politics of Misrecognition*, edited by Simon Thompson and Majid Yar, 87-103. Farnham, UK: Ashgate Publishing, 2011.

Sen, Amartya. *The Idea of Justice*. Cambridge, MA: Harvard University Press, 2009.

Smith, Nicholas H. "Recognition, Culture, and Economy: Honneth's Debate with Fraser." In *Axel Honneth: Critical Essays*, edited by Danielle Petherbridge, 321-344. Leiden: Brill, 2011.

Stout, Martha. *The Sociopath Next Door: The Ruthless Versus the Rest of Us*. New York: Broadway Books, 2005.

Taylor, Charles. "The Politics of Recognition." In *Multiculturalism*, edited by Amy Gutmann, 25-74. Princeton, NJ: Princeton University Press, 1994.

Van Den Brink, Bert. "Recognition, Pluralism, and the Expectation of Harmony," in *Axel Honneth: Critical Essays,* edited by Danielle Petherbridge. Leiden: Brill, 2011.

West, Cornel. *Race Matters*. New York: Random House, 1994.

Williams, Donnie and Wayne Greenhaw. *The Thunder of Angels: The Montgomery Bus Boycott and the People Who Broke the Back of Jim Crow.* Chicago: Chicago Review Press, 2005.

Williams, Patricia. *The Alchemy of Race and Rights*. Cambridge, MA: Harvard University Press, 1991.

Young, Iris. *Justice and the Politics of Difference*. Princeton, NJ: Princeton University Press, 1990.

Zurn, Christopher. *Axel Honneth: A Critical Theory of the Social.* London: Polity, 2015.

Zurn, Christopher. "Social Pathologies as Second-Order Disorders." In *Axel Honneth: Critical Essays*, edited by Danielle Petherbridge, Leiden: Brill, 2011. Kindle.

Printed in Great Britain
by Amazon

16134644R00159